ASSESSING CHANGE IN PSYCHOANALYTIC PSYCHOTHERAPY OF CHILDREN AND ADOLESCENTS

The EFPP Book Series

Series Editors: *Monica Lanyado and Didier Houzel*

OTHER TITLES IN THE SERIES

Chief Editor: John Tsiantis

- *Counter-transference in Psychoanalytic Psychotherapy with Children and Adolescents*
- *Supervision and its Vicissitudes*
- *Psychoanalytic Psychotherapy in Institutional Settings*
- *Psychoanalytic Psychotherapy of the Severely Disturbed Adolescent*
- *Work with Parents: Psychoanalytic Psychotherapy with Children and Adolescents*
- *Psychoanalysis and Psychotherapy: The Controversies and the Future*
- *Research in Psychoanalytic Psychotherapy with Adults*
- *The Therapist at Work: Personal Factors Affecting the Analytic Process*
- *Invisible Boundaries. Psychosis and Autism in Children and Adolescents*
- *The Development of Consciousness: Psychoanalysis, neuroscience and child development*
- *The Analytic Field: A Clinical Concept*
- *Crossing Borders - Integrating Differences: Psychoanaltyic Psychotherapy in Transition*
- *Play and Power*

ASSESSING CHANGE IN PSYCHOANALYTIC PSYCHOTHERAPY OF CHILDREN AND ADOLESCENTS

Today's Challenge

Edited by

John Tsiantis and Judith Trowell

Routledge
Taylor & Francis Group
LONDON AND NEW YORK

First published 2010 by Karnac Books Ltd.

Published 2018 by Routledge
2 Park Square, Milton Park, Abingdon, Oxon OX14 4RN
711 Third Avenue, New York, NY 10017, USA

Routledge is an imprint of the Taylor & Francis Group, an informa business

British Library Cataloguing in Publication Data

A C.I.P. for this book is available from the British Library

ISBN-13: 9781855757080 (pbk)

Typeset by Vikatan Publishing Solutions (P) Ltd., Chennai, India

CONTENTS

ACKNOWLEDGMENTS

This book was conceived during discussions between the first of the editors and the late Professor Issy Kolvin, to whom both John Tsiantis and Judith Trowell express their gratitude. We also wish to express our thanks to the authors of this book who tackle the subject through their knowledge of various theoretical perspectives and clinical experience from both Europe and the USA.

We also wish to express our thanks to the Chief Editors of the series as well as the Executive of EFPP. Finally we express our thanks to Nadia Katsougris and Zetta Iliopoulou, PA's to Professor Tsiantis for their work in preparing this manuscript.

John Tsiantis and Judith Trowell

ABOUT THE AUTHORS

Boëthius Siv Boalt is a licensed clinical psychologist and a psychoanalyst. She is Emeritus Professor at the Department of Education, Stockholm University and former principal of the Erica Foundation, a university college working with psychotherapy for children and adolescents, training programs and research. She was Chairperson of the European Federation for Psychoanalytic Psychotherapy (EFPP) from 2003 to 2007 and now works mainly with research and organisational development in Sweden and at an international level. She has published a large number of articles and books on organisational development, group supervision and psychotherapy research.

Rebecca Burwell, Ph.D., is an Assistant Professor at Westfield State College. She received her M.Phil. in social and developmental psychology from the University of Cambridge and her Ph.D., in child clinical psychology from the University of Denver. Her research deals with cognitive, interpersonal, and emotional vulnerability to depression among children and adolescents.

Gunnar Carlberg, Ph.D., is an associate professor. He is Director of the Erica Foundation in Stockholm, Sweden, an institute providing psychotherapy for children and adolescents, professional training at university level, and research. He is a licensed psychologist and psychotherapist with various publications within psychodynamic developmental psychology and child psychotherapy research. In addition, he is project-leader of the Erica Process and Outcome Study (EPOS).

Tamara Fischmann, Psychoanalyst DPV/IPV. She is a scientist at the Sigmund Freud Institute, Frankfurt, also working in private practice.

Annette Geiser-Elze was born in 1967. She is a psychological psychotherapist, and a research associate in the Heidelberg Study for Psychodynamic Psychotherapy for Children and Adolescents, at the Psychiatric University Hospital Heidelberg.

Jackie Hall is a child and adolescent psychotherapist. She works at the Tavistock Clinic and Family Centre in North London. She has a special interest in the development of Multi Agency work with children and families in the community.

Mechtild Hartmann was born in 1950. She is an analytic child and adolescent psychotherapist in private practice. She is a lecturer at the Institute for Psychoanalytic Therapy for Children and Adolescents, Heidelberg.

Euthymia D. Hibbs, Ph.D., was born in Greece and studied psychology in Europe and the United States. She worked for twenty-five years at the National Institute of Mental Health (NIMH/NIH), as a clinical research psychologist. The last ten years she was the Head of Psychosocial Treatment Research for Child and Adolescent Disorders. She has authored and co-authored a number of peer reviewed research articles, book chapters, and edited books on the topic of mental disorders in children and their families. She has received several professional and civic awards, including one from the American Psychological Association Division 53, for her contributions to the field. She is a diplomat, and Fellow in Psychotherapy, of the American Psychotherapy Association. Since leaving NIMH, she works as adjunct Professor in Psychiatry at the George Washington University, maintains a private practice, and does consulting work.

Hildegard Horn was born in 1945. She is an analytic child and adolescent psychotherapist in private practice. She is also a lecturer at the Institute for Psychoanalytic Therapy for Children and Adolescents, Heidelberg.

Eilis Kennedy is a consultant child and adolescent psychiatrist in the Child and Family Department at the Tavistock Clinic. She has a particular interest in systematic reviews and has been a lead reviewer on two Cochrane systematic reviews as well as undertaking a systematic review of psychoanalytic child psychotherapy and co-editing a review of process and outcome research in child and parent-infant psychotherapy.

Klaus-Thomas Kronmüller, MD was born in 1964. He is an Assistant Medical Director at the Psychiatric University Hospital, Heidelberg. He is also a psychological psychotherapist. His main research fields are depression, eating disorders, schizophrenia and psychotherapy research.

Marianne Leuzinger-Bohleber is Professor for Psychoanalytic Psychology at the University of Kassel, Director of the Sigmund-Freud-Institute, Frankfurt, Training Analyst of the German Psychoanalytic Association (and the Swiss Psychoanalytic Society), and Chair of the Research Committees for Conceptual Research of the IPA. She has published in the areas of clinical, conceptual and empirical research in psychoanalysis, developmental psychology and the interdisciplinary exchange between psychoanalysis and other disciplines (e.g. embodied cognitive science, literature, educational sciences).

Maria Rhode is Professor of Child Psychotherapy at the Tavistock Clinic/University of East London. She is co-editor of *Psychotic States in Children* (1997) and *The Many Faces of Asperger's Syndrome* (2004) in the Tavistock Clinic Book Series, and of *Invisible Boundaries: Autism and Psychosis in Children and Adolescents* (2006), EFPP/Karnac.

Stephen R. Shirk, Ph.D., is a Professor of Psychology and Director of the Clinic for Child and Family Psychology at the University of Denver. Dr. Shirk received his Ph.D. from the New School for Social Research in New York City and completed post-doctoral training at Harvard Medical School. He has served as President of the Society of Clinical Child and Adolescent Psychology of the American

Psychological Association. His current research examines treatment processes, including the therapeutic alliance, that contribute to outcomes in child and adolescent therapy.

Annette Stefini was born in 1971. She is a research associate in the Heidelberg Study for Psychodynamic Psychotherapy for Children and Adolescents and the Study for Psychotherapeutic Treatment of Adolescent Girls and Young Women with Bulimia Nervosa at the Psychiatric University Hospital, Heidelberg.

Judith Trowell is Honorary Consultant Psychiatrist at the Child and Family Department of the Tavistock Clinic, and Professor of Child Mental Health at the West Midlands NIMHE/CSIP. She is a psychoanalyst and child analyst.

John Tsiantis, MD, DPM, FRC Psych., is Professor of Child Psychiatry at the President of European Union of Medical Specialists (UEMS), Section of Child & Adolescent Psychiatry, Previously Chief Editor European Federation Psychoanalytic Psychotherapy Monographs, President of the Hellenic Institute of Psychoanalytic Psychotherapy.

Klaus Winkelmann, MD, was born in 1945. He is a doctor in psychotherapeutic medicine and psychoanalysis, and Head of the Institute for Psychoanalytic Therapy for Children and Adolescents, Heidelberg.

SERIES EDITORS' PREFACE

Monica Lanyado and Didier Houzel

In a previous volume of the EFPP Clinical Monograph Series, devoted to *Research on Psychoanalytic Psychotherapy with Adults* (2004), the editors announced another volume of the Series devoted to research on psychoanalytic psychotherapy with children and adolescents. Here is this volume edited by John Tsiantis and Judith Trowell. The contributions to this volume underline the absolute necessity of assessing the effectiveness of psychoanalytic psychotherapy with children and adolescents, and the important progress that has been made in that field since the beginning of the present century.

In his foreword, Professor Daniel Widlöcher stresses the importance of assessment from a political, an ethical and a scientific point of view. He emphasizes the specific difficulties encountered in this field. How can we fill the gap between the personal experience of a therapeutic relationship, for the patient as well as for the therapist, and the requirement to reach the necessary objectivity of empirical research? This issue is a challenge for clinicians and researchers in their efforts to build appropriate tools to evaluate these treatments.

The contributions to the present volume show us that this challenge is fruitful for both clinician and researcher, and that it is possible to overcome what appears at first to be a paradox. The clinician is required to make the therapeutic process understandable and appropriately quantifiable. The researcher has to recognize the complexity of the therapeutic process and to use new ways of evaluation to take into account that complexity.

This volume presents aspects of research work in psychoanalytic psychotherapy for children and adolescents and demonstrates that it is not only possible to meet this challenge, but that the resolution of this apparent paradox is full of creative opportunities.

FOREWORD

Daniel Widlöcher

The evaluation of the effectiveness of psychoanalytic psychotherapy has become an absolute necessity as with any other sphere of health care. It is a political necessity because the society in charge of these practices has to assess their usefulness and their cost. It is also an ethical necessity because the patients and their families must be assured they will receive the best care possible. Finally it is a scientific necessity because we, as practitioners, must try to ensure we offer our patients the best practice. This book, which I was invited by the editors to read and then to write the preface for, fulfils clearly those three purposes. It brings evidence that, for several decades, research has been carried out in the field of psychoanalytic psychotherapy with children and adolescents and that these research projects help us answer the questions facing us. Nevertheless it is obviously on a scientific level that the book brings us interesting information for our practice, as well as for the research we must develop.

If child and adolescent psychoanalysis seems to have a considerable importance in the field of child psychiatry in Continental Europe since the end of the Second World War, it must be remembered that it is because a great deal of spadework had been going on before and was making considerable progress. It was necessary to build up appropriate facilities, and additionally, while adult psychiatry set up facilities some time ago, there was also a strong need for these to be renewed. As well as this, after the war, more efficient drug therapy was developed in the field of adult mental disorders. It has not been the same for children and adolescents. Over a very long time, psychoanalytically orientated psychotherapists lived and worked like pioneers in the field where they had to clear the way. They were called upon to take charge not only of the children, but also the family, and social and educational structures. In time, the need to undertake thorough assessments of children and adolescents became as important as it had already become, in the field of adult psychopathology. It was necessary to compensate for the delay, and to develop appropriate methods given the complexity of this field. Here we have to think about the importance of the social and educational context and about the fact that psychotherapists address a person who is developing.

We must first raise a question we encounter implicitly or explicitly in most of the contributions we are going to read: to what extent have psychotherapists become aware of the necessity of assessing their practice? We know that the families are concerned with that issue. We know that the authorities wonder as well. But we still observe a strong resistance on the practitioners' part. The reason always offered concerns the feasibility of doing research. The complexity and strength of individual features are invoked. The clinician does his best for each case according to his capabilities and competence, but he is afraid that judgments based on quantitative data will threaten his freedom and his individual responsibility. Without presenting a final solution, this book shows us how to overcome those difficulties. Personally, I think that working in a group of practitioners constitutes a basic method, as in many medical fields by the way. It is one way of developing the critical sense of practitioners and of opening the door to empirical research in institutions or in the networks of private practitioners. Anyway, we must specify here that when we are speaking about assessing treatments and about research, we take into account two fields that have to be carefully distinguished. The first question is whether we know the appropriate place for psychoanalytically oriented psychotherapy with a given pathology compared to other interventions or, which sort of psychoanalytically oriented technique is recommended depending on the diversity of the cases. The second issue is how to test, not the method itself, but the way it is implemented in a particular institution or by a particular practitioner. This issue is even more delicate than any previous one. Reading this book provides the possibility to explore these two questions. On the one hand, there is a comparative process needing interdisciplinary research; it is the chapters on Depression or "Attention-Deficit/Hyperactivity-Disorders". On the other hand, we will enter the life of different institutions and the way the psychotherapists themselves develop this view about their own practice.

But we must notice here that from a methodological standpoint, the emphasis is put on a principle according to which we assess practice: we do not validate methods of treatment arising from *a priori* programs and the concept of evidence. Evidence based medicine seems to have hardly any room in our sphere. A long tradition of practice, clinical and theoretical work, the pluralism of schools of psychoanalysis and psychoanalytic psychotherapy and of institutions requires another kind of reasoning, equally rigorous, and this is which is widely developed in this book.

Another issue concerns the standardization of data. Whatever the aims of an evaluation, it is necessary to collect the data in a way that is as rigorous as possible, and at the same time, to respect the contextual contingencies and individual variations. We are in charge of young people and we have to study cases. Moving from clinical to research, from one side to the other is not easy and needs tact, a will to cooperate and methodological precautions. We talk here about standardization as a tool to classify, as a guide to collect data, and not as an instrument of therapeutic technique. This book is not a handbook of child psychoanalysis but a guide to carry out the assessment of treatment.

Of course, we presuppose that we are speaking about the same theoretical and technical field: helping the young patient to free himself from some pathological issues, taking into account the processes of transference and counter-transference. Many other questions could be raised about the way theoretical and practical bases are implemented according to the cases, the psychoanalytical schools, the institutions and the practitioners themselves. References to psychoanalysis are necessary given that the purpose of the book is to demonstrate the value of psychoanalytically informed interventions.

Although some points could be discussed for example, the point about training of psychotherapists, we must not forget that each time we have to take into account a certain flexibility and the tact of the therapist in the process of evaluation, his competence and his capability are involved by the way the criteria of his training. Personally I have always pleaded for the need for every psychoanalytically oriented psychotherapist to have personal experience of an actual psychoanalysis. As a person having personally acquired such a psychoanalytic experience about himself, the therapist will be able to take advantage of that experience in treating his young patient. It is not only a question of competence, but also a question of personal capability. This capability is not only a question of know-how but is also a necessary precondition to having the possibility of passing this on to his young patient; something of his own sensitivity, of his own capability to associate. This is indeed a point of debate, but it must be stated even if the question of the therapeutic process is not directly dealt with in the empirical field of evaluation.

What is the difference between psychoanalytic psychotherapy and psychoanalysis? The question cannot be excluded by the reader. In spite of, and maybe due to, the reservations I have just given, that question is however an issue the authors are right not to tackle. All through the book the matter is psychoanalysis, even if the authors keep themselves out of the debate in a spirit of caution and reservation. There is no need to make this distinction in a field where it is a matter of knowing what the therapist is allowed by his psychoanalytic experience, to convey to his young patient. Through the question of evaluation, the book testifies to transmission and for that we must be grateful to all the authors who contribute to it.

INTRODUCTION

John Tsiantis

The chapters of this book constitute a selection of papers related to a challenge of today, namely, the field of research in psychoanalytic psychotherapy for children and adolescents.

It is well-known that empirical research on the outcome of psychodynamic child treatment has lagged behind other therapeutic approaches (Target, Slade, Cottrell, Fuggle & Fonagy, 2005). It is also known that changes achieved with psychotherapy are greater than those that emerge without treatment (Kazdin, 1996). Further refinement of these findings, however, requires more detailed studies of both outcome and process variables (Fonagy, 2003; Hibbs & Jensen, 2005). Similarly Fonagy et al. (2002), review critically the treatments for children and adolescents including research on psychodynamic- psychoanalytic psychotherapy, discussing the limitations of their review in detail. Finally they make a summary of their work which contain several assumption and attributes of which I will only mention a few: *the recognition of the multiple causations of childhood disorder (although different orientations may privilege different levels of such an analysis), the recognition that adequate assessment must include information concerning development and knowledge of the population of children showing similar problems (incidence, prevalence, biological factors, system parameters), reliance on a multi-method approach in assessment and treatment, commitment to the comprehensive evaluation of outcomes, the involvement of the family in the treatment, the recognition of the importance of both emotions and cognitions in both causation and treatment, the recognition of the need to develop operational rules (manuals) for the implementation of treatments, the use of techniques specific to client groups and to developmental stages (e.g. preschool, adolescence), a wish to explore the biological, psychological and interpersonal processes that generate change, the recognition of the need for measures of change across a number of domains and a concern with the wider social context of the families, including cultural factors (Fonagy, p. 402).*

A recent multicentre control outcome study on psychodynamic psychotherapy for child depression (Tsiantis et al., 2005; Trowell et al., 2007), indicates that the situation may be changing. Of equal importance, this study demonstrates that empirical methods can be applied effectively to the investigation of child psychodynamic treatment outcomes. On the other hand, numerous case studies involving narrative descriptions of therapy process have contributed to the evaluation of psychodynamic theory and treatment. However, empirical research on therapy with children is markedly limited relative to a substantial body of process research with adults (Shirk & Russel, 1998).

Moreover at the present time, in particular when psychoanalytic psychotherapy and psychoanalysis, especially in the public sector and in particular in work with children and adolescents is being scrutinized and questioned by governments, third-party insurance schemes, and researchers, it is important that we, the professionals who practice psychoanalytically informed therapies, should try to develop research methodologies in order to be able to monitor and evaluate the efficacy of our work.

The first chapter opens with a review of process and outcome psychotherapy in child, adult and parent-infant psychotherapy. The first 'systematic' review focused on effectiveness studies (Kennedy, 2004). This non meta-analytic systematic review categorized studies according to a design hierarchy for studies of effectiveness, i.e. with randomized controlled trials and quasi-randomized trials coming at the top of the design hierarchy, and critically appraised individual studies according to the quality of their design and methodology. The second review of child psychotherapy research (Kennedy & Midgley, 2007) looked more broadly at a wider range of psychoanalytically informed research, i.e. research regarding child psychotherapy process as well as outcome, measures and methods of assessment and parent-infant psychotherapy research. This chapter focuses on the clinical applications of psychoanalytic psychotherapy research with children and adolescents and draws from the findings of recent reviews.

Kennedy in his chapter reviews in a systematic way research on different clinical groups such as children who have experienced maltreatment or neglect, disruptive behavior disorders, personality disorders, emotional disorders, children with a Physical Illness, anorexia nervosa, autism and mixed diagnosis. The author reports a number of studies focused on children presenting in middle childhood with a range of difficulties rather than belonging to a particular diagnostic category.

He also reports on a series of studies regarding the outcome over the long-term such as the Anna Freud Centre long-term follow-up study (Shachter, 2004). This was a part of the Anna Freud Centre long term follow-up study and the outcome of child psychoanalysis which was also examined from the perspective of the patient (Midgley, 2003; Midgley, Target & Smith, 2006).

Kennedy concludes by posing several questions for clinicians and researchers, for example that there are significant benefits from longer more frequent treatments, but one randomized trial comparing treatments of different length found the briefest intervention to be most effective at four year follow up. Does this mean that long treatments are not always a helpful compared to briefer treatment? What are the implications for the patient and the clinician?

Moreover in the Review of Child Psychotherapy of Process and Outcome Research in Child and Adolescent and Parent-infant Psychotherapy: a thematic review (Eillis Kennedy & Midgley, 2007), the editors mention that the richness and diversity of the research challenges the assertion that there is a dearth of "evidence" in the field of research in child and adolescent psychoanalytic psychotherapy. Many of the findings however, seem to provoke further questions for researchers and clinicians alike. For example, particular treatments appear to work in different ways. Family therapy appears to have a highly effective initial impact on childhood depression while the effect of individual child psychotherapy appears to be slower yet possibly sustained.

They go on to mention that:

> "With regards to effectiveness research where the randomized trial is one of the most powerful methodological tools Chalmers caution: It is unclear what the future holds for randomized trial that address issues of no interest to industry but are of great importance to patients and practitioners. It cannot be assumed that the things that get studied in trials, or the way they are studied; necessary reflect the priorities of patients and professionals." (Chalmers, Rouding & Hoch, 2003, p.72).

In the field of General Medicine however, some reviews take a more balanced approach regarding the relative merits of RCT's and observational designs (Ioannidis, Haidich & Lau, 2001). They suggest that empirical studies comparing RCT and observation methodology find comparable treatment effects which criticize the "golden rule" that only RCT's give the accurate assessment of treatment efficacy. It seems that more studies that simultaneously use both approaches are needed in child psychotherapy and elsewhere.

In chapter two, Siv Boalt Boëthius aims to describe a case study which illustrates a strategy for the introduction of research activity into a clinically oriented staff group working with psychoanalytic psychotherapy. The objective is to enable the staff members to develop their clinical work through a systematic collection and analysis of clinical data. The idea is to conduct clinically based research on psychoanalytic psychotherapy directed at showing, for example, what kind of treatment is given to which patients and how the various treatments worked for different categories of patients. This approach can be described as empirical research based on clinical practice, theoretical assumptions regarding child development, and modern psychoanalytic theory. It involves a systematic collection of both quantitative and qualitative data and an analysis of these data aimed at illuminating the specified purposes of the clinical work. This chapter is particularly helpful for clinicians who work in a centre, where the two main tasks in hand have for a long time been psychoanalytic psychotherapeutic treatment and clinically oriented training programmes. If this centre had to embark on a third task, research, then various issues and questions should be taken into consideration in order to accomplish the necessary steps to bridge the three tasks described above. Some of these are: description of the clinical work, preparation for a change including surveying the literature on child psychotherapy, developing an overview of the clinical work of the institute as a whole, identifying staff attitudes and feelings about making research a part of their work, and categorizing facilitating and hindering factors according to the areas of concern.

The author stresses the importance of "*the integration of the different cultures represented by two of the main areas of work in this clinical centre—psychoanalytic psychotherapy and research which can be described as a process of containment of preconceptions regarding potential conflicts, which may threaten to destroy the possibilities for developing creativity both individually and collectively. To create a common integrating culture implies linking various parts of an organisation to each other, while taking into consideration the boundaries surrounding each of the work areas and the interactions between them, as well as the organisational space that encompasses the system as a whole*".

The integration of the different cultures represented by two of the main areas of work in this clinical centre, psychoanalytic psychotherapy and research, can be described as a process of containment of preconceptions regarding potential conflicts, which may threaten to destroy the possibilities for developing creativity both individually and collectively. To create a common, integrated culture implies linking various parts of an organisation to each other, while taking into consideration the boundaries surrounding each of the work areas and the interactions between them, as well as the organisational space that encompasses the system as a whole.

This paper describes very systematically, the steps that are needed to be undertaken by a clinic which is doing psychoanalytically oriented work in order to develop research activity in the same area. I believe that this is a very helpful guide for colleagues working in community child and adolescent mental health services, who wish to start research activities in the area of child and adolescent psychoanalytic psychotherapy.

In chapter three, Judith Trowell, Maria Rhode and Jackie Hall describe and discuss the use of a treatment manual which was used by trained therapists and supervisors for depression in late childhood and early adolescence, in a study that compared individual psychodynamic therapy and family therapy.

The manual starts with an introduction of adolescent depression and describes the psychodynamic framework for understanding depression in young people. It continues by describing the treatment steps to be followed by the therapist, discusses aspects like the intervention in crisis, coexisting marital and family conflicts, the transitions and most importantly, the termination of treatment. It also discusses the management of serious clinical situations, like suicidal young person's violence, substance abuse and self-harming behavior, giving an outline of treatment guidelines and which tasks are the therapists' during the therapeutic work.

The chapter ends by considering technical issues specific to brief work. It is also stated quite clearly in the paper that the manual does not train people how to do psychoanalytic psychotherapy and it is no substitute for a clinical training. Clinicians already trained who have had a personal therapy and are supervised, can use the manual. However the authors do not discuss issues regarding the adherence to the manual by the therapists in different centers.

This manual was written for use during the implementation of a Biomed European, multicentre, randomized, control trial which focused on childhood and early adolescent depression, 10–14 years, comparing focused individual psychodynamic therapy to parallel work with parents and system integrative family therapy. The trial was undertaken in London, Athens and Helsinki (Trowell et al., 2007; Tsiantis et al., 2005).

In chapter four, Gunnar Carlberg stresses that the point of departure is the lack of research in psychodynamic child psychotherapy. This is particularly true for qualitative research. In this chapter, the approach "focused systematic case studies" is presented. This approach implies that data from crucial, data-rich episodes in several child psychotherapies are collected by the same technique to make comparisons possible. Examples from these studies illustrate for example, "the nature of change" and different kinds of "turning points" in child psychotherapy. Results revealed a concordance between the different informants, the psychotherapist, the parental counselor, the supervisor, the child, and even the special educational teacher, regarding the identification of a change, although their opinion on when this change occurred was less clear. Focused systematic case studies turned out to be a fruitful approach for qualitative research. In this fourth chapter, emphasis is given on how it is possible to increase knowledge about processes through the analysis of psychotherapist's experiences of "turning points" in child psychotherapy. Three main questions were formulated concerning "the nature of change", "the content of change" and "factors underlying change". In total, data were collected from 116 psychotherapies, of which 14 were studied intensively. In order to illustrate this approach, data were presented from the findings of a pilot study as follows: 1) the main findings from the study by using vignettes from the therapy of a girl, 2) the nature of change, and 3) a case study based on interviews with different informants who shed light on the process of change in child psychotherapies by using a case example from one of his studies. It can be said that the study of focused systematic case studies turns out to be a creative approach in order to meet one of the aims of psychotherapy which is to create meaning by telling narratives. In this respect, contemporary child and adolescent psychoanalytic psychotherapy is informed by an extensive account of descriptive analysis of therapy process going back to Freud's story of "Little Hans" (Freud, 1909).

Carlberg concludes by emphasizing that therapists have different ways of organizing their experiences of change processes. The important issue is whether the core change processes could be targeted for empirical research work. However, one doubts if one's personal experience could be "measured".

In chapter five, an overview of the Heidelberg Study on the evaluation of psychodynamic psychotherapy for children and adolescents is given by Kronmüller et al. The study design is described and the instruments for the assessment of structural characteristics and the psychotherapeutic process developed and evaluated in the project are presented. In addition, the results regarding treatment outcome are reported. The primary aim of this chapter is to identify the efficacy of short-term psychodynamic psychotherapy in a Randomized Control Trial (RCT) as well to assess the effectiveness of long-term psychoanalysis with a naturalistic study design. The results demonstrate that both short-term psychodynamic psychotherapy and long-term psychoanalysis are highly effective treatments for children and adolescents with mental disorders.

This study is interesting in what it reports but as the authors mention, there are limitations with this study. Some of these are that there was a relatively small sample n = 71, of outpatient children and adolescents, the sample being heterogeneous and therefore not really allowing generalization from the results. It is also known that different disorders do not respond similarly well to short term psychotherapy or psychoanalysis. They also reported that adherence to the manual was not checked. Luborsky and Derubeis (1984) and Hibbs et al., (1997) discuss the usefulness as well as the limitations regarding the use of manuals on psychosocial treatment research.

However, this study is welcomed and has contributed to the field of research in psychoanalytic child and adolescent psychotherapy. The effort of the authors to develop instruments for assessing change in psychoanalytic psychotherapy is important as these instruments can be used and further refined in future studies. Moreover, another merit of the study is that it was implemented within ongoing work in a public child and adolescent mental health community service.

In chapter six, Marianne Leuzinger-Bohleber and Tamara Fischmann describe a study which was carried out in Frankfurt on 5000 kindergarten school children. The authors suggest that Attention-Deficit/Hyperactivity-Disorder (AD/HD) seen from a psychoanalytic perspective, always has to be understood as a product of complex, mostly unconscious interactions, idiosyncratic, biographical, relational, institutional, societal as well as neurophysiological and genetic factors.

The authors discuss in another paper (Leuzinger-Bohleber, Goeppel & Hau, in press) different AD/HD symptoms:

I. Children with a brain organic problem
II. Children with an early emotional neglect
III. AD/HD and trauma
IV. AD/HD and culture
V. AD/HD and extraordinarily talented children
VI. AD/HD and mourning or depression
VII. AD/HD; a compensation for growing up with a "dead mother" (André Green, 1986).

This paper is an excellent study contributing to the issue of children with AD/HD for further discussion in the area regarding etiology and treatment. See also for example, the paper on Attention-Deficit Hyperactivity Disorder pp. 193–226 by Fonagy et al., 2002.

Several treatments were offered to children suffering from AD/HD within the framework of the Frankfurt Prevention study. The authors suggest that psychoanalysis with its unique conceptualizations aimed at understanding psychic realities as products of such complex intertwining of unconscious and reality factors, taking into account biological as well as societal roots of human behavior, could be regarded as one of the best available approaches nowadays capable of dealing theoretically and therapeutically with children suffering from AD/HD.

In chapter seven, Stephen R. Shirk & Rebecca A. Burwell present research issues on therapeutic processes in psychodynamic psychotherapy with children and adolescents. They suggest that the primary aim is to identify core change processes in psychodynamic child therapy that could be targeted for empirical investigation. Three sets of processes are identified as foci for investigation: interpretive interventions, facilitation of reflective function, and the therapeutic alliance. Three researchable hypotheses are considered. The first is that outcome in child psychodynamic therapy should be associated with the interpretive activity of the therapist. The second is that changes in the range and depth of children's symbolic play in therapy should predict better outcomes. Thirdly, the quality of the therapeutic alliance should be associated with the child's engagement in symbolic play or production of symbolic materials such as narrative accounts of personal experiences. Emerging research on play, reflective function, interpretation, and the therapeutic alliance are examined in relation to these hypotheses.

Stephen R. Shirk & Rebecca A. Burwells' work is innovative in that it tries to make proposals for integrating psychodynamic-psychoanalytic thinking and empirical work, something which is very much needed. This research will undoubtedly help clinicians and researchers to answer the question *"Does this treatment work as well as what makes it work?"*

In the last chapter, Euthymia Hibbs indicates that ethical principles in research with children and adolescents became more urgent in the last couple of decades because of the advances in treatment and research coupled with advances in science and technology.

In this chapter the author addresses ethical issues that pertain to the following important areas: a) the involvement of well trained competent therapists in research with young patients, b) the presentation of a patient consent/assent form written in a language that is easily understood by the research participant, and its effect on the research design, c) the protection of the confidentiality of research participants, especially when using computer technology, and when sharing information with parents and the public, d) the examination of the effects of incentives (remuneration) on participation, on the research subjects, and the threats to research design, and finally e) the use of different control groups and their effect on control patients and the research design. In conclusion, this chapter addresses the challenges of carrying out psychosocial research in an ethical manner, while preserving good research design, and treating subjects with honesty and fairness.

This contribution by Euthymia Hibbs is a welcome ending to this book as it raises issues and concerns relevant to maintaining a balance between two aims; protecting child and adolescent research participants and their families from harm and promoting opportunities for advancement of knowledge through scientific endeavors. This is particularly relevant in the field of research on psychoanalytic psychotherapy for children and adolescents.

We hope that this book will be helpful and that it is a small contribution to the gradually growing field regarding the research of child and adolescent psychoanalytic psychotherapy, psychoanalysis for clinicians on child and adolescent psychoanalytic psychotherapy in addition to researchers in the field.

References

Chalmers, I., Rounding, G. & Lock (2003). Descriptive survey of non-commercial randomised controlled trials in the United Kingdom 1980–2002. *British Medical Journal, 327*: 1017.

Fonagy, P. (2003). The research agenda: The vital need for empirical research in child psychotherapy. *Journal of Child Psychotherapy, 29* (2): 129–136.

Fonagy, P. & Moran, G.S. (1990). Studies of the efficacy of child psychoanalysis. *Journal of Consulting & Clinical Psychology, 58* (6): 684–695.

Fonagy, P., Target, M., Cottrell, D., Phillips, J. & Kurtz, Z. (Eds.) (2002). *What Works for Whom? A Critical Review of Treatments for Children and Adolescents*. New York: Guilford Publications.

Fonagy, P., Gerber, A., Higgitt, A. & Bateman, A. (2002). Anna Freud Centre studies 4: The comparison of intensive (5 times weekly), and non-intensive (once weekly), treatment of young adults (AFC4). In: P. Fonagy (Ed.), *An Open Door Review of Outcome Studies in Psychoanalysis* (2nd ed.), (pp. 96–97). London: International Psychoanalytical Association.

Freud, S. (1909). Analysis of a phobia in a five year old boy. In: J. Strachey (Ed.), *The Standard Edition of the Complete Psychological Works of Sigmund Freud, Vol. 10*, (pp. 1–147). London: Hogarth Press.

Green, A. (1986). The dead mother, in *On Private madness* (pp. 222–253). London: The Hogarth Press.

Hibbs, E.D. & Jensen, P. (Eds.) (2005). *Psychosocial Treatments for Children and Adolescent Disorders. Empirically Based Strategies for Clinical Practice* (2nd ed.). Washington DC: American Psychological Association.

Hibbs, E.D., Clarke, G., Hechtman, L., Abikoff, H., Greenhill, L. & Jensen, P. (1997). Development for the treatment of child and adolescent disorders. *Psychopharmacology Bulletin*, 33(4).

Ioannidis, J.P., Haidich, A.B. & Lau, J. (2001). Any causalities in the clash of randomized and observational evidence? *British Medical Journal*, 322: 879–880.

Kazdin, A. (1996). Developing effective treatments for children and adolescents. In: E.D. Hibbs & P. Jensen (Eds.), *Child and Adolescent Disorders. Empirically Based strategies for Clinical Practice* (pp. 9–18). American Psychological Association.

Kennedy, E. (Ed.) (2004). *Child and Adolescent Psychotherapy: A Systematic Review of Psychoanalytic Approaches*. London: North Central London Strategic Health Authority.

Kennedy, E. & Midgley, N. (Eds.) (2007). *Process and Outcome Research in Child, Adolescent and Parent- Infant Psychotherapy: A Thematic Review*. London: NHS London.

Leuzinger-Bohleber M. & Pfeifer R. (2002). Remembering a depressive primary object? Psychoanalysis and Embodied Cognitive Science: A dialogue on memory. *International Journal of Psychoanalysis*, *83*: 3–33.

Leuzinger- Bohleber, Goeppel & Hau, in press.

Luborsky, L. & Derubeis, R.J. (1984). The use of Psychotherapy Treatment Manuals: A Small Revolution in Psychotherapy Research Styles. *Clinical Psychology Review*, 4: 5–14.

Midgley, N. (2003). *Memories of Therapy: A Qualitative Study of Retrospective Accounts of Child Psychoanalysis*. Unpublished Psych. D. thesis, University College London.

Midgley, N., Target, M. & Smith, J.A. (2006). The outcome of child psychoanalysis from the patient's point of view: a qualitative analysis of a long-term follow-up study. *Psychology and Psychotherapy: Theory, Practice, Research*, *79*: 257–269.

Schachter, A. (2004). *The Adult Outcome of Child Psychoanalysis: A Long-term Follow-up Study.* Unpublished PhD thesis, University College London.

Shirk, S.R. & Russell, R.L. (1998). Process issues in child psychotherapy. In: A. Bellack & M. Hersen (Eds.), *Comprehensive Clinical Psychology, (Vol. 15),* (pp. 57–82). Oxford: Pergamon.

Target, M., Fonagy, P., Slade, A.,Cottrell, D. & Fuggle, P. (2005). Psychosocial therapies with children. In: G. Gabbard, J.S. Beck & J. Holmes (Eds.), *Concise Oxford Textbook of Psychotherapy* (pp. 341–352). Oxford, U.K.: Oxford University Press.

Trowell, J., Joffe, I., Campbell, J., Clemente, C., Almqvist, F., Soininen, M., Koskenranta-Aalto, U., Weintraub, S., Kolaitis, G., Tomaras, V., Anastasopoulos, D., Grayson K., Barnes, J. & Tsiantis, J. (2007). Childhood depression: a place for psychotherapy. An outcome study comparing individual Psychodynamic Psychotherapy and Family Therapy. *European Child and Adolescent Psychiatry, 16.*

Tsiantis, J., Kolvin, I., Anastasopoulos, Trowell. J., Tomaras, V., Miles, G., Papadopoulos, R., Soininen, M., Bostrom, C. & Almqvist, F. (2005). Psychotherapy for early adolescent depression: A comparison of two psychotherapeutic interventions in three European countries. In E.D. Hibbs & P.S. Jensen (Eds.), *Psychosocial Treatments for Child and Adolescent Disorders: Empirically Based Strategies for Clinical Practice* (2nd Ed.). American Psychological Association: Washington DC.

CHAPTER ONE

Child and adolescent psychotherapy research: Clinical applications

Eilis Kennedy

There have been two recent reviews of psychoanalytic psychotherapy research with children and adolescents (Kennedy & Midgley, 2007; Kennedy, 2004). The first "systematic" review focused on effectiveness studies (Kennedy, 2004). This non meta-analytic, systematic review, categorized studies according to a design hierarchy for studies of effectiveness, i.e. with randomized controlled trials and quasi-randomized trials coming at the top of the design hierarchy, and critically appraised individual studies according to the quality of their design and methodology. In total, 32 studies were identified of which five were randomized trials and four were quasi-randomized trials. While many of the studies were hampered by limitations in their design, notably small sample size, the overall proportion of RCTs at 15.6%, 34.3% if quasi-randomized studies are included, was relatively high and compares favourably with the proportion of studies using a randomized design when the full range of child mental interventions are examined (7.4%; Fonagy, Target, Cottrell, Philips & Kurtz, 2002). Other strengths of the research included a commitment to involving clinical samples and to long term follow up.

The second review of child psychotherapy research (Kennedy & Midgley, 2007) looked more broadly at a wider range of psychoanalytically informed research, i.e. research regarding child psychotherapy process as well as outcome, measures and methods of assessment and parent-infant psychotherapy research. This chapter will focus on the clinical applications of psychoanalytic psychotherapy research with children and adolescents and will draw from the findings of these recent reviews.

Research with children and young people in different clinical groups

Children who have experienced maltreatment or neglect

This is an area that child psychotherapy researchers have particularly focused on. Some research projects have examined the efficacy of child psychotherapy for children within the care system (Lush, Boston & Grainger, 1991; Boston & Lush, 1993), or for girls who have experienced sexual abuse (Trowell et al., 2002). In addition there is a substantial body of work looking at the impact of abuse on children's development, compared with children who have not had these experiences. This research has also tracked changes in children's development over time in response to the impact of adoptive placements (Hodges & Steele, 2000; Hodges, Steele, Hillman, Henderson & Kaniuk, 2003).

The Tavistock study of children in the care system (Lush, Boston & Grainger, 1991; Boston & Lush, 1993) was originally intended as a pilot study to explore how children in this group would respond to individual psychotherapy as well as looking at the accuracy of therapists' predictions regarding outcome. While the lack of randomisation limits the conclusions that can be made regarding therapeutic efficacy, interesting information is nonetheless generated regarding the outcome of therapy and therapists views on this.

The researchers devised two evaluation forms, one completed following the initial assessment, the other at the end of treatment. The forms focused on personality and emotional development as well as symptomatic improvement and changes in the child's external situation and relationships. Beneficial effects were found to concur broadly with the therapists' predictions of likely progress in therapy. Not surprisingly, there was a tendency for good progress to be related to more stable current placements and good external support of therapy. As part of this study, a more in-depth single case experimental study was undertaken with a boy age ten, who had been taken into care at the age of nine months, but who was presenting with significant difficulty at the time of referral. He had weekly psychotherapy for three years. A range of standardized measures from multiple perspectives were used which recorded his improvement over the four year follow-up period (Lush, Boston, Morgan & Kolvin, 1998).

Trowell et al.'s (2002) intervention study compared the outcome of treatment for girls aged 6–14, who had been sexually abused. Focused, individual, psychodynamic psychotherapy for up to 30 sessions was compared with up to 18 sessions of psycho-educational group psychotherapy. In addition, both groups had parent/carer work. The girls were randomized to one or other treatment and the treatments were manualised. The study revealed the girls to be presenting with high rates of psychiatric disturbance but, there was some amelioration in this for both groups following treatment. Post traumatic stress disorder was most common diagnosis (73%), followed by major depressive disorder (57%) and separation anxiety disorder (58%). Individual psychoanalytic psychotherapy appears to have had a preferential impact on the PTSD scale dimensions of re-experience of traumatic event and persistent avoidance of stimuli (Orvaschel, 1989) compared to group treatment. Generalized anxiety disorder proved the most liable to remit while depressive disorder and separation anxiety disorder were less likely to decrease, although 2/3 of those with depressive disorders and half those with separation anxiety disorders no longer had these one year on.

The numbers in this study were smaller than the study authors had initially planned, 35 received individual therapy and 36 group therapy and the level of abuse the girls experienced high e.g. over 30% had been exposed to multiple perpetrators. This, combined with the fact that two active treatments of a good standard were being compared, ethical approval was declined for a no treatment control group, makes it unsurprising that it was difficult to establish clear differences in outcome between the two groups. Indeed the authors quote Kazdin's observation that alternative models of active therapy tend to be equally effective (Kazdin, 2000).

Another substantial body of work undertaken by Hodges et al. (2004) explores the impact of maltreatment and neglect on children's development. The Story Stem Assessment Profile, formerly known as the "Little Pig" stems, was specifically devised to explore the inner representational world of children age 4–8 who have been subjected to maltreatment or neglect (Hodges, 1990). The Story Stem Assessment Profile battery was developed from the MacArthur Story Stem Battery with the addition of five new stems introduced to look at issues around maltreatment (Hodges, Hillman, Steele & Henderson, 2004).

Hodges and colleagues have looked at the effects of abuse on children's representations as well as changes in these representations following adoptive placement (Hodges, Steele Hillman, Henderson & Kaniuk, 2003). It is hypothesized that children's representations are built up over time in response to expectable interactions with others. The narrative method therefore aims to elicit generic representations of child-parent relationships, because these are, arguably, the most likely to affect later relationships (Hodges & Steele, 2000). The child's play narrative is viewed as an indicator, not so much of reality, but of how "the child reflects upon reality" (Hodges & Steele, 2000, p. 435). The story stem assessments are videotaped, transcribed and rated for the presence or absence of thirty two themes, each theme rated on a three point scale (Hodges, Hillman, Steele & Henderson, 2004). Those trained in the method consistently achieve good levels of reliability.

One of the first studies using the Story Stem Assessment Profile (Hodges & Steele, 2000) compared the narrative assessments of four distinct groups of children: children who had been removed from abusive settings some time earlier and placed in permanent adoptive families (the Coram group), a group of children removed from families in which they had been abused and placed in foster or residential care (the clinical group), and two comparison groups, one comprising of relatively disadvantaged children (matched comparison group) the other a group of predominantly middle class, first born children from the London Parent Child Project (LPCP group). Differences in narrative themes were found between the groups, for instance themes of realistic or pleasurable domestic life were mostly found in the LPCP children and least in the "clinical group". The clinical group more often depicted themes such as: a child being injured or dead, adults as unaware of children's needs or distress, lack of acknowledgement of distress and shifts in a character from being "bad" to "good" or vice versa.

Subsequent research using the Story Stem Assessment Profile with maltreated adopted children (Hodges, Steele Hillman, Henderson & Kaniuk, 2003) looked at changes in children's behaviour and adjustment in relation to numerous variables, including the adoptive parents' attachment organization and the child's maltreatment history over the first two years of a placement. A group of "late placed", maltreated, adopted children was compared with children adopted "early" in infancy. Important differences were identified between the two groups when the children's narrative assessments were compared. For example, those placed for adoption later in childhood were much more likely than the infancy adopted group to try and avoid the story task but this decreased markedly over the first year of the adoptive placement. The late-placed group also showed significantly higher levels of catastrophic fantasy, bizarre-atypical responses and extreme aggression compared with the infancy group which was largely maintained after a year in placement. Compared to the infancy placed children, the late placed children were less likely to show adults helping children and being affectionate and more likely to show adults as aggressive, rejecting and unaware of their needs. At one year changes could be identified in relation to parents helping children although there was little change in terms of parents being represented as affectionate or aggressive. Hodges and colleagues conclusion is that changes in the children's representations over time indicate not erosion but competition: not so much that earlier, negative internal working models fade away, but rather that alternative, competing ones get developed and may even become dominant (Hodges & Steele, 2000). The job of adopters could be seen as the active disconfirmation of existing negative models and building up of competing ones (Hodges & Steele, 2000).

Other interesting findings from this research included the influence of the adoptive parent's attachment style on children's story stem responses (Steele, 2006; Steele, Hodges, Kaniuk, Hillman & Henderson, 2003). As early as three months into an adoptive placement, themes of "aggressiveness" in the children's story stems were significantly more likely to appear in the story completions of children adopted by mothers classified as "insecure" on the Adult

Attachment Interview as opposed to those classified as "secure". Significant differences in themes were also identified in the children's story completions in mothers classified as unresolved with respect to past trauma. The findings suggest that unresolved mourning in a parent may exacerbate the emotional worries of a recently adopted child. Overall, there was a tendency for the children adopted by mothers in this category to appear less able to use an organized strategy to deal with conflict depicted in the story. The researchers note that it is surprising, given the adverse early histories of the children, that so soon after being placed in a new environment, the influence upon the child of the adopter's state of mind with regard to attachment can be discerned.

Further work in this area includes research on the experience of siblings in foster care (Hindle, 2000) and applications of child psychotherapy to work with children in temporary foster care (Philps, 2003).

Disruptive behaviour disorders

The large Anna Freud Centre retrospective case note study ($n = 763$), examined differences in outcome according to diagnostic category (Fonagy & Target, 1996). In general, children with a diagnosis of disruptive disorder were harder to treat, particularly if the diagnosis was of conduct disorder rather than oppositional defiant disorder (Fonagy & Target, 1994) and in comparison, those diagnosed with emotional disorders had a better outcome ($p < 0.0001$). Children with disruptive disorders were difficult to maintain in treatment and more liable to drop out. This prognosis improved for younger children and those in intensive treatment. Indeed, when those children treated intensively for three years were compared, the differences in outcome between those diagnosed with disruptive disorder and those diagnosed with emotional disorder were no longer significant (Fonagy & Target, 1994). Diagnostic variables that predicted improvement in the disruptive disorders group included the presence of an anxiety disorder, absence of co-morbidity and school reported problems. However, the retrospective nature of these studies limits the confidence that can be placed in these findings.

Anderson researched children presenting to Child and Adolescent Mental Health Services with risk taking and dangerous behaviour. Using grounded theory methodology (Glaser & Strauss, 1967), she identified three situations in which such behaviour appears to occur, described as "no haven". "illusory haven" and "perilous haven" (Anderson, 2001, 2004). Each category seems to have a different clinical prognosis and to benefit from particular intervention strategies.

A small (n = 26) German study (Winkelmann et al., 2005) compared children with behavioural disorders treated with psychodynamic short-term psychotherapy (PSTP) with a waiting list control. 31% of the children in the treatment group showed clinically significant improvement compared with 8% of those in the control group.

Personality disorder

An interesting study (Gerber, 2004; Fonagy, Gerber, Higgitt & Bateman, 2002), looks at the efficacy of psychoanalytic psychotherapy as a treatment for young adults with depression, anxiety and personality disorders (mainly cluster B). This quasi-randomized study examined 25 young adults aged 18–24, sequentially assigned to psychoanalysis (n = 14) or psychodynamic psychotherapy (n = 11). The process of psychotherapy was reported using a novel 899 item questionnaire, the Young Adult Weekly Rating Scale. Patients were assessed by an independent psychiatrist at intake, termination and at eighteen month intervals after intake with the Adult Attachment Interview (Main & Goldwyn, 1998) and a range of other symptomatic and diagnostic measures. Over the course of treatment, 6 months to 8 years long, 12 of 19 patients with adequate data, improved symptomatically on an aggregate measure. Ten of the 12 improvers were in the psychoanalysis group, suggesting that this is a more effective treatment in this population.

Fascinatingly, with respect to the Adult Attachment Interview (AAI), the results showed a high proportion of secure classifications at initial assessment, 54%, and in successful treatments, a move towards a preoccupied-entangled attachment pattern which began to resolve by termination. Such changes have not been reported before and challenge the assumption that attachment security is a proxy for therapeutic improvement. Gerber (2004) proposes that in patients with severe character pathology who at first appear to be secure, the transition to a preoccupied-entangled state may be necessary, but not sufficient, for their successful treatment. At or beyond termination of the treatment, a transition back to a secure classification might be expected as evidence of their structural change. Gerber is careful to point out that this was a quasi-randomized study with a small sample size and that many potential confounding variables, such as fewer Axis II subjects in the psychoanalysis group, may explain the results. Further research using the AAI at similar time points during the course of therapy is recommended in a larger sample.

With regard to personality dysfunction in children, a study by Weise and Turber (2004) notes that while narcissistic pathology is a major focus in the adult psychiatric literature, particularly among psychoanalytic clinicians, narcissistic pathology in children has received less attention. They set out to look at correlations between the clinical assessment of narcissistic personality disorder in children and adolescents and underlying self and object relationships. Support for the clinical literature, which describes these children as lacking in empathy or struggling with self esteem regulation and in poor control of their impulses or aggression, was found. Additionally, a tendency to have a vulnerable sense of identity and to be preoccupied with seeking out and developing relationships with others was noted to differentiate these children from peers with similar behavioural and diagnostic profiles.

Suicide and self-harm

A study by Wright and colleagues investigated attachment in suicidal adolescents and explored the phenomenology of different presentations of suicide from a psychodynamic as well as attachment theory perspective (Wright, Briggs & Behringer, 2005). An as yet unpublished study by Briggs and colleagues develops these themes further by identifying risks and protective factors in the "internal worlds" of female adolescents at risk of suicide (Briggs, Grayson & McLean, manuscript in preparation). They set out to look beyond broad attachment categories to focus in more detail on the adolescent's state of mind and patterns of relatedness with respect to suicide.

Emotional disorders

The large Anna Freud Centre study (Fonagy & Target, 1996), identified that when children were grouped according to diagnostic category, in general those children diagnosed with emotional disorders fared better ($p < 0.0001$). Children with emotional disorders proved amenable to psychoanalytic treatment with the vast majority showing a favourable response (Target & Fonagy, 1994). Children within this category designated as being "severely disturbed", were substantially more likely to improve if in intensive treatment (78.7% vs. 26.1%).

These findings indicating a better response for emotional or "internalising" problems are reflected in other studies. A community based audit (Baruch, Fearon & Gerber, 1998; Baruch, 1995) of psychoanalytic treatment for adolescents and young adults presenting with multiple severe difficulties, median number of ICD-10 diagnosis 3, median score for psychosocial stress 4, severe, showed that "internalising" problems were more responsive to treatment. "Externalising" problems were more difficult to treat although the likelihood of improvement increased if the externalising problems were associated with internalising/emotional problems or if the individual was in more frequent treatment.

An Italian quasi-randomized trial (Muratori et al., 2002) of structured-focused psychodynamic psychotherapy (11 sessions) for children age 6–11 years with emotional disorders illustrated that internalising problems were particularly responsive to treatment although externalizing problems also improved. The outcome was better for those children with 'pure' emotional disorders (ICD-10) as opposed to 'mixed' emotional disorders (ICD-10).

A follow up to this study using a larger sample size revealed further interesting findings (Muratori, Picchi, Bruni, Patarnello & Romagnoli, 2003). While both the experimental treatment group and the control group improved on measures of global functioning as assessed by the C-GAS (Shaffer et al., 1983), in the first six months only the experimental group showed evidence of a shift to a non-clinical range maintained at two year follow-up (the researchers hypothesise that the initial therapeutic improvement might be attributable to the assessment that the control group also received). On the other outcome measure used, the CBCL, (Achenbach & Edelbrock, 1983) the researchers note evidence of a "sleeper" effect. No differences between the groups were noted in the first 6 months but at the two year follow up significant changes, including a move into the 'non-clinical' range for internalizing and total problems scales, were noted in the group that received psychodynamic psychotherapy. While internalizing problems improved, so did externalizing problems (ES 0.61 and 0.59, respectively). The improvement in externalizing problems had not been expected. The researchers speculate that the level of clinical disturbance in this sample largely comprised of "intact" Italian families of "middle" socioeconomic status with lower than average mean scores on the CBCL, was such that a short term focused treatment was able to effect change.

A randomized trial in an Indian school setting (Sinha & Kapur, 1999) selected young people who were identified as having emotional problems on the GHQ and who scored high on the internalizing scale and low on the externalizing scale of the YSR. Significant improvements were seen with treatment, ten sessions of Psychodynamic Orientated Supportive Therapy, in this sample which had high levels of internalizing problems. A high percentage, >90%, showed clinically significant improvements in almost all areas of functioning. There was a significant improvement in internalizing problems, adjustment and interpersonal confidence.

Depression

A multi-centre randomized trial by Trowell et al., focused on childhood and early adolescent depression with children and young people aged 10–14 years, comparing focused individual psychodynamic therapy, FIPP which included parallel parent work to systems integrative family therapy, SIFT (Trowell et al., 2007). The trial was undertaken in London, Athens and Helsinki. The researchers planed the study on the basis of preliminary evidence that psychodynamic psychotherapy might be an effective treatment for depressed children and young adolescents (Wrate, 1995; Trowell, Kolvin, Weeramanthri, Berelowitz & Leitch, 1998) as well as the awareness of the importance of family and contextual factors in the aetiology of depression (Tsiantis et al., 2005). In comparing the two treatments, it was hypothesized that individual therapy (FIPP) and family therapy (SIFT) would lead to different responses and outcomes in the participants. Seventy one children were recruited. All of those included met the criteria for major depressive disorder (MDD) and/or dysthymia and were assessed using the Kiddie-SADS (Kaufman et al., 1997) and the Child Depression Inventory (Kovacs, 1992). Treatment was conducted over a nine month period and consisted of eight to fourteen, 90 minute sessions of Family Therapy (mean = 11) or sixteen to thirty, 50 minute sessions of Individual Therapy (mean = 24.7) plus individual parent sessions, one per two sessions of child's therapy, by a separate case worker. There were between 4 and 6 individual therapists and 4 and 6 family therapists in each of the three centres.

Assessments took place prior to treatment, at the end of therapy and at a six month follow up. The mean age of the participants was 12 years and almost two thirds (62%) were male. Just under half, 44%, had a history of maternal psychiatric illness.

At the end of treatment, significant reductions in disorder rates were seen for both groups (Trowell et al., 2007). A total of 74.3% of cases were no longer clinically depressed following Individual Psychotherapy and 75.7% of cases were no longer clinically depressed following Family Therapy. There was also an overall reduction in comorbid conditions across the study. The changes in both treatment groups were persistent and there was ongoing improvement. At follow up six months after treatment had ended, 100% of cases in the Individual Therapy group, and 81% of cases in the Family Therapy group were no longer clinically depressed.

Individual therapy was found to have been effective in cases of Major Depressive Disorder, Dysthymia and "double depression". There were no relapses in the six months following treatment end and in addition, all cases of depression were resolved by follow up, suggestive of a "sleeper effect", i.e. an ongoing response to therapy following completion.

In the family therapy group there were also no relapses in the six months following treatment end and there was further improvement over the follow up period. While response rates appear to have been 20% greater in the Individual Therapy group compared to Family Therapy at follow up, this was influenced by the inclusion of 4 cases lost to follow up in the Family Therapy group, who were all considered in the analysis as unsuccessfully treated cases.

While the final outcome appears to have been similar, a different pattern of response to treatment was noted in the two groups. Family work appeared to have a highly effective initial impact whereas the response to individual work was slower but more sustained. On the Moods and Feelings questionnaire for example (Angold, Costello, Pickles, Winder & Silver, 1987), the family therapy group had a lower score at end of therapy despite having had a higher score than individual therapy at baseline. These differences disappeared at follow up. By follow up many of the family therapy trajectories seemed to have plateaued, while the individual group trajectories suggest the possibility of further improvement.

The results of the study suggest that both individual therapy and family therapy may be more effective in the treatment of depression in this age group than other forms of treatment (Trowell et al., 2007).

A small study by Horn et al., (2005) in Heidelberg looked at the efficacy of psychodynamic short-term psychotherapy (PSTP) for the treatment of depression in children and adolescents compared to a waiting-list control. Twenty children and adolescents fulfilling diagnosis of major depression or dysthymia were included in the research. The treatment group received 25 sessions of psychodynamic psychotherapy. In contrast to the treatment group where 20% of the children showed clinically significant and reliable improvement, no child in the waiting-list control group met this criterion.

Anxiety

Another small study (n = 26) by the Heidelberg group compared psychodynamic short term psychotherapy (PTSP) with a waiting list control (Kronmüller et al., 2005). Whereas 62% of the patients in the treatment group showed clinically significant and reliable improvement at the end of therapy, this was the case for only 8% of the subjects in the waiting list condition.

Children with a physical illness

Moran and colleagues undertook a series of studies looking at psychoanalytic psychotherapy as a means of helping young people with poorly controlled diabetes (Moran & Fonagy, 1987; Moran, Fonagy, Kurtz, Bolton & Brook, 1991; Fonagy & Moran, 1990).

A quasi-randomized study, compared children with unstable, insulin dependent diabetes who received psychoanalytic psychotherapy 3 to 5 times a week for a mean period of 15 weeks with a group of children who had unstable diabetes and who were in receipt of routine psychological input but did not receive individual psychotherapy over this period. The two groups were comparable on most demographic and clinical variables. There were three children in the experimental group with growth failure (height velocity below the third centile), 73% of the experimental group and 63% of the control group having a psychiatric disorder.

At the end of treatment a significant improvement in diabetic control was noted in the experimental compared to control group. This improvement was maintained at one year follow up. All but one subject in the experimental group showed a reduction in glycosylated haemoglobin, a reduction in glycosylated haemoglobin represents good diabetic control, over the course of treatment, whereas only four out of eleven in the control group showed an improvement. At one year follow up nine of the experimental group patients remained below their preadmission average HbA1c levels (glycosylated haemoglobin) in contrast to three of those in the comparison group. Of clinical relevance was the reduction of HbA1c levels to within the "acceptable" range for diabetes in six of the experimental group, whereas none of the comparison group showed such an improvement. Four from the experimental group and eight from the comparison group were readmitted in the year after discharge (Moran et al., 1991).

What makes this study particularly interesting is the researchers stated scepticism about the capacity of conventional psychological outcome measures to capture the kind of change they were looking for, so for this reason, the primary outcome measures selected were physical and related to mainly to the children's diabetic control. As part of this study, three children with diabetes and growth retardation were studied, using a single case experimental design methodology. In all three cases there were gains in height over the predicted height following psychotherapeutic treatment (Fonagy & Moran, 1990).

In a similar vein, another study explored the psychological impact of liver transplantation on children's inner worlds using a psychoanalytic assessment method (Gritti et al., 2001). Eighteen children who had received a liver transplant were compared with an age and gender matched control group.

Anorexia nervosa

Two studies have looked at the effectiveness of psychodynamic psychotherapeutic treatment for Anorexia Nervosa.

One randomized controlled trial (Robin et al., 1999; Robin, Siegel & Moye, 1995) compared Behavioural Family Systems Therapy (BFST) with Ego Orientated Individual Therapy (EOIT) for children aged twelve to nineteen. Both treatments were shown to be effective in the treatment of anorexia. The BFST group showed faster change on some weight measures but more cases from this group required hospitalization. In both groups there were improvements in measures of observed family conflict, illustrating the authors conclude, that family therapy is not necessary in order to bring about a change in parent child interactions as in the EOIT group the adolescents were seen individually and the parents in parallel.

Another further small, non-randomized study (Vilsvik & Vaglum, 1989) looked at the long-term follow up in a group of adolescents who had received individual psychodynamic therapy for Anorexia.

Autism

An ongoing research study is currently assessing the impact of psychoanalytic child psychotherapy for children with autism and their families (Reid, Alvarez & Lee, 2001). The researchers have developed a specialized psychotherapeutic technique that takes into account the particular developmental difficulties of this group of children (Alvarez & Reid, 1999). One component of this approach is to endeavour to work with the intact "non-autistic" parts of the child's personality and to appreciate the individual differences and personal motivation of the children. Close attention is also paid to the impact on families of living with a child with such a profound level of disability. The researchers predict that children and families receiving an extended psychotherapeutic assessment over 6–12 months will show developmental change of a nature and degree significantly different from a control group who do not receive such input. The study is ongoing but preliminary results appear to support this hypothesis.

A single-case study by Alvarez and Lee (2004) aimed to identify early forms of interpersonal relatedness in a 4 year old child with autism and to examine changes in this over a three year period while the child was in psychotherapy. The child was severely autistic, scoring 38.0 on the Childhood Autism Rating Scale (CARS, Schopler, Reichler & Rennedr, 1986). His mother was interviewed using the Autism Diagnostic Interview (ADI-R, Lord, Storoschuk, Rutter

& Pickles, 1993) which confirmed and detailed further the child's impairment in the areas of reciprocal social interaction and communication and repetitive, stereotyped behaviours. The child received psychotherapy three times a week over 42 months and all of these sessions were videotaped. Ratings were made from videotapes twice yearly for the three years of treatment.

Over the course of treatment, the clinical observations demonstrated an improvement in the child's capacity to engage in more developed forms of dyadic relating. In addition there was a reduction in the child's level of excitement and agitation, an increased capacity to maintain attention and evidence of an emerging "personality". The formal ratings demonstrated not just that components of dyadic relatedness could be reliably measured, but that these forms changed over time. There was however, no conclusive evidence for change in the level of triadic relating, a triadic episode implying that the child "understands" that the other person holds in mind an attitude towards the shared item i.e. person-person-object, forms of relating that serve to integrate a common world between two individuals.

An ongoing study by Rhode and colleagues looks at the impact of therapeutic infant observation on children identified as having difficulties as assessed by the Checklist for Autism in Toddlers or CHAT (Baron-Cohen et al., 1996), (Rhode, in press).

Obsessive compulsive disorder

A small Israeli study, showed improvements in young people with OCD treated with psychotherapy who had previously failed to comply with behavioural treatment (Apter, Bernhout & Tyano, 1984). The small study size and non randomized design, limits the conclusions that can be drawn.

Children with learning difficulties

A study by Heinicke & Ramsay Klee (1986) looked at boys aged 7–10 years referred with reading retardation and associated emotional disturbance. The children were given psychoanalytic psychotherapy over a period of two years. All of the children improved with treatment but those seen more frequently, four times a week for one or two years, improved most, particularly with regard to self esteem, flexible adaptation, capacity for forming and maintaining relationships, frustration tolerance and ability to work. A smaller pilot study by the same group had similar findings (Heinicke, 1965). One non-controlled study focused on a small sample of very young children, mean age 3 yrs and 8 months, with developmental delay, oppositional defiant disorder or in some cases pervasive developmental disorder and showed gains in I.Q level following psychoanalytically based treatments (Zelman, Samuels & Abrams, 1985).

Mixed diagnoses

A number of studies have focused on children presenting in middle childhood with a range of difficulties rather than belonging to a particular diagnostic category.

One randomized trial (Smyrios & Kirby, 1993) looked at children age 5–9 with "disturbances of emotion specific to childhood" (WHO, 1978), who had sought assistance from the Child & Family centre where the study was based. Quite stringent exclusion criteria were applied i.e. exclusion of single parent families, those with a history of mental illness and children with a previous history, suggesting that the families involved in the study were a less disadvantaged group. This study randomized participants to three groups of psychoanalytically informed family and individual treatment of different lengths; time limited, time unlimited and a minimal contact control. All three groups did well on a variety of outcome measures at four year follow up, although the group seen least did rather better.

The researchers speculate that the four session "minimal contact control" group may have proved most effective because the families own capacities for coping and resilience had been harnessed.

A further study by Szapocznik et al. (1989) looked at Hispanic boys age 6–12 years presenting with a range of diagnoses, e.g. 32% ODD, 30% anxiety disorder, 16% conduct disorder. The participants in this study were recruited through a media campaign and school counsellors rather than being clinically referred. The inclusion criteria were quite stringent; those not living in a two parent family were excluded as were families with a history of mental health care or those who had not been living in the US for more than 3 years.

This study compared structural family therapy with individual psychodynamic child psychotherapy and a 'recreational' control.

Attrition was greatest in the control group, 43%, and greater in the family therapy group as compared to the individual therapy, 16% vs. 4%. Both family therapy and individual psychodynamic therapy were similar in reducing behavioural and emotional problems on a variety of outcome measures, including family systems and individual psychodynamic rating scales. These improvements were maintained at one year follow up. On measures of family functioning, the control group stayed the same, the family therapy group improved but those receiving individual psychodynamic psychotherapy showed deterioration at one year follow up. This finding may possibly be biased as an "intention to treat" analysis was not carried out despite variable drop outs in the three groups. However, it also may be attributable to the fact that the individual psychodynamic child therapy was undertaken in the absence of any parallel parent work, contrary to usual practice. This study underlines the importance of working with the wider family system in conjunction with individual work with the child.

Two German studies (Petrie & Thieme, 1978; Winkelmann et al., 2000) involved the naturalistic follow up of children and adolescents with a range of difficulties, referred to clinics specializing in psychoanalytic psychotherapy. One of these studies (Winkelmann et al., 2000) noted that improvement in the period after treatment seldom occurred if difficulties were not resolved in the therapy itself but improvements seen during therapy continued after therapy.

Outcomes over the long-term

(a) The Anna Freud Centre long-term follow up study

The Anna Freud Centre long-term follow up study examined outcomes of child psychotherapy from childhood into adulthood (Schachter, 2004; Shachter & Target, in press; Target & Fonagy, 2002). This study was designed to provide a life-span perspective on a group of children with childhood disorders, specifically to examine whether gains in treatment in childhood are maintained into adulthood and help to "forestall some of the negative risk factors associated with early psychiatric disturbance" (Champion, Goodall & Rutter, 1995).

This study compared children who had received treatment at the Anna Freud Centre as children between 1952 and 1991, with the siblings of those who received treatment. Initially it had been planned to have another comparison group of children referred with apparently similar psychopathology who did not receive treatment, but for mainly ethical reasons, it proved impossible to trace and contact such a group.

In all, 34 former patients and 11 siblings of former patients participated in the study. These subjects were interviewed in depth and completed a range of outcome measures. Those that had received treatment in childhood were found to be functioning well and reported low levels of adversity, relatively few severe life events and good health with minimal use of medical services. They displayed adequate personality functioning across a range of domains and a low rate of personality disorders. The participant's level of functioning as adults was significantly related to attachment security, with secure attachment being associated with better coping and functioning. A key finding of the study was that the best predictor of adult outcome was a child's overall level of functioning as identified using the Hampstead Child Adaptation Measure (HCAM score; Schneider, 2000) before receiving treatment. The number of co-morbid diagnoses at the end of treatment also appeared to be linked to a long-term adverse outcome. A secure adult attachment status was common to those who moved from poor functioning as children to high functioning as adults.

Interestingly, while adversity in childhood was greater in the treated siblings, the untreated siblings were found to experience more negative life events in adulthood. In relation to personality functioning, the entire sample appeared to be doing well in the work domain and in the area of intimate relationships. Those children successfully treated in childhood appeared to be doing better than their untreated siblings. Possible adverse effects of treatment were highlighted in relation to attachment security where it was noted that if the immediate outcome of treatment was good, the treated children did as well as their siblings in adulthood. However, if the treatment had been unsuccessful, their attachment style was predominantly preoccupied/entangled. Those in the sample who did not receive psychoanalytic treatment were predominantly dismissing in their attachment style. Treated subjects demonstrated a balanced and accurate memory of their childhood experiences, however, in contrast to their siblings, their memories tended to be more painful. This study also found that there was relatively high agreement between the adult recall of events and the childhood case note recordings.

The researchers point out that the small, unrepresentative size of this sample means that the findings can only be tentative. However, the study is unique in terms of the length of follow up and the development of an interview protocol for the long term assessment of psychoanalytic treatment.

(b) Outcomes from childhood into adulthood from the perspective of the patient

As part of the Anna Freud long-term follow up study, the outcome of child psychoanalysis was also examined from the perspective of the patient (Midgley, 2003; Midgley, Target & Smith, 2006). This study explored the memories of adults who were in analysis as children and looks at what meaning the participants have given to the experience of therapy in the context of their later lives; not only how they understood what therapy was about, but also how they feel it has affected their lives both as children and adults. All adults who were referred as children to the Anna Freud Centre between 1952 and 1980 were invited to take part the follow up study. Of those whose whereabouts were established, 42% agreed to be interviewed. A total of 27 adults in this group had received intensive, i.e. four or five times per week child analysis, and this group was selected to be interviewed in depth. The average age of the participants was 36. Five had been under 6 at the time of childhood referral, sixteen had been between 6 and 12, with six referred in adolescence. The mean time in treatment was two years and nine months. This study used the "memories of therapy" semi-structured interview, developed specifically for the project. Interpretative phenomenological analysis was found to be particularly helpful in analyzing the data because of its focus on a detailed exploration of the participants' view of the topic under investigation (Smith, Jarman & Osborn, 1999).

A large number of the participants found it difficult to state with certainty whether the therapy had helped them or not because of the problem of knowing how things might have turned out if they had not received treatment. One former child patient described this vividly by stating "And if it did help me, I'm very grateful but how do

I establish that, because unless there was another clone of me, sitting next to me that didn't come...."

Two thirds of those who took part were able to describe some aspect of the experience of child psychoanalysis that they felt to be helpful at the time. Some were more confident about the positive impact than others. Several of the participants described how being able to talk and "unburden" themselves was helpful. One described how the treatment provided a "sort of canvas" to "express myself in a way that I wouldn't necessarily have been able to talk to anyone else about these problems." Some noted how the therapist's attention made them feel more confident. Talking appeared to enable some to see things differently.

Nine participants, mainly men, went beyond describing how the therapy helped them to *see* things differently by describing how it enabled them to *deal* with things differently as children and in particular, how it helped in managing feeling states, especially stress and anxiety. One participant noted how "even if the problems didn't go away I was certainly able to deal with them in a much more constructive manner and I didn't allow these worries to affect me."

The ability to better cope with feelings was associated, for six of the interviewees, with a feeling that they developed "the tools for self-analysis". One interviewee recalled how his therapist once said to him "the point of this, the point of the treatment, is for you to be able to do what you're doing without me, on your own." While this ability was mostly seen as helpful, one participant talked of feeling that it might have made him "a bit more likely to be introspective... to analyse a bit too much" and that he thought "it can put too much emphasis on the individual to solve the problem." Others also questioned the potentially negative impact of the therapy.

Interestingly, the majority of negative comments were made by women rather than men and they were all latency age or older at the time of being referred for therapy. Such comments included feelings that the therapy was "pointless" and had made no difference or that it had set them apart from others, as one observed "the last thing I wanted was to feel different". For some, this sense of being different created or exacerbated a sense that they were somehow "damaged". Two of the participants described feeling that there was "something wrong" with them and for one this had confirmed her anxieties about being "mad".

While most of the participants struggled with how to evaluate the impact of psychotherapy on their lives, the majority, two thirds, did feel that the therapy had been helpful for them. The emphasis placed by many on the importance of the experience of being listened to and understood by the therapist, appears to echo the importance that children in family therapy research place on "being heard". There is support too for the idea that the therapy enabled the children to "see" things differently and in this way enhanced resilience and coping.

Conclusions

Many of the findings from the studies described above raise interesting questions for researchers and clinicians alike. How for instance, do we understand the finding that a shift from secure to insecure attachment is associated with improvement in the treatment of young adults with personality and affective disorders? Benefits are noted to accrue from longer more frequent treatments in many studies, yet one randomized trial comparing treatments of different lengths found the briefest intervention to be most effective at four year follow up. What are the implications of this? Indeed brief interventions appear to be effective for certain groups, but depending on the diagnosis or type of difficulty, differences in outcome are associated with the frequency and length of treatment. How can the length and intensity of treatment be tailored to the presenting problem?

Particular treatments appear to work in different ways: family therapy appears to have a highly effective initial impact on childhood depression while the effect of individual child psychotherapy appears to be slower yet possibly more sustained. What determines these different patterns of response? Individual psychotherapy for the child in the absence of work with the parents or family seems to lead to poor outcomes for the family, whereas parent work undertaken in conjunction with individual work has been shown to have an impact on family functioning. What then is the best combination of treatments and in what order for any given clinical situation? An ongoing response to treatment or "sleeper effect" is noted by several studies. What is the mechanism by which this occurs?

The complexity of the process of change is highlighted by looking at the subtleties of shifts in previously maltreated children's representations of family life in response to adoptive placements. The interplay between parental states of mind and the child's representations is apparent as early as three months following the placement. Can further research similarly capture these kinds of processes?

Perhaps some of the most interesting questions are asked by former patients themselves. For any given individual, how can the impact of a therapeutic intervention be fully assessed? As well as the many benefits thought to be attributable to psychotherapeutic treatment, what are the possible adverse effects? How commonly do children in treatment feel that they are damaged in some way, that there is something wrong with them? Or as one former child patient ventured, is there "too much emphasis on the individual" to solve the problem'? These studies may hopefully stimulate future research as well as developing clinical thinking.

At the same time while outcome studies are informative about the potential for beneficial or adverse outcomes over time and with particular groups of patients, for the practicing clinician, retaining a focus on the process and short term goals of psychotherapeutic treatment and not just the expected 'end result' is of central importance. Gerber quotes Anna Freud "*it is very much like driving somewhere. Your aim is to arrive, and if instead of looking at the road, you think how nice it will be when you arrive, you will probably have an accident*" (Sandler, Kennedy & Tyson, 1980, p. 251; Gerber, 2004).

References

Achenback, T.M. & Edelbrock, C. (1983). *Manual for the Child Behaviour Checklist and Revised Child Behaviour Profile.* Burlington, Vermont: Queen City Printers.

Alvarez, A. & Reid, S. (1999). *Autism and personality: Findings from the Tavistock autism workshop.* London: Routledge.

Alvarez, A. & Lee, A. (2004). Early forms of relatedness in autism: a longitudinal clinical and quantitative single-case study. *Clinical Child Psychology and Psychiatry, 9* (4), 499–518.

Anderson, J. (2001). *Risk-taking, dangerous behaviour in childhood.* Thesis, University of East London.

Anderson, J. (2004). Risk-taking, dangerous behaviour in childhood: child protection and clinical strategies. *Journal of Social Work Practice, 18* (1), 19–32.

Angold, A., Costello, E., Pickles, A., Winder, F. & Silver, D. (1987). *Moods and Feeling Questionnaire: the development of a questionnaire for use in epidemiological studies of depression in children and adolescents.* London: Institute of Psychiatry.

Apter, A., Bernhout, E. & Tyano, S. (1984). Severe obsessive compulsive disorder in adolescence: a report of cases. *Journal of Adolescence, 7,* 349–358.

Baron-Cohen, S., Cox, A., Baird, G., Swettenham, J., Nightingale, N., Morgan, K., Drew, A. & Charman, T. (1996). Psychological markers in the detection of autism in infancy in a large population. *British Journal of Psychiatry, 168,* 158–163.

Baruch, G. (1995). Evaluating the outcome of a community-based psychoanalytic psychotherapy service for young people between 12–25 years old: work in progress. *Psychoanalytic Psychotherapy, 9* (3), 243–267.

Baruch, G., Fearon, P. & Gerber, A. (1998). Evaluating the outcome of a community–based psychoanalytic psychotherapy service for young people: one year repeated follow up. In: R. Davenhill & M. Patrick (Eds.), *Rethinking clinical audit* (pp.157–182). London: Routledge.

Boston, M. & Lush, D. (1993). Can child psychotherapists predict and assess their own work? A research note. *Association for Child Psychology and Psychiatry Review & Newsletter, 15* (3), 112–119.

Briggs, S., Grayson, K. & McLean, L. (manuscript in preparation). Risks and protective factors in the internal worlds of suicidal adolescents: a study of female adolescents at risk of suicide. Unpublished manuscript in preparation.

Champion, L., Goodall, G. & Rutter, M. (1995). Behavioural problems in childhood and stressors in early adult life: I. A 20 year follow up of London school children. *Psychological Medicine, 25,* 231–246.

Fonagy, P. & Moran, G.S. (1990). Studies of the efficacy of child psychoanalysis. *Journal of Consulting & Clinical Psychology, 58* (6), 684–695.

Fonagy, P. & Target, M. (1994). The efficacy of psychoanalysis for children with disruptive disorders. *Journal of the American Academy of Child & Adolescent Psychiatry, 33* (1), 45–55.

Fonagy, P. & Target, M. (1996). Predictors of outcome in child psychoanalysis: a retrospective study of 793 cases at the Anna Freud Centre. *Journal of the American Psychoanalytic Association, 44* (1), 27–77.

Fonagy, P., Target, M., Cottrell, D., Phillips, J. & Kurtz, Z. (2002). *What works for whom? A critical review of treatments for children and adolescents.* New York: Guilford Publications.

Fonagy, P., Gerber, A., Higgitt, A. & Bateman, A. (2002). Anna Freud Centre studies 4: The comparison of intensive (5 times weekly), and non-intensive (once weekly), treatment of young adults (AFC4) In P. Fonagy (Ed.), *An open door review of outcome studies in psychoanalysis* (2nd Edition), (pp. 96–97). London: International Psychoanalytical Association.

Gerber, A. (2004). *Structural and symptomatic change in psychoanalysis and psychodynamic psychotherapy: a quantitative study of process, outcome and attachment*. Unpublished PhD thesis, University College London.

Glaser, B.G. & Strauss, A.L. (1967). *Discovery of grounded theory. Strategies for qualitative research*. Weidenfeld & Nicolson.

Griiti, A., Di Sarno, A.M., Comito, M., De Vincenzo, A., De Paola, P. & Vajro, P. (2001). Psychological impact of liver transplantation on children's inner worlds. *Paediatric Transplantation, 5*, 37–43.

Heinicke, C.M. (1965). Frequency of psychotherapeutic session as a factor affecting the child's developmental status. *Psychoanalytic Study of the Child, 20*, 42–98.

Heinicke, C.M. & Ramsay-Klee. D.M. (1986). Outcome of child psychotherapy as a function of frequency of session. *Journal of the American Academy of Child & Adolescent Psychiatry, 25* (2), 247–253.

Hindle, D. (2000). An intensive assessment of a small sample of siblings placed together in foster care, PhD thesis, University of East London/Tavistock Clinic.

Hodges, J. (1990). *Rating manual for the 'Little Pig' story stem assessment*. Unpublished manuscript, London: The Anna Freud Centre.

Hodges, J. & Steele, M. (2000). Effects of abuse on attachment representations; Narrative assessments of abused children. *Journal of Child Psychotherapy, 26* (3), 433–455.

Hodges, J., Steele, M., Hillman, S., Henderson, K. & Kaniuk, J. (2003). Changes in attachment representations over the first year of adoptive placement: narratives of maltreated children. *Clinical Child Psychology and Psychiatry, 8* (3), 351–368.

Hodges, J., Hillman, S., Steele, M. & Henderson, K. (2004). *Story stem assessment profile rating manual*. Unpublished manuscript, London: The Anna Freud Centre.

Horn, H., Geiser-Elze, A., Reck, C., Hartmann, M., Stefini, A., Victor, D., Winkelmann, K. & Kronmüller, K.T. (2005). Efficacy of short term psychotherapy for children and adolescents with depression. *Praxis Kinderpsychol Kinderpsychiatr, 54* (7), 578–97.

Kaufman, J., Birmaher, B., Brent, D., Rao, U., Flynn, C., Moreci, P., Williamson, D. & Ryan, N. (1997). Schedule for affective disorders and schizophrenia for school-age children-present and lifetime version (K-SADS-PL): Initial reliability and validity data. *Journal of the American Academy of Child and Adolescent Psychiatry, 36* (7), 980–988.

Kazdin, A.E. (2000). *Psychotherapy for children and adolescents. Directions for research and practice*. New York: Oxford University Press.

Kennedy, E. (2004). *Child and adolescent psychotherapy: A systematic review of psychoanalytic approaches*. London: North Central London Strategic Health Authority.

Kennedy, E. & Midgley, N. (2007). *Process and outcome research in child, adolescent and parent-infant psychotherapy: A thematic review*. London: NHS London.

Kovacs, M. (1981). Rating scales to assess depression in school age children. *Acta paedopsychiatrica, 46*, 305–15.

Kronmüller, K., Postelnicu, I., Hartmann, M., Stefini, A., Geiser-Elze, A., Gerhold, M., Hildegard, H. & Winkelmann, K. (2005). Efficacy of psychodynamic short term psychotherapy for children and adolescents with anxiety disorders. *Praxis Kinderpsychol Kinderpsychiatr, 54* (7), 559–577.

Lord, C., Storoschuk, S., Rutter, M. & Pickles, A. (1993). Using the ADI-R to diagnose autism in preschool children. *Infant Mental Health Journal, 14*, 234–252.

Lush, D., Boston, M. & Grainger, E. (1991). Evaluation of psychoanalytic psychotherapy with children: therapists' assessments and predictions. *Psychoanalytic Psychotherapy, 5* (3), 191–234.

Lush, D., Boston, M., Morgan, J. & Kolvin, I. (1998). Psychoanalytic psychotherapy with disturbed adopted and foster children: a single case follow-up study. *Clinical Child Psychology & Psychiatry, 3* (1), 51–69.

Main, M. & Goldwyn, R. (1998). *Adult attachment scoring and classification system*. Unpublished manuscript. Berkeley, CA: University of California.

Midgley, N. (2003). *Memories of therapy: A qualitative study of retrospective accounts of child psychoanalysis*. Unpublished Psych D thesis, University College London.

Midgley, N. & Target, M. (2005). Recollections of being in child psychoanalysis: a qualitative study of a long-term follow-up study. *Psychoanalytic Study of the Child, 60*, 157–177.

Midgley, N., Target, M. & Smith, J.A. (2006). The outcome of child psychoanalysis from the patient's point of view: a qualitative analysis of a long-term follow-up study. *Psychology and Psychotherapy: Theory, Practice, Research, 79*, 257–269.

Moran, G. & Fonagy, P. (1987). Psychoanalysis and diabetic control: a single-case study. *British Journal of Medical Psychology, 60*, 357–372.

Moran, G.S., Fonagy, P., Kurtz, A., Bolton, A.M. & Brook, C. (1991). A controlled study of the psychoanalytic treatment of brittle diabetes. *Journal of the American Academy of Child & Adolescent Psychiatry, 30* (6), 926–935.

Muratori, F., Picchi, L., Casella, C., Tancredi, R., Milone, A. & Patarnello, M.G. (2002). Efficacy of brief dynamic psychotherapy for children with emotional disorders. *Psychotherapy and Psychosomatics, 71* (1), 28–38.

Muratori, F., Picchi, L., Bruni, G., Patarnello, M. & Romagnoli, G. (2003). A two-year follow-up of psychodynamic psychotherapy for internalizing disorders in children. *Journal of the American Academy of Child and Adolescent Psychiatry, 42* (3), 331–339.

Orvaschel, H. (1989). *Kiddies SADS-E Section. Designed to assess PTSD.* Philadelphia, PA: Medical College of Pennsylvania.

Petrie, H. & Thieme, E. (1978). Katamnese zur analytischen psychotherapie im kindes und jugendalter. *Psyche 1*, 21–54.

Philps, J. (2003). *Applications of child psychotherapy to work with children in temporary foster care.* Unpublished Psych.D. thesis. University of East London.

Reid, S., Alvarez, A. & Lee, A. (2001). The Tavistock autism workshop approach: Assessment, treatment and research. In: J. Richer. & S. Coates (Eds.), *Autism-the search for coherence* (pp. 182–192). London: Jessica Kingsley.

Rhode, M. (2007). Helping toddlers to communicate: infant observation as an outreach intervention. In: S. Acquarone (Ed.), *Autism in Infants Detection and Early Intervention.* London: Karnac.

Robin, A., Siegel, T. & Moye, A. (1995). Family versus individual therapy for anorexia: Impact on family conflict. *International Journal of Eating Disorders, 17* (4), 313–322.

Robin, A., Siegel, P., Moye, A., Gilroy, M., Dennis, A.B. & Sikand, A. (1999). A controlled comparison of family versus individual psychotherapy for adolescents with anorexia nervosa. *Journal of the American Academy of Child and Adolescent Psychiatry, 38* (12), 1482–1489.

Sandler, J., Kennedy, H. & Tyson, R.L. (1980). *The technique of child psychoanalysis: Discussions with Anna Freud.* London: Karnac Books.

Schachter, A. (2004). *The adult outcome of child psychoanalysis: A long-term follow-up study.* Unpublished PhD thesis, University College London.

Schachter, A. & Target, M. (in press). The history and current status of outcome research at the Anna Freud Centre. In: N. Midgley, J. Anderson, E. Grainger, T. Nesic-Vuckovic & C. Urwin (Eds.), *Child psychotherapy and research: new approaches, emerging findings.* London: Routledge.

Schopler, E., Reichler, R.J. & Renner, B.R. (1986). *The Childhood Autism Rating Scale (CARS), for diagnostic screening and classification of autism.* New York: Irvington.

Schneider, T. (2000). *Measuring adaptation in middle childhood: the development of the Hampstead Child Adaptation Measure.* Unpublished PhD thesis, University College London.

Shaffer, D., Gould, M.S., Brasie, J., Ambrosini, P., Fisher, P., Bird, H. & Aluwahlia, S. (1983). A children's global assessment scale (C-GAS). *Archive of General Psychiatry, 40*, 1228–1231.

Sinha, U.K. & Kapur, M. (1999). Psychotherapy with emotionally disturbed adolescent boys: Outcome and process study, *National Institute of Mental Health & Neuro Sciences Journal (NIMHANS), 17* (2), 113–30.

Smith, J., Jarman, M. & Osborn, M. (1999). Doing interpretative phenomenological analysis. In: M. Murray & K. Chamberlein (Eds.), *Qualitative health psychology: Theories and methods* (pp. 218–240). London: Sage.

Smyrnios, K.X. & Kirby, R.J. (1993). Long term comparison of brief versus unlimited psychodynamic treatments with children and their parents. *Journal of Consulting & Clinical Psychology, 61* (6), 1030–1027.

Steele, M., Hodges, J., Kaniuk, J., Hillman, S. & Henderson, K. (2003). Attachment representations and adoption: associations between maternal states of mind and emotion narratives in previously maltreated children. *Journal of Child Psychotherapy, 29* (2), 187–205.

Steele, M. (2006). The 'added value' of attachment theory and research for clinical work in adoption and foster care. In: J. Kendrick, C. Lindsey & L. Tollemarche (Eds.), *Creating new families: therapeutic approaches to fostering adoption and kinship care.* London: Karnac Books.

Szapocznik, J., Murray, E., Scopetta, M., Hervis, O., Rio, A., Cohen, R., Rivas-Vazquez, A., Posada, V. & Kurtines, W. (1989). Structural family versus psychodynamic child therapy for problematic Hispanic boys. *Journal of Consulting and Clinical Psychology, 57* (5), 571–578.

Target, M. & Fonagy, P. (1994). The efficacy of psycho-analysis for children with emotional disorders. *Journal of the American Academy of Child & Adolescent Psychiatry, 33* (3), 361–71.

Target, M. & Fonagy, P. (2002). Anna Freud Centre studies 3: The long-term follow-up of child analytic treatments (AFC3). In: P. Fonagy (Ed.), *An open door review of outcome studies in psychoanalysis* (2nd Ed.), (pp. 141–146). London: International Psychoanalytic Association.

Trowell, J., Kolvin, I., Weeramanthri, T., Sadowski, H., Berelowitz, M., Glasser, D. & Leitch, I. (2002). Psychotherapy for sexually abused girls: psychopathological outcome findings and patterns of change. *British Journal of Psychiatry, 180*, 234–247.

Trowell, J., Joffe, I., Campbell, J., Clemente, C., Almqvist, F., Soininen, M., Koskenranta-Aalto, U., Weintraub, S., Kolaitis, G., Tomaras, V., Anastasopoulos, D., Grayson K., Barnes, J. & Tsiantis, J. (2007).

Childhood depression: a place for psychotherapy. An outcome study comparing individual Psychodynamic Psychotherapy and Family Therapy. *European Child and Adolescent Psychiatry, 16.*

Tsiantis, J., Kolvin, I., Anastasopoulos., Trowell. J., Tomaras, V., Miles, G., Papadoploulos, R., Soininen, M., Bostrom, C. & Almqvist, F. (2005). Psychotherapy for early adolescent depression: A comparison of two psychotherapeutic interventions in three European countries. In: E.D. Hibbs & P.S. Jensen (Eds.), *Psychosocial treatments for child and adolescent disorders: Empirically based strategies for clinical practice.* 2nd Edition. American Psychological Association: Washington DC.

Vilvisk, S.O. & Vaglum, P. (1990). Teenage anorexia nervosa: A 1–9 year follow up after psychodynamic treatment. *Nord Psykiatr Tidsskr, 44,* 249–255.

Weise, K. & Tuber, S (2004). The self and object representations of narcissistically disturbed children. An empirical investigation. *Psychoanalytic Psychology, 21* (2), 244–258.

World Health Organization. (1978). Mental disorders: Glossary and guide to their classification in accordance with the Ninth revision of the International Classification of Diseases. Switzerland: Geneva.

Winkelmann, K., Hartmann, M., Neumann, K., Hennch, C., Reck, C., Victor, D., Horn, H., Uebel, T. & Kronmüller, K.T. (2000). Stability of therapeutic outcome after child and adolescent psychoanalytical therapy. *Praxis Kinderpsychol Kinderpsychiatr 49,* 315–328.

Winkelmann, K., Stefini, A., Hartmann, M., Geiser-Elze, A., Kronmüller, A., Schenkenbach, C., Hildegard, H. & Kronmüller, K.T. (2005). Efficacy of psychodynamic short-term psychotherapy for children and adolescents with behaviour disorders. *Prax Kinderpsychol Kinderpsychiatr, 54* (7), 598–614.

Wrate, R., Kolvin, I., Garside, R., Wolstenholme, F., Humbert, C.M. & Leitch, I. (1995). Helping seriously disturbed children. In R. Nichol (Ed.), *Longitudinal studies in child psychology and psychiatry* (pp. 265–318). Chichester, England: Wiley.

Wright, J., Briggs, S. & Behringer, J. (2005). Attachment and the body in suicidal adolescents: A pilot study. *Clinical Child Psychology and Psychiatry, 10* (4), 477–491.

Zelmann, A.B., Samuels, S. & Abrams, D. (1985). I.Q. Changes in young children following intensive long-term psychotherapy. *American Journal of Psychotherapy, 39* (2), 215–227.

CHAPTER TWO

Integrating research in a clinical setting for child psychotherapy: A case study about facilitating and hindering factors in psychoanalytic psychotherapy

Siv Boalt Boëthius[1]

The aim of this chapter is to describe a case study, which illustrates a strategy for introducing research activity into a clinically oriented staff group working with psychoanalytic psychotherapy. Prior to the start of this project, the staff members had been engaged mainly in clinical work with children and their parents, and in training programmes focusing on psychotherapeutic treatment and supervision. The objective was to enable staff members to develop their clinical work through the systematic collection and analysis of clinical data. The idea was to conduct clinically based research on psychoanalytic psychotherapy directed at showing, for example, what kind of treatment was given to which patients and how the various treatments worked for different categories of patients. This approach can be described as empirical research based on clinical practice, theoretical assumptions regarding child development and modern psychoanalytic theory. It involves the

[1] *Acknowledgement.* Many thanks to professor Carl-Otto Jonsson, Stockholm University and professor Dorothy Stock Whitaker, Leeds University, UK for stimulating cooperation and constructive comments.

systematic collection of both quantitative and qualitative data and an analysis of these data aimed at illuminating the specified purposes of the clinical work.

On a general level, research on child psychotherapy has shown that psychoanalytic psychotherapy is effective for children with a wide range of psychological disorders (Kennedy, 2004; Midgley, Anderson, Grainger, Nesic & Urwin, 2009; Muratori, Picchi, Bruni, Patarnello & Romagnoli, 2003; Shirk & Russel, 1992). Further refinement of these findings, however, requires more detailed studies of both outcome and process variables (Fonagy, 2003; Hibbs & Jensen, 2005; Urwin, 2007). It is noteworthy that in the available body of published research, the participation of psychotherapists who work with children and their parents is more or less missing (Boalt Boëthius & Berggren, 2000; Midgely, 2004). There are probably many reasons for this, one being that it takes time and resources to engage in this type of research. Psychotherapists who are willing to do so are dependent on the support of their clinical centre, and they must have the required training in research methodology as well as a strong personal motivation. However, it is assumed by the author and others (e.g., Midgely, 2004; Whitaker, 2001; Whitaker & Archer, 1994), that research which is planned and conducted by practitioners and based on their own curiosities and practice experience will stimulate and increase the quality of their psychotherapeutic work, while contributing also to an increased understanding of, and knowledge about psychotherapy on a more general level.

The troubled relationship between researchers and psychotherapists has been well documented in the literature (Elliot & Morrow-Bradley, 1994; Fonagy, 2003; Hibbs & Jensen, 2005). As in every troubled relationship, this lack of communication has two sides. Researchers blame therapists for not utilizing research findings and for being biased or antiscientific. On the other hand, therapists blame researchers for not investigating common or clinically relevant treatments or populations and for being irrelevant. This gap is especially troublesome for psychoanalytic child psychotherapy compared to both the research on other treatment models for children and research on psychoanalytic psychotherapy for adults. In a summary of existing evidence of the effectiveness of psychoanalytic psychotherapy for adults, Fonagy (2003) points out the relevance of these findings to research on child psychotherapy.

According to Fonagy (2003p. 133), the agenda for research on psychoanalytic child psychotherapy implies that:

> "First we require evidence concerning *specific patient groups* who uniquely benefit from our interventions, and related to this, assessment systems that help to identify these individuals, either in terms of diagnosis and symptomatology, or in terms of characteristic modes of mental functioning or even social conditions. Second, we need *sensitive measurement systems* to identify changes that may go beyond symptomatic improvement and indicate benefits of relative freedom from future difficulties. Third, we need to develop new *adaptions of psychoanalytic therapy* that extend and improve upon existing applications in the direction of both greater generalisability across clinical groups and more powerful impact on them either in terms of symptom relief or prevention."

These demands are not easy to fulfil, and in comparison to treatment models based on behaviour and learning theory, research on psychoanalytic psychotherapy is faced with a more complex task (Elliot & Anderson, 1994; Fonagy, 2003). However, the situation is changing and since the beginning of this century considerable progress has been made. As pointed out by Hibbs and Jensen (2005), in their informative and detailed survey of current research on child psychotherapy, a number of promising studies are in progress and seem likely to provide compelling evidence for the effectiveness of psychoanalytic psychotherapy. One example of a current study based on time-limited individual psychodynamic psychotherapy and family psychotherapy is the three-centre prospective outcome and process study of childhood depression based on data from England, Finland and Greece (Trowell, Joffe, Campbell, Clemente, Almquist, Soinenen, Koskenranta-Aalto, Weintraub, Kolaitis, Tomaras, Anastasopoulos, Grayson, Barnes & Tsiantis, 2007; Tsiantis, Kolvin, Anastasopoulos, Trowell, Tomaras, Miles, Papadopoulos, Soininen, Boström & Almqvist, 2005). Other examples are a study of psychotherapy for sexually abused girls (Trowell, Kolvin & Weeramanthri, 2002) and a study of goal directed, time-limited child psychotherapy with parallel parental counselling (Carlberg, 2009).

The effort to be described in this study was conducted at the Erica Foundation in Stockholm, a university college, which was founded in 1934 and has a long tradition of clinical work and training. The study was conducted during a three-year period when the author was Director of the institute. From the outset, research had been one of the institute's main tasks, in addition to different training programmes and psychoanalytic psychotherapy for children and adolescents. The Government financed the training programmes, and the clinical work was financed through the County Council of Stockholm. However, financial support for research had to be applied for in the form of grants from various research funds, which were difficult to get.

Concomitant with this approach, there was also a considerable interest in using systematically collected qualitative data (Stiles, 1994), i.e. narratives from the patients and their parents as well as the therapists, for broader purposes. One objective was to describe processes of psychotherapy in such a way that people outside of our field, without any prior knowledge about psychotherapy, would be able to understand what child psychotherapy is about. This meant, for example, describing psychotherapeutic processes in discussions with the public as well as in articles or books about child psychotherapy.

In the following, these two approaches are called, respectively, clinically based research and developmental work with regard to psychoanalytic psychotherapy. Concerning the first line of action, clinically based research, the formulating of research questions was the main starting point for developing projects of relevance for psychotherapeutic work with children and their families (Boalt Boëthius & Berggren, 2000; Carlberg, 1997). Regarding the second line of action, projects describing psychoanalytic psychotherapy to "non-informed persons," e.g., politicians, administrators, teachers, etc., a systematic collection of mainly qualitative data was necessary in order to give the potential authors a genuine grasp of the material they wanted to talk or write about (Cleve, 2000; Cleve, 2002; Orrenius, 1997).

Psychoanalytic psychotherapy and research are marked by distinctive cultures

The case study presented in this chapter is based on an analysis of the work carried out in a clinical centre, where the two main tasks had for a long time been psychoanalytic psychotherapeutic treatment and clinically oriented training programmes. The third task to be added was research. The introduction of research into the daily work of the organisation was conceived as a meeting between two cultures, which differ in terms of required skills, norms and value systems. However, the long-term goal, to increase the understanding of how psychoanalytic child psychotherapy works, is the same in both cultures (Carlberg, Eresund & Boalt Boëthius, 2009; Hibbs & Jensen, 2005).

The concept of culture is used here to describe the weave of interactions, attitudes and values that characterises any area of human activity that can be delineated in relation to other areas of activity. A culture can be seen as consisting of more or less dynamic systems of meaning, which interact in a weave tied together by a group of people belonging to the same ethnic group, profession or work organisation (Hannerz, 1993). To belong to a certain culture implies that people feel connected to each other due to similar knowledge, skills, values or experiences. It is assumed that the culture of an organisation influences its members' perception of reality, not by distorting it, but by giving rise to a special model for interpretation. For example, if something is perceived as too new or threatening, it cannot be integrated and has to be kept apart, at least for some time. This does not imply that people belonging to the same culture act in the same way. However, the culture can be assumed to govern a number of possible strategies for action, and therefore, some degree of similarity in the reactions of group members can be expected.

In relation to clinical work and psychoanalytic psychotherapy with children, the specific culture is manifest by the way clinicians interact with the children and their parents and how they respond to the activities of the patients, both individually and collectively. The culture is also manifest in the way data are documented and reported, verbally and in writing. Moreover, it expresses itself in the interaction between colleagues, and in the group's relations with other organisations and the outside world. The culture, which develops in a clinical centre, is also influenced by the type of training the various professionals working in the clinic have had, as well as by the attitudes that are expressed, more or less openly, towards other theoretical orientations and organisations. This implies, for instance, those clinicians' earlier experiences from other professional training programmes or similar contextual situations, where strong cultural influences are exerted, can be important for an understanding of the culture of a particular organisation.

There are similarities between the cultures represented by psychotherapy research and clinical practice. These include, for instance, the use of one's creativity and intuition with regard to possible interventions in a psychotherapeutic session, and with regard to the formulation of plausible hypotheses in the search for a good enough understanding of certain phenomena of interest. There are also important differences between the two cultures. On a general level, the aims as well as the methods differ, and the results tend to be presented differently. Research is not primarily concerned with the wellbeing of the individual patient, but with the attainment of a general knowledge, which will hopefully contribute to improving clinical practice in the long run. The role of the researcher differs also from that of the psychotherapist, and latent conflicts are often linked to different views of what constitutes results. Are results only something that can be observed and measured, or can they also consist of experiences that are reported verbally or in notes from a session? Furthermore, psychotherapeutic work is based on a close interaction between the child and the therapist, and this relationship unfolds in what can be called the "rationality of individual space." Research, on the other hand, is about looking into things and achieving a certain control through impartial checking by a third party, an activity that can be referred to as being part of the so called "rationality of official space" (Janson, 1999).

Description of the clinical centre

The staff group of the studied centre consisted of about 25 persons with professional backgrounds as psychologists, child psychiatrists, social workers, and pre-school teachers. About half of the members of the clinical staff were psychologists, and both they and the psychiatrists and social workers were trained as psychotherapists. The majority had also had training in supervision of psychotherapy.

The clinicians at the Erica Foundation were experienced and well trained psychotherapists who worked with children, adolescents and adults mainly in long-term individual psychoanalytic psychotherapy. There was a strong desire among staff members to share their knowledge with others, primarily through supervision and teaching. There was also a manifest need for increased personal and professional stimulation through contacts with colleagues working with similar tasks in Sweden and abroad, and through studies of relevant literature.

As mentioned above, research had been one of the main stipulated tasks of the institute from the start, and during certain periods over the years, research activity had indeed been given priority. However, the research projects had always been the responsibility of a single person or a small group of persons. The research had never involved the whole institute, which meant that there had never been sufficient opportunities to develop any kind of culture that would encompass more than the clinical practice and the teaching/supervision, even though several studies had been published in the name of the institute.

However, some years before the activity described in the present case study began, there had been an effort to engage part of the staff in a research project involving group treatment for preschool children with autism and other forms of early contact disorders. The project had involved a lot of documentation, e.g., videotaped psychotherapy sessions and written documentation of the supervised sessions with trainees who conducted the psychotherapy. From a clinical point of view, the project was a success, as the group treatment became an integrated part of the clinical practice of the institute. But the output of the research, which entailed a tremendous amount of work for some clinicians and trainees, was meagre. Research was once again the work of a few persons, and not integrated in the activities of the institute.

Partly due to these experiences there was, among the staff, in parallel with a genuine interest in developing the clinical practice through research and a hope that I as the principal would be able to contribute to this change, a certain amount of ambivalence towards the idea of engaging in clinically oriented research projects. However, there was a clear awareness of the need for research projects, focusing on psychoanalytic psychotherapy, with well defined goals, based on a systematic collection and analysis of clinical data. It was also perceived as important to win acceptance for new ideas and suggestions both among the clinical and the administrative staff, the latter because they would also be involved in the projects by being assigned responsibility either for managing various types of data or for handling finances in case the projects received support through research grants.

Preparing for change

Surveying the literature on child psychotherapy

As a first step, a survey was made of the wishes and demands of the clinicians with regard to the development of the collective knowledge of the institute. The most common desire was to get an overview of what had been written specifically about child psychotherapy, focusing on different types of research projects as well as case reports describing psychotherapy processes with individual children and their parents. This resulted in our collecting all the books and journals on child psychotherapy which were available at the clinic at that time. The material was then distributed to individual clinicians according to their personal interests. All of us wrote brief comments on the articles and books we were responsible for. The result of this work was summarised in a booklet that provided a good overview. This work, which was based on the interests and knowledge of the individual clinicians, was carried out fairly quickly and it had an amazingly stimulating effect. Individual clinicians developed a better grasp of how their own way of working could fit in into the larger context of psychotherapeutic work. In a general sense, this survey gave support to the clinical work being done and provided clinicians with new ideas that could be tried out.

Identifying staff attitudes and feelings about making research a part of their work

It has already been noted that a research culture and a practice culture carry with them different assumptions, attitudes and feelings. As expected, there were mixed feelings amongst the staff about embarking on research activity. As Director of the Erica Foundation, I considered that it would be important to make these sentiments explicit, so that they could be acknowledged, and, if possible, addressed. To assist in this, as a second step, Professor Dorothy Stock Whitaker from the University of York in England was invited as a visiting professor. She was initially invited for a month in order to facilitate and encourage the development of a new way of thinking about research on psychoanalytic child psychotherapy that could be integrated into the clinical practice and the training programmes. Earlier contacts with her had indicated her personal interest in this kind of research-related work in cooperation with clinicians. She had also carried out similar work in the UK previously (Whitaker & Archer, 1990; Whitaker & Archer, 1994). Professor Whitaker's overarching assignment was to assist in the work of creating a culture that integrated clinical practice and clinical training programmes with research. Later, as the work progressed, she returned for briefer periods to assist in the guiding of research efforts.

As part of her consultancy, the two of us, she in the role of an external research consultant and myself in the role of principal, would work together to get an understanding of the conscious or unconscious feelings and attitudes which this endeavour evoked among the staff.

Professor Whitaker's first task was to assist the staff in articulating their attitudes and feelings concerning the objective of making research a part of their work. This required examining the more or less contradictory perceptions, attitudes, interests and wishes of the clinicians, which were likely to either stimulate or hinder their efforts in formulating relevant research questions. New ideas and potential projects were discussed and this part of the work can be described in terms of a force-field analysis (Lewin, 1965; Whitaker & Archer, 1990). The general idea was to define the various stimulating or inhibiting factors that individual staff members identified in relation to the project of incorporating research into the work of the organisation, and to use them in a force-field analysis as described by Lewin (Whitaker & Archer, 1990). It was assumed that strategies for facilitating the planned change in the organisation as a whole could be developed through a content analysis of the data generated by the force-field analysis. Thus, the force-field analysis was an important preparatory step. How it worked out in practice at the Erica Foundation is described in the next section.

The force-field analysis in practice

Identifying facilitating and hindering factors

The aim of the force-field analysis was, as mentioned above, to acquire an understanding of the kind of issues that individual staff members perceived as affecting their ability to formulate relevant research questions. The gathering of data for the force field analysis was carried out during a half-day seminar. The clinicians were divided into groups consisting of 3–4 persons. In each group the members listed issues, which they perceived as either stimulating or inhibiting with regard to their engagement in a potential research project. The discussions in the small groups had the character of brainstorming: nothing was judged as being right or wrong and all suggestions were taken into consideration. Flip charts were used to enable a sharing of experiences when the papers of all the groups were put on a wall. Some issues could be both stimulating and inhibiting, depending on what aspect was focused upon.

An overview of the issues in this analysis is shown in Fig. 1. The line in the middle shows the *Actual Level,* which can be described as the present level for the developmental work and the line at the top indicates the *Wished for Level.* The idea is to illustrate what type of stimulating issues are pushing the line indicating Actual Level upwards, towards the Wished for Level, and which hindering issues are pushing it downwards, away from the Wished for Level.

The figure illustrates Lewin's (1965) theory that the main principle for achieving the Wished for Level is to decrease the pressure from the hindering issues (above the middle line). This was assumed to be more important than to increase the number of stimulating issues (below the middle line indicating the Actual Level). The underlying idea is that the stimulating factors tend to develop more or less automatically as hindering factors are removed or decreased, provided that the general framework is adequate.

Categorising the facilitating and hindering factors according to the focus of an issue and its associated emotional loading

The issues were then divided into three main categories depending on whether they could be seen as mainly related to the individual member of staff, to a work group, or to the organisation as a whole.

Wished for level			
Stimulating issues			*Inhibiting issues*
Personal development	→	←	Lack of time and money
Personal interests	→	←	Lack of secretarial services
Developing new parts of the work	→	←	Earlier negative
A wish to withdraw	→		experiences
Nice to think about what I am		←	Lack of knowledge about
doing	→		how to do research
Stimulating to learn new things	→	←	Fear of not being
Improving my competence as a			able to manage more
clinician	→		responsibilities
Positive support by the principal	→	←	Forgotten what I once
Good access to library resources	→		knew
Increase of status	→	←	Importance of ethical
Wanting recognition for our work	→		questions
Improving the capacity to answer		←	Need for confidentiality
questions from the outside world	→	←	Competitions and rivalry
Improving communication with		←	Undermining the clinical
others	→		identity
Improving the image of the		←	Interference with the work
institute	→		with patients
Actual level			

Figure 1. Force field analysis according to Lewin (1965).

Dorothy Whitaker and the author sorted the issues into the three categories, independently at first, then jointly, with a high degree of agreement. The next step involved selecting the areas of concern that were considered most important, i.e., that had the highest negative or positive weight according to the clinicians. The members in each of the small groups were asked to indicate how emotionally loaded the different issues were on a three point scale.

Categorising the facilitating and hindering factors according to area of concern

Five areas of concern were identified through a content analysis procedure conducted by professor Whitaker and the author. Each of us made our judgements independently and we then resolved any differences through discussion.

The five main areas of concern arrived at by this procedure were labelled: (a) impact on relationships among colleagues; (b) impact on the organisational structure; (c) impact on clinical work, patients, and self as practitioner; (d) practical issues regarding time, money and space, and finally: (e) concerns related to the formulation of research question and methodological issues. Each of these areas of concern merits separate discussion.

The first three categories, which involved psychological and organizational issues and which could be seen as reflecting the legitimacy of one's work in relation to the outer world, were perceived as more important according to the weighing of factors that the initial small groups of members of staff had done. Practical and administrative issues as well as issues related to the content of actual projects were given relatively lower priority. All the areas of concern contained both positively and negatively loaded issues.

a. Impact on relationships among colleagues

When a new task is to be integrated into the everyday work of a clinical centre, it is to be expected that a number of obstacles, both conscious and unconscious, will appear. The different tasks have to be distributed and this distribution has to be negotiated and agreed upon in some way. Even if individual clinicians have different preferences, some tasks will generally be perceived as more interesting, challenging or demanding than others. Various questions regarding competition, envy and rivalry were raised. Fear of failing was raised along with the negative experiences of the earlier research project mentioned above. There were also questions about who would get what kind of gratification for what type of activity, or what kind of support for ideas could be expected, etc.

The discussion of the issues within this area seemed to indicate that psychotherapists who spent time on a research project could expect a lot of support initially. However, if the project were to take time from the clinical work and a therapy session perhaps be cancelled due to a research conference, it was expected that solidarity would decrease and that negative reactions would emerge. There was awareness that the role of researcher would imply a partly different way of thinking about psychotherapeutic work compared to the role of psychotherapist. One fairly common reflection was that research would entail a certain emotional distance to the patients involved in a study, something that would be impossible in clinical work. However, a major positive factor concerned the possibilities for a deepened professional development, for learning something new and perhaps getting an opportunity to withdraw a little from the clinic and do some thinking on one's own.

b. Impact on organisational structure

The organisational frame of the institute provided a degree of legitimacy in relation to the external world. It had an influence on how the different tasks of the institute such as the clinical work, training programmes and research projects were presented formally in documents, in reports to official authorities and at national and international conferences. There was total agreement among the staff regarding the need to gain a clearer picture of when and for whom psychoanalytic psychotherapy would be a good choice of treatment, although there were differences in opinion about how this should be done. However, the possibility of creating a situation that would permit thinking about a more careful and systematic evaluation of the clinical work was met with hopefulness by most of the clinicians. It was also evident that an evaluation of the psychotherapeutic practice that made sense both to the clinicians and to people outside of the institute was perceived as an important form of quality assurance (Fonagy, 2003; Hibbs & Jensen, 2005, Midgley et al., 2009). Having an integrated ongoing research program was seen as a way of being able to answer questions from the outside world and as a way of improving the image of the institute.

Other organisational issues of importance concerned how various aspects of the work at the Erica Foundation as a whole could be integrated as well as how to contain the increasing complexity of tasks (Boalt Boëthius, 1999b; Obholzer & Zagier Roberts, 1996). It was evident for the members of staff that the organisation of the daily work in the institute would have to be changed to some extent, if there was to be a real integration of the research activity. For example, time would have to be set aside for discussions of various research ideas, and some form of supervision or consultation about research projects would have to be integrated in the work of the clinic, just as opportunities for supervision were a permanent feature of the clinical work. (Hibbs & Jensen, 2005; Trowell, Kolvin & Weeramanthri, 2002).

c. Impact on clinical work, patients, and self as practitioner

A feeling expressed by some clinicians was that the research orientation might undermine their "identity as clinicians." There was a sense of threat involved in taking on a new task the implication being that research activities might take over "the real work" with the patients. The issue of confidentiality and of how to write about a patient without anybody, besides those involved in the psychotherapy, being able to identify the persons concerned, was also regarded as very important. Prior negative experiences of the above mentioned research project, which had involved several persons but generated few publications, which were also of limited clinical interest, were still in the minds of some members of staff. There was a fear that something similar might happen again, that this work would involve an impressive collection of data but that there would not be enough time or other resources to pull the threads together and finish the project.

As described in connection with the force-field analysis, some of the concerns expressed by staff were infused by reservations about undertaking research, and fears about possible negative consequences of research. As far as possible, these concerns were dealt with by discussion as they arose.

d. Practical issues regarding administration, money, time and space

With regard to practical issues, the demands from the Government and the County Council for detailed information about the activities of the institute had increased over time. For a long time there had been different opinions about what information the County Council, for example, should be given in order for it to understand the content of the work at the clinic. Clinicians expressed a wish for arriving at a mutual understanding with outside authorities about what kind of information was relevant, and indicated that they believed that a research project could contribute towards this aim. The need for grants to cover the costs for planning such a project and getting it started was evident.

Lack of time was a powerful and stressful aspect and there were doubts about if there would be time enough to permit the kind of rethinking about the therapeutic work that would be needed. Time was also an important aspect of long-term child psychotherapy. There was a fear that therapy sessions might have to be cancelled, with undesirable effects on the psychotherapeutic process as well as on the working relationship with the persons upholding the contact with the parents. This fear could be dealt with by careful scheduling, done well in advance. The wish for more space for research was also expressed concretely as a need for separate rooms that would allow the clinicians to keep the clinical work and the research work apart, and to have a legitimate place reserved for both types of work.

e. Concerns about formulation of research questions and methodological issues

The questions and problems that individual clinicians wished to gain a better understanding of were generally stated and fairly complex, which is a well-known phenomenon in clinical settings and important to work with on a continuous basis. Clinicians engaged in psychoanalytic psychotherapy are used to working with very complex phenomena and it takes time before they realize that this may not be the best approach within a research context. There were also many questions about research design and methodology, and about ethical questions and confidentiality, as mentioned above. Questions concerning how to collect data without disturbing or influencing the psychotherapeutic process too much were discussed, as well as what data to register in the computerised system that was being developed.

Group discussions about research methodology for practitioners

Parallel to the work with the force-field analysis, a series of group discussions about research methodology were introduced. The group discussions were conducted through a series of seminars, based on the ideas of potential projects suggested by individual clinicians and following a model developed by professor Whitaker and a co-worker (Whitaker & Archer, 1990).

The first step was to assist each staff member in stating his or her own particular interest or curiosity in the form of one or more questions. The approach used in this context was to start with the specific research questions the clinicians had. It was evident that the formulation of clinically relevant research questions was seen as important. This part of this course was devoted to thinking about the questions individual clinicians had, while further discussion made it possible to reformulate the initially generally stated questions. Staff members were encouraged to express their interests in rather specific terms, and/or to formulate a sub-set of questions, which were contained within the question as originally stated. For many clinicians, this process of cutting down clinically relevant questions in size so that they became manageable implied a new way of thinking about what part of the clinical work they wanted to go deeper into.

To give an example, one clinician expressed a wish to get a more thorough understanding of how to work psychotherapeutically with adopted children. This is a relevant question, but it has to be more specific in order to allow for some useful answers. In this case, the focus of interest turned out to be a description and analysis of self-images in a limited number of clinical cases.

It was evident to the participants that this way of thinking about "research" was different from what they had experienced before during their years at the university and in connection with the previously mentioned project on group treatment of children with early contact disorders. The focus on how to formulate clinically relevant questions which could be answered through a process of collecting and analysing clinical data, and the attention given to methodological issues was appreciated. The approach was perceived as effective in that it helped the individual clinicians to clarify their own purposes. In a broad sense, this can be described as a way of supporting the clinicians in their efforts to place their clinical experiences within a methodological frame of reference, and this had a clearly stimulating effect.

The second step was to develop a research design that would fit the specific research questions which had been identified in the first step. The fact that the research questions had been specified made it possible to design specific studies that would suit each question or set of questions. Would a single case study or multiple case studies be the best choice, for example? Should the study be quantitative, qualitative or a mix of both? Should there be pre- and post- assessments? Would some processes have to be tracked over time? Would control groups be indicated or possible? Would it be preferable to have direct contact with the patients, or would it be better to ask parents or teachers, etc.? The answers would differ depending on which group one asked. Thoughts about how to get access to the kind of information one was interested in were discussed, and the advantages and disadvantages of different ways of designing a study were explored.

The third step was to think about ways of collecting data. Different methods for collecting data such as interviews, questionnaires, and observations were discussed and tried out. The advantages and disadvantages of qualitative and quantitative approaches were discussed based on what kind of questions a specific study aimed at exploring.

As a fourth step, different ways of analysing the data were introduced. Did the data lend themselves to a quantitative analysis, to vignette descriptions of episodes during practice sessions or to content analysis of interviews, etc.? Examples of different ways of analysing data were given and discussed.

A fifth and final step consisted of discussing how to write up the research for publication or distribution, or prepare it for verbal communication. In discussing this issue, it was important to keep in mind the intention mentioned at the beginning of this chapter. The objective was to describe processes of psychotherapy in such a way that people outside of our field, without any prior knowledge about psychotherapy, would be able to understand what child psychotherapy is about.

To summarise, this approach enabled clinicians to gain an understanding of how to formulate research questions, choose a design, and develop methods for collecting and treating data that were in accordance with their specific needs. This way of presenting methodological issues was perceived as very different from the approach used in most other similar courses or research seminars. It was also evident that it had an encouraging effect on the members of staff and that they felt as if they had something to contribute in the process of integrating research with clinical work. As the seminars proceeded, staff members developed their own ideas about how to conduct their research, while acquiring at the same time some of the necessary theoretical knowledge about research designs and methods.

A longer-term strategy for continuing to develop and maintain research-orientation in the clinical setting

Judging by the amount of stimulating and hindering issues presented in Fig. 1, a very tentative interpretation of the content of this force-field analysis would indicate that there was a certain balance between issues perceived as stimulating and hindering. According to Lewin (1965), in order to get a change in a preferred direction it is preferable to decrease the strength of hindering issues, rather than increase the stimulating forces. This diminishes the pressure of the ambitions of the clinical staff. For instance, putting pressure on staff members to undertake research might generate counter-forces and prove ineffective, or even make matters worse (Whitaker & Archer, 1990). With this in mind, a long-term strategy for achieving a higher degree of research-orientation was developed.

The general principles governing the development of strategies which had been agreed upon by me as the principal and the members of staff at the outset can be summarised in nine points: (1) focusing on relevant issues; (2) defining the research questions; (3) encouraging time-limited projects; (4) following up of each project continuously in conferences; (5) making sure that all projects would be anchored in the whole staff group, i.e., that everybody would have some knowledge about what was going on even if they were not involved in any projects; (6) inviting guest lecturers and researchers to serve as role models; (7) identifying and solving administrative problems, e.g., providing access to functional data programs and good tape recorders, getting interviews transcribed, etc.; (8) submitting applications for economic support/grants for specific projects, and (9) striving to create an increased awareness of organisational and psychological factors as well as of the content of the studies.

A general conclusion, which could be drawn from the force-field analysis, was that the research activity would increase the complexity of the work situation. It would be necessary to make priorities among the new tasks to be taken on and to find a balance with regard to the established tasks that were already part of the daily work. Moreover, differences between the various areas of work could be expected to emerge, depending on the different cultures created by the specific conditions of clinical work and research, respectively.

The tendency to develop divergent norms and attitudes in relation to different tasks had to be kept in mind, in order to avoid the risk of splitting and projection among the members of staff (Boalt Boëthius, 2002; Obholzer & Zagier Robert, 1996).

Another dimension of clinical practice that has been described in other studies (Boalt Boëthius, 1999a; Obholzer & Zagier Roberts, 1996) was the influence of the clinical work on members of staff. Psychotherapeutic work with severely disturbed patients tends to evoke feelings of doubt and insecurity regarding the value of one's work. This is often a necessary part of the psychotherapeutic process, which affects the therapist in his or her role, but such feelings can easily spread to other areas where the clinician may feel insecure; in this case, this other area would be research. This could be expected to happen since many members of staff felt that they had insufficient knowledge about research and that the training they had once had was more or less forgotten. The opposite of low self-esteem would be feelings of omnipotence, which can also be seen as part of the psychotherapeutic process. Sometimes one has to rely on such feelings in order to take on certain cases, and this can also affect how one judges one's capacity in other work areas. These examples are given just to illustrate that it may take time to find a realistic balance between one's aspirations and one's capacity.

Discussion

This case study suggests that the lack of involvement in research and developmental work that characterizes many psychotherapeutic work places focusing on psychoanalytic psychotherapy is not just a result of the different natures of research and psychotherapeutic work, which many researchers as well as clinicians have described (Hibbs & Jensen, 2005; Fonagy, 2003; Kazdin, Bass, Ayers & Rogers, 1990). It is also caused by psychological and organisational factors connected to the culture of the clinical setting (Boalt Boëthius, 1999a; Whitaker, 2001).

As mentioned above, the five main areas of concern can be described in terms of psychological, organisational, person-role, administrative/practical and research-related issues. Of these, the first three were significantly more emotionally loaded than the latter two. The issues concerning administrative and practical matters related to specific projects as well as the research-related ones were the kind of questions that arise in any research project.

The most interesting result in this case study was that staff-oriented psychological and organisational issues were seen as so much more important and emotionally loaded than research-oriented and administrative issues. This suggests that psychological and organisational aspects should be seen as critical factors, which are necessary to attend to before going into ordinary research-related planning when the research is aimed at psychoanalytic psychotherapy.

It could be argued that the chances for real change are limited, unless conscious and unconscious processes related to the interaction within and between different staff groups, including relations with the head of the institute and the outside world, are taken into consideration. If these psychological issues remain unacknowledged and unaddressed, they are likely to operate covertly, showing themselves in various forms of resistance to the research effort. This point cannot be over-emphasized in connection with research on psychoanalytic psychotherapy for children. But, to the best of my knowledge, it is so far not a phenomenon that has been the object of much interest or even less of any systematic analysis.

These findings point to the need to be aware of various expressions of feelings and thoughts indicating, for example, competition, rivalry or envy, as well as admiration and idealisation. In this case study, feelings emerged which could be related to attitudes about research in comparison with psychotherapy for instance, the idea that research is done for the benefit of the career of the individual researcher, while psychotherapy is for the benefit of the patients. However, these results are actually in line with Fonagy´s (2003, p. 131) argument that child psychotherapists need to change their attitudes "from a culture of knowing and certainty to one of questioning, uncertainty and progress". This implies in many ways a need for using the same approach to the research-related work as the individual clinician uses in relation to his or her psychotherapeutic work.

In a similar way, organisational processes linked to leadership and organisational frames are likely to be influenced when a new task is taken on. The change caused by the integration of a new task is likely to alter or even upset the balance between the different areas of work. The potential conflict between the role of psychotherapist and the role of researcher can be assumed to remain latent as long as the organisational structure remains the same, i.e., as long as there is no attempt to introduce a new element, in this case, research activity, into the clinical centre's work. But when this structure changes and the possibility of research activity is introduced, earlier latent conflicts might become manifest (Boalt Boëthius, 1999a; Janson, 1999).

The need to deal with these processes can be described in terms of containment, which implies a joint responsibility of the staff group as well as those in leadership roles. Final responsibility, however, lies with the head of the organisation. By containment is meant a capacity to listen to and take in questions, critiques, anger, frustrations and disappointment as well as hopefulness, wishes and idealisation, whether realistic or not, and then to digest these feelings and reactions in a process of metabolisation, in order to eventually give them back in a less fragmented form that can be accepted by the members of the organisation (see, e.g., Obholzer & Zagier Roberts, 1996).

As to the outcomes of this project, subsequent to the force-field analysis, which was followed by renewed visits by Dorothy Whitaker over a number of years and a considerable amount of work with different projects, the general attitude towards clinically based research changed radically. The most important outcome can be described as a clearly increased awareness of the need for systematic documentation of the clinical work, along with a realisation that this type of change depends on the interaction between the staff and the head of the institute. Without continuous attention from the head, the systematic collection of clinical data will diminish, and without the efforts of engaged and motivated members of staff, the data will be lacking in both quality and quantity. Looking back it seems likely that this type of institutional change process has to be based on a mutual trust between members of staff and the head of the institute, and that the support of the head is of fundamental importance if the integration of research is to be carried further (Whitaker & Archer, 1990).

With respect to the participation of members of staff, it can also be noted that several successful research projects have been completed. Some members of staff have been more active than others in terms of formulating research questions and collecting and analysing data, whereas others have contributed with interviews or independent judgements of narratives describing psychotherapeutic processes.

It was important that this be acknowledged within the staff group as both understandable and acceptable. To this end, it was essential that the head of the organisation value every staff member, whatever role he or she took on with respect to research, and however enthusiastic or non-enthusiastic he or she was.

Furthermore, it is evident that the degree of competition among staff members both for recognition and space for action has increased over time. Perhaps it would be more correct to say that the nature of the need for recognition and gratification has changed, and that there is a continuous pressure on persons in leadership roles to provide enough containment to handle these forces. This, in turn, has led to a higher level of creativity, which actually seems to have increased the quality of the clinical work. Another impression is that the general atmosphere has become more open and less defensive with regard to both internal and external relations, resulting in a clear interest in other ways of working and in other theoretical models for psychotherapeutic work with children (Boalt Boëthius, 2002; Fonagy, 2003).

As to the research output, one doctoral thesis and six major projects have been published and presented internationally, and about ten minor projects plus a number of books and reports aimed at non-professional readers have been completed over a period of about ten years. In addition, a number of new projects are under way. The investigated subjects have included focus interviews with psychotherapists working with autistic children, an analysis of the role of course tutor, the integration of infant observations in a psychotherapy training programme, working with parents, turning points in child psychotherapy and focused systematic case studies. (Boalt Boëthius, 1999a; Carlberg, 2009; Carlberg, 2010; Cleve, 2002).

A general conclusion is that a force-field analysis is an interesting and stimulating instrument for developing strategies for change, in this case towards a more research-oriented culture in a clinical centre working with psychoanalytic psychotherapy. This procedure gives individual members of staff an opportunity to clarify the purpose of their work and to express personal, sometimes contradictory, opinions; it legitimises all feelings and points of view and puts the various opinions and experiences into a new meaningful perspective. It is also evident that this kind of approach may have permanent effects on the staff and the work if it is maintained for a considerable amount of time. In this specific case, for example, it was clear that individual staff members developed extensive skills in conducting research on individual psychoanalytic child psychotherapy as well as other types of developmental work such as writing for non-professional audiences and participating in debates.

The integration of the different cultures represented by two of the main areas of work in this clinical centre, psychoanalytic psychotherapy and research, can be described as a process of containment of preconceptions regarding potential conflicts which may threaten to destroy the possibilities for developing creativity both individually and collectively. To create a common integrating culture implies linking various parts of an organisation to each other, while taking into consideration the boundaries surrounding each of the work areas and the interactions between them, as well as the organisational space that encompasses the system as a whole.

References

Boalt Boëthius, S. (1999a). Kulturmöten vid förändringsarbete inom en behandlingsinstitution. [Meetings between Different Cultures and Organisational Change]. In: B. Qvarsell (Ed.), *Pedagoger om kultur.* [Pedagogues on culture], (p. 45–58). Rapport nr 62. Pedagogiska Institutionen, Stockholms Universitet.

Boalt Boëthius, S. (1999b). In the Nick of Time. Recharging an Organization through Leader-initiated Interaction with Staff. In: R. Vince & R. French (Eds.), *Group Relations, Organizations and Management.* (pp. 173–189). Oxford: University Press.

Boalt Boëthius, S. & Berggren, G. (2000). *Forskning om psykoterapi med barn och ungdomar. En kunskapsöversikt. [Child and Adolescent Psychotherapy Research. An Overview of Current Research].* Ericastiftelsen: Stockholm.

Boalt Boëthius, S. (2002). Developing Strategies for Change through an Analysis of Conflicting Interests and Needs in Groups and Organizations. Presentation at the International Group Relations Conference "Exploring Being in Global Systems", Melbourne, Australia, June 25–29.

Carlberg, G. (1997). Laughter Opens the Door. Turning Points in Child Psychotherapy. *Journal of Child Psychotherapy, 23*: 331–349.

Carlberg, G. (2009). Exploring Change Processes in Psychodynamic Child Psychotherapy: the Therapists´ Perspective. In: N. Midgley,

J. Anderson, E. Grainger, T. Nesic-Vuckovic & C. Urwin. (Eds.), *Child Psychotherapy and Research: New Approaches, Emerging Findings, London: Routledge.*

Carlberg, G. (2010). Focused Systematic Case Studies. An Approach Linking Clinical Work and Research. In: J. Tsiantis & J. Trowell (Eds.), *Assessing Change in Psychoanalytic Psychotherapy of Children and Adolescents: Today's Challenge*. EFPP Book Series, London: Karnac.

Carlberg, G., Eresund, P. & Boalt Boëthius, S., (2009). *Child and Adolescent Psychotherapy Research. Workshop for Clinicians and Researchers at the Erica Foundation* October 2008. Stockholm: The Erica Foundation.

Cleve, E. (2000). *From Chaos to Coherence. Psychotherapy with a Little Boy with ADHD*. London: Karnac Books.

Cleve, E. (2002). *A Big and a Little One is Gone. Crisis Psychotherapy with a Two-year Old Boy*. London: Karnac Books.

Elliot, R. & Andersson, C. (1994). Simplicity and Complexity in Psychotherapy Research. In: R. Russel (Ed.), *Reasessing Psychotherapy*. (pp. 65–113). New York: The Guilford Press.

Elliot, R. & Morrow-Bradley, C. (1994). Developing Working Marriage between Psychotherapists and Psychotherapy Researchers: Identifying Shared Purposes. In: P. Talley, H. Strupp & S. Butler (Eds.), *Psychotherapy Research and Practice: Bridging the Gap*. (pp 124–142). New York: Basic Books.

Fonagy, P. (2003). The Research Agenda: The Vital Need for Empirical Research in Child Psychotherapy. *Journal of Child Psychotherapy, 29* (2): 129–136.

Hannerz, U. (1993). *Cultural Complexity. Studies in the Social Organization of Meaning*. New York: Columbia University Press.

Hibbs, E & Jensen, P. (Eds.) (2005). *Psychosocial Treatments for Children and Adolescent Disorders. Empirically Based Strategies for Clinical Practice*. Second edition. Washington DC: American Psychological Association.

Janson, U. (1999). Forskning om praktik och praktiker som forskare. [Research on Practice and Practitioners as Researchers]. In: B. Qvarsell (Ed.), *Pedagoger om kultur*. [Pedagogues on culture]. (pp. 59–67). Rapport nr 62. Department of Education, Stockholm University.

Kazdin, A., Bass, D., Ayers, W. & Rogers, A. (1990). Empirical and Clinical Focus of Child and Adolescent Psychotherapy Research. *Journal of Consulting and Clinical Psychology, 58*: 729–740.

Kennedy, E. (2004). *Child and Adolescent Psychotherapy. A Systematic Review of Psychoanalytic Approaches*. Anna Freud Centre: London.

Lewin, K. (1965). Group Decisions and Social Change. In H. Proshansky & B. Seidenberg (Eds.). *Basic studies in social psychology*. (pp. 423–37). New York: Holt, Rinehart and Winston.

Midgley, N. (2004). Sailing between Scylla and Charybdis: Incorporating Qualitative Approaches in Child Psychotherapy Research. *Journal of Child Psychotherapy, 30* (1): 89–111.

Midgley, N., Anderson, J., Grainger, E., Nesic, T. & Urwin, C., (Eds.) (2009). *Child Psychotherapy and Research: New Approaches, Emerging Findings*, London: Routledge.

Muratori, F., Picchi, L., Bruni, G., Patarnello & Romagnoli, G. (2003). A Two-year Follow-up of Psychodynamic Psychotherapy for Internalizing Disorders in Children. *Journal of the American Academy of Child and Adolescent Psychiatry, 42* (3): 331–339.

Obholzer, A. & Zagier Roberts, V. (Eds.), (1996). *The Unconscious at Work: Individual and Organizational Stress in the Human Services*. London: Tavistock Publications.

Orrenius, A. (1997). *Föräldrakärlek - livsviktig men förrädisk. [Parental Love – Vital but Treacherous]*. Stockholm: Wahlström & Widstrand.

Shirk, S.R. & Russel, R.L. (1992). A Re-evaluation of Estimates of Child Therapy Effectiveness. *Journal of the American Academy of Child and Adolescent Psychiatry, 36*: 609–615.

Stiles, W. (1994). Views of the Chasm between Psychotherapy Research and Practice. In: R. Russel (Ed.). *Reassessing Psychotherapy Research*. (pp. 154–166). New York: The Guilford Press.

Trowell, J., Kolvin, I. & Weeramanthri, T. (2002). Psychotherapy for Sexually Abused Girls: Psychopathological Outcome Findings and Patterns of Change. *British Journal of Psychiatry, 180* (3): 234–247.

Trowell, J., Joffe, I., Campbell, J., Clemente, C., Almquist, F., Soinenen, M., Koskenranta-Aalto, U., Weintraub, S., Kolaitis, G., Tomaras, V., Anastasopoulos, D., Grayson, K., Barnes, J. & Tsiantis, J. (2007). Childhood Depression: A Place for Psychotherapy. An Outcome Study Comparing Individual Psychodynamic Psychotherapy and Family Therapy. *European Child and Adolescent Psychiatry, 16*: 157–167.

Tsiantis, J., Kolvin, I., Anastasopoulos, D., Trowell, J., Tomaras, V., Miles, G., Papadopoulos, R., Soininen, M., Boström, C. & Almqvist, F. (2005). Psychotherapy for Early Adolescent Depression: A Comparison of Two Psychotherapeutic Interventions in Three European Countries. In: E. Hibbs & P. Jensen (Eds.), *Psychosocial Treatments for Child and Adolescent Disorders. Empirically Based Strategies for Clinical Practice.* Second Edition. (pp. 267–293). Washington DC: American Psychological Association.

Urwin, C. (2007). Revisiting "What works for Whom?": A Qualitative Framework for Evaluating Clinical Effectiveness in Child Psychotherapy. *Journal of Child Psychotherapy, 33*: 134–160.

Whitaker, D.S. (2001). *Using Groups to Help People*. Second Edition. Philadelphia: Brunner-Routledge.

Whitaker, D.S. & Archer, L. (1990). Using Practice Research for Change. *Social Work & Social Sciences Review, 2* (1): 9–21.

Whitaker, D.S. & Archer, L. (1994). Partner Research and its Contributions to Learning and to Team-building. *Social Work Education, 13* (3): 39–59.

CHAPTER THREE

What does a manual contribute?

Judith Trowell, Maria Rhode and Jackie Hall

Introduction

This chapter discusses the role of a manual for individual psychoanalytic psychotherapy for depression in late childhood and early adolescence. The manual to be discussed was written by Judith Trowell and Maria Rhode with comments and additions from Margaret Rustin, Consultant Child Psychotherapist Tavistock clinic, John Tsiantis, Professor of Child Psychiatry Athens, Effie Lignos, Consultant Child Psychotherapist, Athens and Olga Maratos, Psychoanalyst and Lead Clinical Research Psychologist. The manual was written as part of the Biomed EU research funded Childhood Depression study conducted in Athens, Helsinki and London.

The contribution of the manual

The value of the manual is that it brings together, for front line trainees and newly qualified psychotherapists, a rationale for a way of working.

In order to develop the skills required to become a therapist, trainees have their own personal therapy, undertake an infant observation and take intensive, long-term cases under supervision. This prepares them for the intensity and demands of working with very troubled children and families. In addition, they learn about child development, psychopathology assessment, termination issues and psychoanalytic theory. These are learnt in a range of settings for example, Community CAMHS, hospitals, paediatric liaison, schools and special schools, adolescent units, under fives services and learning difficulties services.

After this training, additional help is needed to feel confident when offering a relatively brief intervention. The manual provides guidance and makes suggestions so that the frontline professional can be helped to reflect and think about situations as they arise.

It also discusses different types of depression to assist professionals in their understanding of their task and some key concepts. It goes on to explain the focus of the work and to explore what particular problems are likely to be. Issues of risk are identified and these are raised to alert professionals so they can seek advice to act promptly. The more usual dilemmas are discussed with the expectation that the professional can manage them.

The therapists' task and the setting required are explained, along with some of the research issues and constraints of this form of intervention. The manual also provides clarification of what therapists can expect to achieve within the time limits of the therapy. In addition, a number of issues are examined that are specific to psychoanalytic work with depressed children and adolescents.

It is important to stipulate that audiotapes of the sessions and supervisions are needed to monitor compliance with the manual. Besides these, the usual process notes taken to supervision are essential as the use of the tapes and notes can be very helpful in understanding what is happening psychodynamically between therapist and patient.

The tape recorder's presence may be unsettling for the therapists at first but most children and young people do not object and its presence is useful in some therapies. In most cases, it is ignored.

What the manual does not do

The manual does not tell people how to do psychoanalytic psychotherapy. It is no substitute for a clinical training. Trained clinicians, who have had personal therapy, have flair and intuition and are regularly supervised, could use the manual.

The manual does not cover all the theoretical orientations: it is limited to those of the authors which are Kleinian, post Kleinian and independent ideas and hypotheses about the issues and ways of working with depressed children and adolescents.

The Manual does communicate what happens in therapy, and that what makes this intervention different from other forms of treatment is the use of transference and counter-transference. It also communicates the theoretical, technical and managerial issues that the newly qualified or senior trainee needs to be aware of, and provides a review of this information that is useful to more experienced colleagues, in refreshing and checking their skills. It in no way replaces consultation and supervision.

The crucial area of work with parents is also addressed. The intergenerational issues prove to be very important, and the need for parental projections to be taken back and for the young person to be freed up, was often the key to improvement. The internal worlds of the parents, as well as their external worlds, were often chaotic and some help with this was essential.

This issue of what the therapists felt to be premature termination was a difficulty that had to be addressed in each case. But given that most young people managed well, that puberty was in full swing for most, that time limited work was often more acceptable to the clients and that the improvement was ongoing post termination (the sleeper effect), there was recognition and perhaps reassurance that up to 30sessions can be effective for young people.

Thinking about the manual and what contribution it made after our study, we are very aware that the cases selected by the CDI, (Kovacs, 1981) the K-SADS (Chambers et al., 1985) and the Moods and Feelings Questionnaire (Angold et al., 1987) presented as very empty, with a very fragile sense of self. If depression is seen as related to the failure to manage aggression, which is either externalised as behaviour problems or internalised as a self-destructive super-ego, then the young people in our study who were severely depressed, appeared to have lost their identity and sexual identity, at least in part, in a self destructive internal world.

The manual

This manual concerns the application of psychoanalytic psychotherapy to the treatment of young people between nine and fifteen years of age. These young people were seriously depressed, as measured by their performance on a number of instruments during the intake process. They were offered once-weekly therapy for up to thirty sessions of fifty minutes' duration; their carers were offered parallel work once a fortnight with a separate parent worker.

Introduction: Adolescent depression

Relatively little is known about adolescent depression in comparison to depression in adults. Depression is diagnosed in adolescents using the same criteria as in adults, but there may be some developmental variations in its manifestations.

Harrington (1993) states in that about 20% of young people with depressive disorders also have a conduct disorder, and nearly 50% suffer from high levels of anxiety. Depressed adolescents show many of the psychosocial defects associated with depression in adults, such as poor self-esteem, negative and irrational cognitive distortions, social withdrawal and impaired social ability. These deficits make it difficult for depressed adolescents to cope with the developmental challenges posed by peers in the social, academic and interpersonal spheres.

Experiencing a depressive episode in early life may have long-lasting consequences. Studies indicate that people of all ages who have had an episode of depression are at substantially greater risk for the further recurrence of depression and for the development of other psychological difficulties (Kandel & Davies, 1986; Kovacs et al., 1984a, 1984b; Lewinsohn, Hoberman & Rosenbaum, 1988). Many depressed adolescents are undetected and untreated: their depression is viewed as "normal adolescent turmoil". There is evidence that depression may actually be more prevalent among young people (Klerman & Weissman, 1989). It also seems likely that individuals who become depressed early in life may experience a more severe form of the disorder (Birmaher et al., 1996; Kolvin and Sadowski, 2001). Although the parasuicide and suicide rate in this age group has increased substantially during the last twenty years

(Birmaher et al., 1996, Kolvin and Sadowski, 2001), most depressed adolescents do not receive treatment.

Brent et al., (1997) and Birmaher et al., (2000) have looked at young people randomly allocated to CBT, systemic behavioural family therapy and non-directive supportive therapy. In their first study, positive outcomes by the end of therapy were 60% with CBT, 29% with family therapy and 36% with non-directive supportive therapy. They all had between 12 and16 weekly sessions; they were aged between 13 and 18 years, and 76% were female. About one-third were recruited via a newspaper article, but the comparability with referrals to CAMHS services is difficult to assess. The diagnosis of Major Depressive Disorder, MDD, as distinct from dysthymia, was made according to the criteria of DSM-III. In the first study, 60% of young people receiving CBT had improved, as compared to 29% of those receiving family therapy and 36% of those receiving non-directive supportive therapy. The second study was a two year follow up, which showed that most participants, 80%, had recovered: there were no differences between the interventions. However, 30% of the total sample suffered a recurrence post recovery; 57% were on SSRI medication, and 62 of the 78 had had booster sessions.

In the TADS (Treatment for Adolescents with Depression Study, Marsh, 2004), a non-clinical volunteer sample aged between 12–17 with a primary DSM IV diagnosis of MDD were given 12 weeks of (a) Fluoxetine, (b) CBT, (c) CBT plus Fluoxetine, or (d) placebo. The response with Fluoxetine plus CBT was 71%, Fluoxetine alone was 60.6%, CBT alone was 43.2% and placebo 34.8%. Suicidal thinking was present in 29% of total sample at the start and improved in all treatment groups, with Fluoxetine plus CBT showing the greatest reduction. Seven patients attempted suicide out of the total of 439 but none completed suicide.

These two studies show that interventions are helpful, but questions still remain about how to safely treat depressed young people. The NICE guidelines recommend that a psychological therapy be tried initially after a period of watchful waiting. If the initial CBT, interpersonal or short-term family therapy does not help, then they recommend additional therapy and parent work and then to consider the use of Fluoxetine medication. One of the additional therapies suggested is Individual Psychodynamic therapy and the aim of this manual is to support and enable this.

Professionals can easily feel helpless when faced with such levels of depression. Medication for depression has not been shown to be effective in the ten-to-fourteen-year-old age group (Birmaher et al., 1996; Kolvin & Sadowski 2001), thus other treatment approaches are required. A recent study of mild to moderate depression in adults has shown six sessions of counselling to be 80% effective in alleviating symptoms, a success rate identical to that achieved with medication. Moreover, most clients preferred a "talking cure" (Chilvers et al., 2001). Various authors have also reported encouraging outcomes to single-case studies of depressed children and adolescents treated with once-weekly psychotherapy (Harris, 1965; Youell, 1997). The present study therefore, investigates the outcome of time-limited individual psychoanalytic psychotherapy for severe depression in young people between the ages of ten and fourteen.

A psychodynamic framework for understanding depression in young people

Different types of depression

Depression is diagnosed with reference to the presenting problems and symptomatology. From a psychodynamic viewpoint, one may distinguish normal depression, neurotic depression, borderline depression and "psychotic" depression. Individuals with overt psychotic symptoms were excluded from this study.

1 Normal depression

Throughout the life cycle, each developmental step forward entails both gains and losses. Individuation and maturation imply separation and loss: relationships change and some must be relinquished. Sadness, distress and a measure of guilt will be associated with these changes. The adolescent's life task of becoming more independent may cause anxiety and pain, both because of the adolescent's loss of the protected state of childhood with the sense of parents taking responsibility, and also because the adolescent may feel that the parents are not ready to allow the child to move away. In sensitive individuals, or in vulnerable families, these normal "life event" developments can lead to sadness or depression that exceeds the normal range and may give rise to symptoms. The conflicts at issue may not be abnormally severe or go beyond the usual development difficulties, but the individual's unique temperament and particular involvement with the family composition and structure may be such that the result is pathological.

2 Normal depression associated with trauma

A life event such as parental illness can be experienced traumatically, particularly if it appears to confirm a fantasy entertained by the young person (Garland, 1991; Cecchi, 1990). Such a fantasy might not have seemed dangerous in the absence of "confirmation" by a real event, but if confirmed, can lead to the young person's serious anxiety about their own destructiveness and therefore to an important degree of inhibition. Working over the fantasy with the therapist can help the young person to understand the difference between fantasy and reality.

3 Neurotic depression

In neurotic depression, the individual has reached a developmental state of being able to function adequately in certain areas of their lives, while at the same time having become stuck, fixed or regressed in other areas. Areas of unresolved conflict have become extended, resulting in significant problems and symptoms. The individual's mental state is fluid and flexible in certain aspects, but in others, has become fixed into a "psychic retreat" (Steiner, 1993) designed to evade emotional conflict, particularly feelings of guilt, which can seem impossible to resolve. This can result in a severe restriction in the ability to engage in fulfilling personal relationships and important tasks.

4 Borderline depression

The individual functions predominantly at a "paranoid schizoid" level rather than a "depressive" one (Klein, 1935; 1940). This means that the main defences against anxiety are projection, splitting, projective identification, denial and manic flight.

When conflicts are dealt with primarily by these mechanisms, there is little capacity to make reparation, mourn or seek resolution of conflicts in an objective, rational manner. The client may feel empty, futile and cut off from emotions. However, people in this group are capable of moving towards the more developmentally advanced state of "the depressive position" (Klein, 1935; 1940) at some times or in some areas of their functioning. Given the usual clinical population, it is likely that most cases of adolescents or young adults will fall into this category or into Category 5.

5 Depression with "psychotic' anxieties"

Note: "psychotic" as used here is a psychoanalytic term, and does not imply psychiatrically suffering delusions or hallucinations, as would be the case in psychosis.

In this most severe category, clients feel to an extreme degree that their situation is hopeless and that life is pointless. They are typically preoccupied with the fear that the inner world of their mind is peopled by dead figures whom there seems to be no hope of reviving. Clients may feel that they lack the physical or mental equipment that is essential for living life properly; that they are perpetually on the edge of an abyss; that a barrier or a wall of glass cuts them off from other people; that they live in a bubble. Many suffer from existential anxieties about losing their identity and from fears about spilling out or falling forever that have been described by Winnicott (1949) and Tustin (1986).

Diagnosis

There are many sad, distressed young people where the diagnosis of depression can be made with a careful, thorough assessment. The symptomatology of childhood depression and dysthymia varies according to the individual child, and can affect many different aspects of the child's functioning for example, affective, cognitive, social and somatic. Based on the DSM-IV description, symptoms can be grouped under the following categories:

Symptoms expressed through the body

- psychomotor retardation/psychomotor agitation
- appetite disturbance, leading to weight loss/weight gain

- insomnia/hypersomnia
- feelings of fatigue (loss of energy)
- other somatic complaints and symptoms

Symptoms referring to mood or affect

- depressive mood/irritability
- thoughts about death/suicide
- diminished levels of interest/pleasure
- feelings of hopelessness
- feelings of guilt and worthlessness

Symptoms involving cognitive processes and performance

- impaired ability to think
- impaired ability to concentrate
- indecisiveness
- low school performance
- low self-esteem

Symptoms involving socialisation and relatedness

- poor social interaction
- lack of close friends (peer group problems)
- shyness
- difficulty in relating to others (relatedness)

Theoretical concepts

Freud pointed out in "Mourning and Melancholia" (Freud, 1917) that the severely depressed, melancholic person's self-reproaches were such as might make sense if they were directed against a significant other in the patient's life. He conceptualised depression as a situation in which the patient's superego, the internalised primitive conscience derived from parental figures, cruelly reproaches and oppresses the ego: "The shadow of the object fell upon the ego." (Freud 1917, p. 249) In other words, depression results from destructive relationships between parts of the self, some of which were derived from internalised parental figures.

Abraham (May, 2001) was the first psychoanalyst to highlight the particular importance in depression of hostile elements in the early relationship to the mother, a perspective that was developed by Melanie Klein. Klein (1935) proposed that the first months of life were characterised by the "paranoid-schizoid" defences against anxiety, in which the prime concern is for the survival of the self. Splitting of good and bad is necessary to overcome confusion, but when taken to extremes can lead to an excessively black-and-white worldview and an impoverishment of the personality. In the depressive position, which follows developmentally, good and bad aspects of the self and significant others begin to be integrated, which leads to guilt concerning attacks against loved people. The main concern is for the survival of loved figures, both externally and internally, implying that someone who has not overcome the anxieties of the depressive position may be preoccupied with loss and be frightened of forming attachments. These depressive anxieties, not the same as a state of depression, are resolved by making reparation during the working-through of the depressive position. Someone for whom guilt is intolerable, may regress to the paranoid-schizoid position or adopt a psychic retreat (Steiner, 1993).

Winnicott's Age of Concern is very similar to Klein's (1935, 1940) depressive position. He mapped out ways in which the quality of maternal provision can impinge on the individual's sense of self and well-being, including the development of a "False Self" when the baby is forced to pay premature attention to the mother's state of mind (Winnicott, 1948; 1960). His description of maternal mirroring and its effect on a sense of identity is highly relevant to the sense of alienation and futility often reported by depressed people (Winnicott, 1963). Andre Green in France, working with adults, has highlighted the fundamental importance of the fantasy of "the dead mother" (Green, 1980).

In general, psychoanalytic authors are in agreement that depression is associated with fears about the consequences of aggression, with resulting hopelessness and despair. There follows a tendency to turn aggression against the self, and a failure to elaborate issues of identity in a satisfactory manner. The psychosomatic symptoms listed above, would be conceptualised in terms of an inadequate provision of the emotional containment (Bion, 1962) that is necessary if the individual is to develop the capacity to think about emotional experiences and to present with feelings rather than with sensations (Tustin, 1981; 1986).

Technique: A rationale

Many different levels at which childhood depression may be understood are all considered as highly relevant when the team is working towards the formulation of a case. The reader is referred to the Manual for Systems Integrative Family Therapy for an exposition (Depression in the context of the referral: why now? the social/cultural context; family context: factors precipitating/maintaining depression; the hereditary component). However, the actual individual treatment of the child is concerned with his or her personal experience, as it is revealed in the relationship with the therapist.

The aim of psychoanalytic psychotherapy is to provide an opportunity for the client to understand his own personality and his model of the world by exploring his relationship with a therapist about whom he has little factual information. This means that much of the way he experiences the therapist will be influenced by his expectations of people's behaviour, what Attachment Theorists call his Internalised Working Models. Exploring these together with the therapist provides the client with an emotionally convincing experience of the way in which his perceptions may be governed by unrealistic expectations. Having his experience verbalised by the therapist may also provide him with a sense of his own legitimacy.

It will be clear that there are some points of overlap with cognitive behavioural therapy. One main difference is that psychoanalytic psychotherapy addresses underlying personality structure rather than individual problematic situations, so that improvements can generalise over a wide area. Another important difference is that the focus is on the emotional relationship between client and therapist, so that the transference/counter-transference (Heimann, 1950; Money-Kyrle, 1956; Brenman Pick, 1985) is the prime tool. By remaining open to emotional communications from the young person, and continuing to process these, the therapist provides the experience that frightening emotions can be managed in the context of a relationship with a separate, dependable person. With young people like the very depressed ones in the present study, where the disturbance of the relationship to the self and others is the principal problem, this deficit is addressed directly through providing a relationship in which "Working through in the counter-transference" (Brenman Pick, 1985) is possible.

Mediating variables

According to psychodynamic theoretical models, problems and symptoms, including depression, may result from dysfunction in various fundamental areas of psychic life. These areas include the management of libidinal instincts and of aggression; the adequate structuring of the personality, fantasy life, object relations and self-representation.

A mediating variable could be defined as the area that lies between these dysfunctional fundamental psychic areas and the symptom. The mediating variable is expressed through the child's play, dreams, drawing, acts and verbal productions, and is therefore the area which the therapist can reach through verbal intervention. A psychodynamically orientated therapeutic approach would effect change through the interpretation of mediating variables as they become apparent during therapy. For example, working on the reasons for emotional inhibition would be expected to lead to greater freedom in communicating emotions and a lessened need to resort to somatic symptoms. The therapist might explore emotional inhibition both in terms of defences and in terms of deficits (Alvarez 1992). As always, this exploration will occur within the framework of the relationship with the therapist; what are the feared consequences of emotional expression? Does the client expect the therapist to be cold/hostile/indifferent/unresponsive/vengeful/easily damaged? Does the client not expect a gratifying response? Does the client expect the therapist to see him or her as useless/unlovable/incompetent? This focus on the patient's relationship with the therapist and expectations of response delineates one of the main differences in approach between psychoanalytic psychotherapy and cognitive behavioural therapy.

Outline of the therapeutic process

With acknowledgements to:

Mufson L., Moreau D., Weissman M. M., and Klerman G. L., Interpersonal Psychotherapy for Depressed Adolescents.

Introduction to therapy and therapist

After the assessment and administration of research instruments, the therapist and parent worker would:

1. Explain the duration and frequency of sessions and that the aim is to help the young person with their worries and concerns. The young person may wish to discuss and explore this.
2. The need for regular attendance and the issues of confidentiality and what will be shared should be clarified. It is important to explain that if concerns are acute, they will need to be shared.
3. Discuss the parallel work with the parent(s), and the implications for the young person's treatment.
4. Explore and take seriously what precipitated the referral, i.e. what was the particular issue and why now. It is also important not to imply that all problems, conflicts, concerns can be resolved. This is brief focused work.
5. If there are major life events, these are likely to be significant, so it can be helpful to explore these. Possible such issues could include:

   Bereavement }
   Separation } with significant others
   Serious Illness } family, friends
   Serious Dispute }

   Transitions
   (such as change of school, birth of sibling, new partner for parent, sibling leaving home, parental divorce).

6. Some data from the questionnaires given during the research assessment may assist at this stage.

The treatment

1. The therapist will work on the topics raised by the young person, particularly focusing on what happens in the room and in the relationship with the therapist that links with the topic or material identified in the introductory session.
2. The therapist will need to monitor the young person's symptoms to detect any deterioration.
3. The therapist will need to meet the parents before the beginning of treatment, and be available should any serious problems arise, while at the same time taking care to maintain confidentiality. Communication with the parent worker is essential, and is discussed further below.

4. The evolution of the relationship with the therapist is key as is the therapist's capacity to face negative feelings, both within the young person and in the young person's attitude to the therapist. The capacity to acknowledge all these negatives, pain, rage, destructiveness and self destructiveness, to put them into words and to be able to tolerate them without the need to "to look on the bright side", is crucial. This links with the psychoanalytic theoretical model of depression, according to which problems or the fear of problems, in managing aggression in an interpersonal context can lead to aggression being turned against the self.
5. Crises may occur: the depression or anger may escalate. It is important to anticipate these crises and to be able to think about them and put them into words. This will help the young person consider realistically what might be the consequences of, for instance, a suicidal attempt or serious acting out. If a crisis occurs, it must be taken seriously. The therapist may need to raise with the young person the need for other responsible adults to be consulted, even though it may not be possible for the requirements of confidentiality to be upheld completely. The young person may need to realise that in an extreme situation, the therapist will fulfil their duty as a responsible citizen to protect their client in consultation with others.
6. The time frame needs constant reiteration.
7. Particular Problems:

    a. **Abnormal Grief:** delayed chronic
    This may require special attention if the young person is in a fixed state and is either very preoccupied and talks of nothing else, or refuses to talk and avoids the topic completely.

    b. **Marital and family conflict:**
    Whilst hearing and understanding the conflict in the external world, it will be important to think about the links with earlier internal conflicts and to try and help the young person gain a sense of what is external reality and what is internal, deriving from the here and now or from earlier experience.

    Certain disputes may be such that coming to terms with the situation is what is required.

c. **Transitions:**
   These can arouse fear, rage, betrayal, and rivalry. Anxiety about being unable to manage the problems of transitions needs to be addressed.

8. Some of the young people may have considerable problems with interpersonal relationships. There could be problems in expressing feelings, initiating relationships, maintaining relationships and poor communication. Exploring their identity and establishing their capacity to relate to others is a key aspect of adolescence and needs careful, sensitive work. Friendships, group pressures and social isolation need to be addressed.
9. Early Termination:
   It will be important to clarify if this is by agreement, the young person's choice, or a parental decision.

Termination

1. Separation and loss are likely to have been central for this client group. The termination phase provides the opportunity to work on this in the here and now, as this is a planned ending. Previous losses and separations are likely to emerge. Sadness and anxiety are frequent. Reflecting on the process of the treatment will be helpful, as will reviewing what has been worked on and achieved. This will be a particular feature of the last ten sessions, during which the client will be prepared for separating from the therapist and for the repeat research assessments.
2. It will be important to link again with the parent/s. There will have been once a term review meetings with carers, but an end of treatment meeting with them is essential. There will need to be discussion with the young person about whether it is appropriate for them to be present.
3. Further treatment may be needed. If possible, leaving a gap to allow the full impact of the therapy to emerge will be helpful for the young person and their family. This will be reviewed at follow up.

Serious clinical situations

These must be monitored closely and discussed with the supervisor and clinical case manager, but may need a rapid response.

a. Suicidal Young Person
b. Violence
c. School Refusal
d. Substance Abuse
e. Child Abuse — Sexual Abuse; Physical Abuse
f. Self-harming behaviour
g. Running Away
h. Pregnancy (self or partner)

Clinical dilemmas

1. The young person needs parenting. The limits of the therapeutic relationship must be clarified.
2. Frequent missed sessions or lateness. These need to be discussed with the supervisor and parent worker, and the use of telephone calls and letters should be considered. In general, sessions that are missed because of a good reason are not counted towards the thirty sessions allocated. Examples include illness of the child, illness of the parent if the child cannot come independently or a strike on public transport if the family depends on this. If a parent had an urgent work commitment and could not make alternative arrangements for the child to be brought, that session would not be counted but if it were obvious that alternative arrangements could have been made and were not, then that session would be counted. Sometimes a decision may be problematic, for example, a child who misses the last session of term because of conjunctivitis which appears to be related to grief about endings, but which the family would not recognise as such. This session would be made up on the grounds that the family would have been completely unaware of the meaning of their behaviour. The general principle is that missed sessions are counted if they are missed for reasons that are to do with acting out, either on the child's part or on the caregiver's.

The structure of the therapist's task

The psychoanalytically based individual therapy offered as part of this research project can be carried out by medical or non-medical practitioners who have trained in child analysis or in psychoanalytic child psychotherapy. Outlines of the training requirements of one of the recognised UK training schools for child psychotherapists and of training for child psychiatrists can be obtained from the appropriate institutions.

Because of the severity of the distress suffered by the young people in this project and their families, the provision of fortnightly supervision is an essential aspect of processing and containing it. This is particularly so because much communication will take place by non-verbal means, and an important part of the therapists' work will lie in making use of their counter-transference experience. Supervision can be an important safeguard against unsubstantiated, "wild" interpretations.

Therapists can feel disturbed by the time limits on the treatment they are able to offer very troubled young people. It can feel as though they are being tantalising or cruel by stopping treatment when fundamental issues come up, often at the end of treatment, such as issues of identity or sexual identity. The fact that most therapists will have been trained to provide long-term treatment can make it difficult for them to address adequately the negative transference, and particularly the negative feelings aroused by termination. In a previous study with girls who had suffered sexual abuse (Long and Trowell, 2001), good outcome was associated with the therapist's ability to deal with the negative transference as well as with the parents' willingness to engage. Supervisors can help to contain the therapists' anxiety and guilt about termination by reminding them of these findings, and in this way counteract the temptation to avoid the negative transference.

Treatment guidelines

Duration and frequency of therapy

In adulthood, improvement has been shown to be related to duration of dynamic therapy, this being proportionately greater in early sessions, the improvement then proceeding more slowly as the number of sessions increase. (Howard et al., 1986) This has led to the suggestion that when comparing two different forms of therapy which are intrinsically different, the duration of therapy should be controlled. However, such arguments are negated by the fact that different therapies are likely to differ in the timing and frequency of their optimal effects at different points of intensity and time (Kolvin et al., 1988; Bell et al., 1989).

Thus, a firm prescription of the number of sessions could be counterproductive for those therapies that appear to peak earlier. Furthermore, it may well be that each form of therapy has its own momentum, at least in the shorter term (Trowell et al., 1996).

A limit of thirty sessions can feel like a cruel imposition, as discussed above. However, if the therapist can view it as an extended therapeutic assessment, it can provide an opportunity for work on crucial issues of separation and the management of aggression. This can happen much more readily in a setting where future access to therapy is a realistic option. The positive side of the limit on thirty sessions is that many young adolescents would fear being trapped in a long-term commitment, whereas a limited contract can allow them to become acquainted with what therapy can offer.

The therapeutic setting

The predictability and reliability of the setting are essential if deep-lying fears are to be dealt with, including fears of abandonment as well as fears of the young person's own destructiveness. The sessions take place:

- at regular intervals (once weekly)
- on the same day of the week
- at the same time of day
- with the same therapist
- in the same room, which provides a protected, private setting.

Equipment used in therapy

The room will contain:

- table(s)
- chairs (and, where possible, a couch)
- a pillow

- a blanket
- a waste bin
- a source of water (where possible)

The standard set of toys comprises:

- pipe cleaner doll families
- families of wild and farm animals
- fences
- bricks
- toy cars and lorries
- paper
- ordinary and coloured pencils
- felt-tipped pens
- plasticine
- ruler
- scissors
- rubber
- Sellotape and glue
- sharpener
- sponge ball
- string
- beaker

This standard equipment may need to be modified, as some of the older children in the age range 10–14 years may feel that toys are infantilising. For these young people, a limited range of materials, e.g. drawing materials only, can be more appropriate.

Technical issues of particular concern

a. Physical contact should only be allowed in order to:

  - restrain from self-harm
  - prevent harm to the therapist
  - prevent exploration of therapist's body
  - prevent young person from exposing themselves (genitals, breasts)
  - protect the therapy room and furniture from damage.

b. Leaving the room
   Where the young person continues to insist on this after discussion, they should be accompanied into the care of the appropriate adult.
c. Disclosure of suicidal thoughts and plans or abuse
   This needs to be shared with the case manager, who will then decide on what should be communicated to the relevant carers and statutory services (see Institutional Guidelines).

Treatment guidelines

Prior reading to complement psychoanalytic texts: Gilbert, Paul (1992). *Counselling for Depression*: Sage. This provides an excellent, clear introduction to depression. It then describes, in detail, Cognitive Behavioural counselling. However, the relationship with the therapist and topics considered as they emerge may help in both understanding and focusing on issues likely to emerge with this client group. This book is aimed at those working with adults so this needs to be borne in mind.

The patient will have been assessed formally. It will be important to clarify the framework of the whole project, including what is available and what will be offered to the young person (see earlier in this chapter: Outline of the Therapeutic Process).

As described in that section, once the therapist and patient have been introduced, the treatment alliance needs to be established. The length of the treatment and the repeat assessments will need to be explained, as will issues of confidentiality and of what might be shared with the parents at reviews. In addition, it is possible that this client group could bring up seriously worrying issues, such as suicidal intentions or self-harming behaviour that could not justifiably be kept as confidential within the research and treatment team, and might need to be shared with the responsible adults if the patient is at risk of harm.

The therapist will attempt to convey to the child/young person that the method of work involves developing an understanding of the meaning of all communications between them. What is said is only one part of the communication: all the external areas that enter the therapy will also be considered in this way including missed sessions, reluctance to come and reluctance to leave. All this work will take place within the boundary of the therapy room. Over time, the therapist will help the child/young person to see the deeper unconscious meaning of all these communications, verbal and non-verbal, and the links between this and past and present areas of conflict and difficulty.

The therapeutic work

The therapist's task includes:

1. Enabling the child/young person to express himself, whether by means of words, play, drawings or actions within the therapeutic setting;
2. Finding a way to give meaning to the child's communication, and of communicating that meaning in a way that will make sense to the child/young person;
3. Selecting from the mass of verbal, non-verbal and unconscious communication, those areas which can be most helpfully addressed, whether by comment, by description, by clarification or by interpretation; for example:

    a. Comment: "It's as though you couldn't imagine being able to enjoy school."
    b. Description: "The mother doll doesn't seem to be taking any notice of the baby."
    c. Clarification: "Why isn't the mother doll paying any attention when the baby cries?"
    d. Interpretation:

        - "Maybe you can't believe I'm on your side if I'm not around during the week."
        - "Perhaps when you're cross with your parents you can't believe they won't get hurt or angry, and perhaps when you are cross with me you can't believe I won't either."

4. Observing and reflecting on his/her own reactions to the child and young person; striving to be aware of the transference and counter-transference, as distinct from any of the therapist's own emotional issues which may be triggered by the treatment;
5. Remaining aware of the time limited and focused nature of the treatment;

6. Implementing the research project requirements:
   a. For data recording
   b. For supervision. Aspects of the need for this have already been discussed above.

Therapeutic technique

Therapists will be expected to follow the usual analytic technique, and to refrain, for instance, from self-disclosure and reassurance.

Topics addressed will be those raised by the young person: the therapy is child-led and proceeds at the child's pace. However, the therapist needs to be aware of the time-limited nature of the treatment, and to keep in mind the need to address issues that are being avoided or denied when the child's behaviour or play indicate this to be appropriate.

All the issues that arise will have some bearing on the transference and counter-transference and will need, at least to some extent, to be addressed in relation to the therapist. It will be important to get the balance and timing right in dealing with the transference on the one hand, and in making links with current and past external experiences, on the other.

For example, if a child describes an uncaring teacher who does not like children, it might feel insensitive and invalidating for the therapist not to acknowledge the emotional reality of this experience before making a transference interpretation. On the other hand, appropriate transference interpretations will be crucial to the degree to which the therapy becomes a lasting internal resource. Thus, a girl in her last session said she hoped that when she had stopped all the progress would not get lost, but that she would not want further treatment if it were available because she had a lot to do at school. She then went on to describe a good time she had had with friends, and how sad it had been coming back to a darkened house; her mother was probably depressed and had just gone to bed. The therapist took up how important it was for this girl to feel that the therapist was prepared to let her go but thought, on reflection, that it would have been useful to link the girl's fear of losing the improvements she had made with the fear that these left her mother and therapist in the depressed state she herself had been in previously, which would not feel like a secure foundation to build on.

Establishing contact with the young person

In order to establish contact it may be important for the therapist to verbalise the client's doubts, fears and anxieties, which will include their possible reluctance to engage in therapy. Their hopes for the therapy may need addressing, as will lack of hope and disappointment.

The child/young person may become angry, hostile or rude and this will need to be acknowledged together with any subsequent guilt.

Therapeutic boundaries may need to be re-iterated.

Some important issues: A rating scale

The following issues are among those that may be expected to arise during treatment. They form the basis of a rating scale filled in by therapists every week.

1 *Trust/Hope/Betrayal*

Is the child trying to think about hope or trust in relation to mother, father, therapist or any other significant person or is the child thinking about betrayal by these people?

2 *Emptiness*

Is there a sense that the child feels he has nothing inside him, or is trying to work on internal losses?

3 *Mindlessness*

Is the child in a state of mindless non-reflection? Is there any evidence of his actively breaking mental links or attachments, or getting rid of experiences in order to avoid painful thoughts?

4 *Basic assumption/Splitting (inside/outside)*

Is the child struggling with issues about getting inside an object? Are they defining their worth through being inside an object or group?

5 Disintegration

Is the child trying to hold himself together, struggling not to fall to pieces emotionally?

6 Chaos and confusion

Is the child filled with inner chaos and confusion, and therefore unable to make sense of life experiences?

7 Group identity

Is the child exploring relationships with peers?

8 Academic functioning

Is the child exploring their capacities and involvement in school and work?

9 Fantasy/play/creativity

Is the child able to use their imaginative capacity as a form of communication to express their inner state? Can they symbolise their feelings and thoughts through play or drawings/creative productions?

10 Dreams/day dreams

Is there evidence from dreams; how is this evidence used or thought about by the child?

11 Knowing/not knowing

Does the child have an awareness of why he is coming, that he needs help, and have some understanding of his situation? Is the child trying to struggle with this, to think what may have felt unthinkable, to make connections and links?

12 Acting out/enactment

Are there events, feelings or behaviours that are not symbolic, but concretely represent the child's distress? For example, a boy took an overdose during a holiday break, and later told his therapist about it in such a way as to convey that it had happened a long time before. When this kind of event takes place, there needs to be a careful review of possible risk in view of the potentially misleading communication. As in this case, the inaccuracy can often only be picked up in team meetings.

13 Mother

Is the child exploring his relationship with his mother? Internal or external?

14 Father

Is the child exploring his relationship with his father? Internal or external?

15 Other

Is the child exploring his feelings and relationship with this person e.g. step-parent, grandparent, significant other?

16 Oedipal

Is the child struggling with thoughts and feelings about the triangular relationship, being left out, not being left out, usurping one parent's place in sexual relationships, e.g. triumph or guilt arising from this?

17 Siblings

Is the child working on feelings about siblings, natural or step?

18 Loss

Is the child working on loss? This can include loss of experience of own bodily or mental integrity; loss of childhood; loss of parent/s, siblings, grandparents, friends etc.

19 Who am i?/identity

Is the child working on issues to do with an emerging sense of who they are? This includes trying to make sense of events in their lives and of their own thoughts and feelings, as well as of their strengths and weaknesses and range of attributes.

20 Sexuality

Is the child trying to think about their own sexual feelings in the past, now or in the future? Is the child thinking about parental sexuality or about peer sexuality?

21 Body language

Is the body used to convey the child's emotional state? Does observation of the body language provide information about transference and counter-transference?

22 Boundaries

Is the child working on issues of boundaries, not only his own body boundaries, but also boundaries in other areas, e.g. the room, the toy box, the therapist's body personal space or a sense of time?

Recording sessions

a. The therapist will make detailed process recording notes of every session, and will hand these to the Project Co-ordinator. These notes form the basis for discussion in supervision, where particular attention will be given to the first and final sessions, and to sessions around holiday breaks.
b. Every session will be audio taped. It is expected that the therapy with subjects between the ages of ten and fourteen will be largely verbal, and that an audio taped record will be suitable for research purposes i.e. therapist competence and adherence to the manual. However, the process recordings are to be made from memory, not from the tapes.
c. Data sheets will be completed:

   1. the weekly theme check list, and
   2. therapist ratings every fourth week (i.e. 1 st, 2nd, 6th, 10th, 14th, 18th, 22nd, 26th, 29th and 30th).

Ending treatment

The child/young person will be aware throughout of the length of the treatment and the expectation of completion of the session package. The therapy will have been child-led, in that the topics will have been covered in the order they emerge for the child/young person. The therapist will have worked to build up a "narrative" to help the child make sense of past experiences, significant events, loss, trauma, separation, and key relationships.

However, over the last 10sessions, particular attention will be paid to the issue of termination, reworking previous topics, reviewing the work and preparing for the separation from the therapist and the repeat research assessments. The phase of ending is likely to encourage thoughts of the future, of what may come next, and encourage the client to think about what kind of person he or she might develop into; a form of "anticipatory identification" (Alvarez, 1992). Wittenberg (1988) has discussed the importance of endings and the opportunities which arise to consolidate the work of therapy.

In addition to the once a term review meetings with the carers, there will need to be an end of treatment review meeting. The therapist will discuss this with the child/young person so that they can help to decide whether or not they should be present at this meeting.

Some technical issues specific to brief work with this client group

The young people in this project can be expected to suffer from severe disturbance, and to have major difficulties in the areas of relationships, academic performance, and their sense of identity. The despair and sense of futility which they communicate can be hard for their therapists to bear, as can the suspicion, contempt and anger with which some treat any adult they encounter. These feelings are doubly hard to sustain when they are complicated by the therapists' own feelings of powerlessness and guilt at having only thirty sessions to offer (Long & Trowell, 2001). They may sometimes feel that they are abandoning their client just at the point when he or she is beginning to tackle central issues, that of sexual identity, for example.

Because of this, as already discussed, support from regular supervision is essential, particularly in enabling the therapists to make appropriate use of their counter-transference and to take up the client's negative feelings about the ending. Working in a clinic setting in which further help can be offered once the research follow-up assessments have been completed, can provide vital backup for the therapists. Linking with the parent workers and outside agencies is essential, as indeed is true of all child psychotherapy.

In addition, some technical points that are relevant to clients who are very disturbed and/or very wary of involvement are useful to bear in mind. Many of these points derive from Bion's (1962) work on containment. They have been elaborated by Alvarez (1992) in relation to children who have been traumatised or abused, or who suffer from psychosis or borderline psychosis. For whatever reason, they have insufficient symbolic capacity to make use of the kind of verbal interpretations that would be helpful with more neurotic children.

This lack of symbolic capacity means that such clients often have difficulty in sustaining transference work, since they can find it difficult to distinguish adequately between the situation with the therapist and with their families. A clumsily phrased transference interpretation can feel to them as though they were being asked to take responsibility, not just for what they feel towards the therapist at that particular moment, but for everything that had gone wrong in their lives: as though anger towards the therapist, for instance, meant that their anger was to blame for the family problems. This is not to say that transference interpretations should be avoided. They are the essential currency of the therapy. However, it does mean that they must be tactfully timed, dosed and phrased, that due acknowledgement must be made of actual external circumstances, and that the ground must be prepared through the use of other techniques (Rhode 1997).

- **Using description/mirroring:** A descriptive commentary on play sequences serves the essential function of making the young person realise that he or she is being attended to and thought about. Similarly, a simple reflection of the events and feelings they describe can provide validation of their viewpoint, emotions and indeed of their identity. With a client group such as this, work of this kind needs to underpin the interpretation of unconscious conflict that would be appropriate with less disturbed children.

- **Holding projections/working in the counter-transference:** Therapists working with this kind of client, like those working with severely deprived children (Boston & Szur, 1983) need to be able to manage communications of despair, worthlessness, exclusion and so on. Very often a comment such as, "Perhaps I need to understand what it feels like to be completely useless/helpless/no good" can be particularly helpful, and will often need to precede any kind of implication that the feeling in question actually belongs to the child. When this kind of attribution is made prematurely, the child may misinterpret the therapist's comment as though the therapist were attempting to fix them in an unendurable position, and may react by becoming manic, destructive or impervious.
- **Approaching the transference:** With children who are particularly frightened of their own aggression, as very depressed children are likely to be, the negative transference during treatment will need tactful handling. This can often be achieved by a description of what kind of qualities they feel the therapist would need to have in order for them to feel safe. This implicitly recognises their fear that the therapist might not have them, while at the same time demonstrating the therapist's understanding of their needs and fears.
- **Interpretations in displacement:** With some children who are particularly frightened of a direct relationship with the therapist, it can be particularly useful to ascribe feelings to characters in their play without immediately relating them to the child and the therapist. An extension of this technique relates to describing feelings in the room without immediately attempting to locate them in either the child or the therapist, i.e., "It feels as though finishing for today can be really difficult". Steiner (1993) has discussed criteria for choosing a "client-centred" or an "analyst-centred" interpretation in terms of how much of his own experience a client is equipped to own at a given time. Others (Casaula et al., 1997) have usefully distinguished the mental work necessary for the formulation of an interpretation from the choice of appropriate means for communicating it to the client.

- **Phrasing interpretations:** Without providing reassurance, it may be helpful to re-phrase negative-sounding interpretations that the child may otherwise feel trapped in. Alvarez (1992) gives the example of avoiding, "You can't believe you and I will survive the weekend" in favour of: "It's really important to be sure we'll see each other again on Monday". Similarly, she emphasises the importance with severely depressed children, of not undermining the beginnings of potency and hope by interpreting them as omnipotent or manic defences.

The manual: How does it help?

The reflections of a therapist who used the manual

As this chapter has made clear, the manual cannot substitute for regular supervision with experienced clinicians. Nevertheless, as already described, for the senior trainee and newly qualified psychotherapist for whom this manual is most clearly suited, it offers specific guidance in working in a time limited way with young people that is not available in any other area of the child psychotherapy training at present. Although trainees will have conducted brief interventions as part of their training experience such as extended assessments, planned and delimited pieces of work of this kind are not usual. The conditions of this form of treatment, with its necessary focus on ending, requires a significant departure from the more open-ended approach to therapy, normally adopted by therapists in their once weekly work with patients.

As noted in the preceding sections, this focus on ending can engender considerable anxiety in the therapists undertaking this work, especially, as is quite likely to be the case, if they have not yet experienced an ending in their own personal therapy. The manual in these circumstances provides a reliable, concrete form of support, available at any time for consultation and reference when problems and questions arise but, perhaps most crucially, when experiences and emotions are evoked in the therapy for the therapist and/or the patient that might feel particularly overwhelming and uncertain. Of course, supervision will also provide this essential support, but the usefulness and value of the manual is that it clearly sets out a way of working that can help the therapist anticipate and think about some of the difficulties that are likely to emerge regarding the "technical issues specific to brief work with this client group", as described above, and is "at hand" to help the therapist manage the gap between the supervision sessions, when these can be addressed more directly.

It perhaps needs to be stressed how different this form of therapy is from the child and adolescent psychotherapist's usual mode of working and how hard the dual demands are of thinking of the work with the young person as an "extended assessment", allowing on the one hand for the therapy to be "child led" and to proceed at the "child's pace", whilst on the other, also emphasising the necessity for the therapist to maintain awareness in the therapy of the time limited nature of the treatment.

One of the main consequences of offering time limited therapy is the pressure the therapist might feel to overwork, attempting to address and interpret the difficulties and dilemmas that the patient brings to the sessions too quickly and directly. Although the manual does make clear that further therapeutic work can be offered to a patient once the time limited work is completed, if this indicated, this can be quite difficult for the therapist to hold in mind, especially when the young people's disturbance can seem severe and the feelings they communicate of futility and despair and, perhaps, more actively, of "suspicion, contempt and anger" (p. 26) can be so hard to tolerate and receive. The manual recognises that the therapists "can feel disturbed by the time limits of the treatment they are able to offer very troubled young people", but makes clear that this is an inevitable outcome and that the ability to bear the negative transference whilst also recognising the limits of what can be achieved in such a relatively short period of time, is at the heart of the study's rationale and research-based hopes for change.

More than any other form of therapeutic training, the manual, and the supervision which informs it, instructs and supports the therapist to "hold" the patient's projections, without responding to an inner clamour to make an interpretation as a panic reaction to the anxiety the attack induces, that would return these feelings to the young person in a premature and unprocessed way. In response to a remark of searing rejection or contempt, for example, the manual suggests that the therapist needs to accept those feelings and reflect on their experience, at that moment, of what it feels like "to be completely useless/helpless/no good...". Perhaps, right at the beginning, it is enough just to respect the patient's feeling and allow it to exist: "So that's how you feel at the moment ... maybe we need to get to know each other a little bit before anything might feel different".

The unendurability of these feelings can be powerfully communicated to the therapist in the countertransference. Supervision is essential for providing the emotional containment and understanding that the therapist needs to manage and respond to these communications in a way that is helpful to the young person, but the recognition of the need to hold these projections, which is intrinsic to working with these patients in a time limited way, is underpinned in the thinking of the manual.

Therapeutically, there is a real sense from using the manual, with its specific guidance and focus on technique in brief work with this client group, that "less is more". Allowing feelings to exist in the room without precipitous attribution and emphasising the importance of description and mirroring before any interpretation of unconscious conflict is attempted, slows down the process of the interaction so a much greater attention can be given to transitory, often momentary, barely perceptible changes to the patient's feeling states and sense of agency.

As described above, the feeling of paralysis and sense of futility that these patients communicate can be very great. Describing play sequences, as well as "serving the essential function of making the young person realise that he or she is being attended to and thought about" and that their "viewpoint, emotions and ... identity" are validated (p. 27), also allows the therapist to notice not just despairing or destructive feelings and actions, but subtle variations in the play or drawings where the presentation of a sense of agency or hopefulness may be fleetingly apparent. The therapist describing and remarking when a patient throws a ball on target or draws a picture of a figure doing something lively when the young person themselves might be very lifeless and flat, for example, acknowledges and affirms a sense of potency that might run counter to the general presentation but, is nevertheless manifest. This noticing and affirmation of change in the present, which stems from the attentive acts of describing and mirroring, is very different from reassuring the patient that things will be better. It is an aspect of technique that might be assumed to be in practice in psychotherapeutic work but is not always encouraged or commented on in the ordinary currency of training. The manual makes clear that it is particularly helpful to a client group of this kind.

The importance of affirmation of the patient's feelings is also addressed in the manual's guidance on "Phrasing Interpretations", giving the example of Alvarez's work (1992) in highlighting the importance of what should happen rather than emphasising the anxiety of what might not: "It's really important to be sure we'll see each other again on Monday". Recognising the patient's entitlement to feel anger at impending separation also affirms a potency and sense of justness to their feelings (Alvarez, 1992) without evading the inevitable pain of ending the therapy, anticipated and agreed to in the contract of the work from the outset.

Finally, the task of rating specific features in the sessions which the manual describes in detail, forces the therapist to carefully reflect on the sessions, to notice and measure any changes they believe have to have occurred on the range of scales employed. Analysing separate elements in this way is unusual for a child and adolescent psychotherapist but far from breaking down and reducing the overall sense or experience of an individual session, this practice had the effect of honing observational and assessment skills, bringing to light interrelationships between different areas of the patient's emotional and social experience which may not have otherwise been thought about or observed. In a climate where therapies are increasingly required to evidence their effectiveness, these abilities to differentiate between various aspects of a patient's inner world and mode of relating and to quantify the degree of change to these features in the course of the therapeutic relationship, seem very important in enhancing our understanding of what takes place in our work, formulating the difficulties and needs of our individual patients and, in identifying gains, justifying the relevance of time limited child psychotherapy as a treatment that can bring about developments and progress with this client group.

Based on the unpublished

Manual for Individual Child Psychotherapy Trowell, J. Rhode, M., with comments from Rustin, M. Work with Parents Trowell, J. and Miles, G. 1999.

References

Alvarez, A. (1992). *Live Company*. London/New York: Routledge.

Angold A., Costello, E.J., Messer, S.C., Pickles, A., Winder, F., Silva, D. (1995). The development of a short questionnaire for use in epidemiological studies of depression in children and adolescents. *International Journal of Methods in Psychiatric Research, 5*: 237–249.

Bell, V., Lyne, S. & Kolvin, I. (1989). Play group therapy: Processes and patterns and delayed effects. In: M.H. Schmidt and H. Remschmidt (Eds.), *Needs and Prospects of Child and Adolescent Psychiatry*. Hogrefe & Huber.

Bion, W. R. (1962). *Learning from Experience*. London: Heinemann. Reprinted, London: Karnac Books, 1984.

Bion W. R. (1967). *Second Thoughts*. New York: Jason Aronson.

Birmaher, B., Williamson, D.E., Dahl, R., Alexson, D., Kaufman, J., Dorn, L. & Ryan, N. (1996). Childhood and adolescent depression: A review of the past ten years. Part I. *Journal of the American Academy of Child and Adolescent Psychiatry, 35*: 1427–39.

Birmaher, B., Brent, D., Kolko, D., Baugher, M., Bridge, J., Holder, D., Iyengar, S. & Ulloa, R. (2000). Clinical Outcome after short term Psychotherapy for adolescents with major depressive disorder. *Archives of General Psychiatry, Vol. 57*: 23–36.

Boston, M. & Szur, R. (Eds.), (1983). *Psychotherapy with Severely Deprived Children*, London/New York: Routledge, Reprinted, London: Karnac Books, 1984.

Brenman Pick, I. (1985). Working through in the counter-transference. In E.B. Spillius, (Ed.), *Melanie Klein Today. Vol 2: Mainly Practice*. London/New York: Routledge, 1988.

Brent, D., Holder, D., Kolko, D., Birmaher, B., Baugher, M., Roth, C., Iyengar, S. & Johnson, B. (1997). A clinical psychiatry trial for adolescent depression comparing cognitive, family and supportive treatments. *Archives of General Psychiatry, 547*: 877–885.

Casaula, E., Coloma, J., Colzani, F. & Jordan, J. F. (1997). Bi-logic of interpretation. *Journal of Melanie Klein and Object Relations, 15*: 563–74.

Cecchi, V. (1990). The analysis of a little girl with an autistic syndrome. *International Journal of Psychoanalysis, 71*: 403–410.

Chambers, W., Puig-Antich, J., Hirsh, M., Paez, P., Ambrosinium, P., Tabrizi, M., Davies, M. (1985). The Assessment of affective disorders in children and adolescents by semi-structured interview: Test-retest reliability of the schedule for affective disorders and schizophrenia for school-age children present episode version. *General Psychiatry*, 42: 696–702.

Chivers, C., Dewey, M., Fielding, K., Gretton, V., Miller, P., Palmer, B., Weller, D., Churchill, R., Williams, I., Bedi, N., Duggan, C., Lee, A. & Harrison, G. (2001). Antidepressant drugs and generic counselling for treatment of major depression in primary care: randomised trial with patient preference arms. *British Medical Journal, 322*: 772–775.

Davenloo, H. (1978). Basic principles and techniques in short term dynamic psychotherapy. New York: Spectrum Publications.

Fombonne, E. (1998). Interpersonal Psychotherapy for Adolescent Depression. *Child Psychology and Psychiatry Review, 3:* No. 4.

Freud, S. (1900). *The Interpretation of Dreams*, SE IV, SEV, Hogarth Press & IPA: London.

Freud, S. (1917). *Mourning and Melancholia*, SE XIV, Hogarth Press & IPA: London.

Freud, S. (1920). *Beyond the pleasure principle*, SE XVIII, Hogarth Press & IPA: London.

Freud, S. (1923). *The ego and the id*, SE XIX, Hogarth Press and IPA: London.

Garland, C. (1991). External disasters and the internal world: An approach to the psychotherapeutic understanding of survivors. In: J. Holmes, (Ed.), *Textbook of Psychotherapy in Psychiatric Practice*. London: Churchill Livingstone.

Gilbert, P. (1992). *Counselling for Depression*. London: Sage.

Green, A. (1980). The dead mother. In *On Private Madness*. London: Hogarth, 1986 (reprinted, London: Karnac Books, 1997).

Harrington, R.C. (1993). *Depressive disorder in Childhood and Adolescence*. Rutter, M. & Wiley series on studies in Child Psychiatry, Wiley: Chichester.

Harrington, R.C. (1994). Depressive disorder in Adolescence, *Focus on Depression, 2*; (2): 6–9 Lundbeck.

Harris, M. (1965). Depression and the depressive position in an adolescent boy. In: M. Harris Williams, (Ed.), *The Collected Papers of Martha Harris and Esther Bick*, Strath Tay: Clunie Press (1987).

Heimann, P. (1950). On Counter-transference. *International Journal of Psychoanalysis, 31*: 81–84.

Howard, K.I., Krause, M.S. & Orlinsky, D.E.. (1986). The attrition dilemma: Toward a new strategy for psychotherapy research. *Journal of Consulting & Clinical Psychology, 54(1)*: 106–110. American Psychological Association, US.

Kandel, D.B. & Davies, M. (1986). Adult sequelae of adolescent depression, *Archives of General Psychiatry*, (1984) 43: 255–262.

Klein, M. (1935). A contribution to the pathogenesis of manic-depressive states. In: *The Writings of Melanie Klein Vol. 1*. London: Hogarth (1975).

Klein, M. (1940). Mourning and its relation to manic-depressive states. *Ibid.*

Kolvin, I., MacMillan, A., Nicol, A.R. &d Wrate, R.M. (1988). Psychotherapy is Effective. *Journal of the Royal Society of Medicine, 81:* 261–266.

Kolvin, I. & Sadowski, H. (2001). Childhood depression: clinical phenomenology and classification. In: I.M. Goodyer, (Ed.), *The Depressed Child and Adolescent.* Cambridge Child and Adolescent Psychiatry. 119–142. New York.

Kovacs, M. & Finkelstein, R., (1984). Depressive disorders in childhood. (a) A longitudinal prospective study of characteristics and recovery, *Archives of General Psychiatry, 41*: 229–237.

Kovacs, M., Feinberg, T.L., Crouse-Novak, M., Paulauska, S.L., Pollock, M. & Finkelstein, R. (1984). Depressive disorders in childhood, (b) A longitudinal study of the risk for subsequent major depression. *Archives of General Psychiatry, 41 (7):* 643–649.

Kovacs, M. (1981). Rating scales to assess depression in school aged children. *Acta Paedopsychiatr, 46:* 305–315.

Klerman, G.L. & Weissman, M.M. (1989). Increasing rates of depression, *Journal of American Medical Association, 261 (15):* 2229–2235.

Kashani, J.H., Curlson, S.A., Beck, N.C., Hooper, E.W., Corcoran, C.M., McAllister, J.A., Fallahi, C., Rosenberg, T.K. & Reid, J.C. (1987). Depression, depressive symptoms and depressed mood among a community sample of adolescents. *American Journal of Psychiatry, 144:* 931–34.

Lewinsohn, P.M., Hops, H., Roberts, R.E. & Seeley, J.R. (1984). *The prevalence of affective and other disorders among older adolescents,* Eugene Oregon: *Oregon Research Institute—unpublished.*

Lewinsohn, P.M., Hoberman, M. & Rosenbaum, M. (1988). A prospective study of risk factors for unipolar depression. *Journal of Abnormal Psychology, 97(3):* 251–264.

Lewinsohn, P., Rohde, P., Hops, H. & Clarke, G. (1991). Adolescent coping with depression course. *Castalia Publishing Company, Eugene DR:* 97–440.

Long, J. & Trowell, J. (2001). Individual brief psychotherapy with sexually abused girls: What can we learn from the process notes? *Psychoanalytic Psychotherapy, 15*: 39–59.

Luborsky, L. (1984). *Principles of Psychoanalytic Psychology. A manual for supportive—expressive treatment,* Basic Books.

Malan, D.H. & Osimo, F. (1992). *Psychodynamics, training and outcome in brief psychotherapy.* London: Butterworth.

Marsh, J., Silva, S., Petryck, I, S., Curry, J., Wells, K., Fairbank, J., Burns, B., Domino, M., McNulty, S., Vitiello, B., Severe, J. (2004). Treatment for

Adolescents with Depression Study (TADS) Team; Fluoxetine, cognitive–behaviour therapy and their combination for adolescents with depression. Treatment for Adolescents Depression Study (TADS) randomised controlled trial. *JAMA 18* (7): 807–820.

May, U. (2001). Abraham's discovery of the "bad mother": a contribution to the history of the theory of depression. *International Journal of Psychoanalysis 82*: 283–306.

Money-Kyrle, R.E. (1956). Normal countertransference and some of its deviations. In *The Collected Papers of R.E. Money-Kyrle*, Strath Tay: Clunie Press: 1978.

Mutson, L., Moreau D., Weissman, W. & Klerman, G. (1993), *Interpersonal Psychotherapy for Depressed Adolescents*. N.Y.: Guidford Press.

NICE Clinical Guideline 28 September 2005. Depression in children and young people. *National Institute for Health & Clinical Excellence*. Developed by the National Collaborating Centre for Mental Health.

Rhode, M. (1997). Discussion [of papers in Section II] In: M. Rustin, M. Rhode, A. Dubinsky & H. Dubinsky, (Eds.), *Psychotic States in Children*. London: Duckworth.

Scharff, D. (1996). *Object relations theory and practice*. Aronson: New York.

Steiner, J. (1993). *Psychic Retreats*. New Library of Psychoanalysis: London/New York: Routledge.

Trowell, J. (1996). Thoughts on Counter-transference and Observation. In: J. Tsiantis, A.M. Sandler, D. Anastopoulos & B. Martindale (Eds.), *Counter-transference in Psychoanalytic Psychotherapy with Children and Adolescents*. Clinical Monograph Series. Karnac: London.

Tustin, F. (1981). *Autistic States in Children*. London/New York: Routledge (second revised edition, 1992).

Tustin, F. (1986). *Autistic Barriers in Neurotic Patients*. London: Karnac Books (second revised edition, 1994).

Winnicott, D.W. (1947). Hate in the Counter-transference. In: Collected Papers, *Through Paediatrics to Psychoanalysis* (1958), Tavistock Publications: London.

Winnicott, D.W. (1948). Reparation in respect of mother's organised defence against depression. In: *Through Paediatrics to Psychoanalysis*. London: Tavistock, 1958. (Reprinted, London: Hogarth, 1975).

Winnicott, D.W. (1949). Birth memories, birth trauma and anxiety. In: *Through Paediatrics to Psychoanalysis*, London: Tavistock, 1958. (Reprinted, London: Hogarth, 1975).

Winnicott, D.W. (1951). Transitional Object and Transitional Phenomena. In: Collected Papers, *Through Paediatrics to Psychoanalysis* (1958), Tavistock Publications, London.

Winnicott, D.W. (1956). Primary Maternal Preoccupation, In: Collected Papers, *Through Paediatrics to Psychoanalysis* (1958), Tavistock Publications, London.

Winnicott, D.W. (1960). Ego distortion in terms of true and false self. In: *The Maturational Process and the Facilitating Environment*. London: Hogarth, 1965. (Reprinted, London: Karnac Books, 1990).

Winnicott, D.W. (1963). The Mentally Ill in your caseload. In: *The Maturational Process and the Facilitating Environment*. London: Hogarth, 1965. (Reprinted, London: Karnac Books, 1990).

Wittenberg, I. (1988). Ending therapy. *Journal of Child Psychotherapy, 25*: 339–56.

Youell, B. (1997). Psychodynamic Psychotherapy. In: K.N. Dwivedi & V.P. Varma, (Eds.), *Depression in Children and Adolescents*. London: Whurr Publications.

CHAPTER FOUR

Focused systematic case studies: An approach linking clinical work and research

Gunnar Carlberg

The lack of research on processes in psychoanalytic child psychotherapy is evident (Fonagy, Target, Cottrell, Phillips & Kurtz, 2002; Kazdin, 2004; Kennedy 2004; Midgley, Anderson, Grainger, Nesic & Urwin, 2009). This is particularly true regarding qualitative research (Carlberg, Eresund & Boalt Boëthius, 2009; Fonagy, 2003; Kennedy & Midgley, 2007; Midgley, 2004). In this chapter I will present some thoughts concerning the obstructive factors which underlie this lack of research. I also wish to present and exemplify a way of undertaking research with the aim of deepening our knowledge of change processes in individual psychodynamic child psychotherapy. What I have recognized as "focused systematic case studies" has turned out to be a fruitful approach and one which has captured the interest of psychotherapists. The latter is important as we try to link clinical work and research.

The psychotherapist as a researcher

Being a psychotherapist has much in common with being a researcher. It is possible to combine the two roles. One can even look upon "psychotherapy *as* research". The therapist

> collects, from a neutral position, data from the patient,
> silently formulates hypotheses,
> presents the hypotheses in the form of interventions,
> waits for a verification or falsification of the hypotheses and
> formulates new hypotheses and so on ...

The psychotherapist has certain knowledge that makes him or her particularly suited to become a researcher. The therapist is trained to reflect and search for the hidden meaning. Focus is directed towards the patient but, in the same moment, towards him or herself. The therapist's own analysis and many years of supervision have provided training in the use of free association and countertransference as therapeutic tools. Considered in this way, being a trained psychotherapist can be an advantage when doing research.

However, when the psychotherapist becomes a researcher, a certain stringency is required that may come into conflict with the therapeutic attitude. The "free floating attention" might be threatened. On the other hand, the psychotherapist's "knowledge from within" and "preconceptions" might make him or her "blind" as a researcher. Therefore, scientific training is useful in stimulating critical thinking and facilitating seeing things from the outside.

When the two roles are combined, one important question emerges: "How can I, as a psychotherapist and researcher, utilise my clinical experience and 'knowledge from within' without losing the ability to cast a critical eye over what is taking place?"

The psychotherapist as an informant

Let us consider the psychotherapist as an informant. By this I mean "the one who informs the researcher". Among clinicians we find experience-near knowledge about psychotherapy. However, this knowledge is seldom formulated. We might call it "implicit knowledge" (Schneider, Barwinsky & Fäh, 1992). One important task for the researcher is to visualise clinicians' experiences (Safran, Greenberg & Rice, 1988) the implication being that we must explore how clinicians think by having them tell how they think.

Many studies explore psychotherapies that vaguely resemble therapies the clinicians are engaged in. One dilemma is therefore that therapists seldom recognise themselves in research results. Comparatively few studies explore the process of psychotherapy (Shirk & Karver, 2003) even though it is processes that interest clinicians the most. Also the researchers themselves question whether the results from controlled laboratory situations can be generalised to clinical reality (Kazdin, 2000; Weiss, Catron, Harris & Phung, 1999; Weisz, Weiss & Donenberg, 1992). Researchers striving for high internal validity, control, do so at the expense of a low external validity, generalisability.

We also need studies of naturalistically conducted psychotherapies, and in order to capture the interest of psychotherapists, we need research methods in harmony with psychotherapy. In the long run, these kinds of studies can create the basis for studies with a higher degree of control and more quantitative approaches.

Focused systematic case studies

The research approach used in the studies that will be presented here may be described as "focused systematic case studies". The ambition was to retain the richness of the case study whilst at the same time making it possible to compare cases and create a space for critical thinking. This approach differs from the case studies we usually meet in the psychotherapy and psychoanalysis literature, in which one or more cases are described in order to illustrate a theoretical concept or a question of technique.

In this case, a focused systematic case study implies that data from crucial, data-rich episodes in several child psychotherapies have been collected by the same technique to make comparisons possible. Focus is on one phenomenon in its context. In this case the phenomenon was "turning points" identified by the therapists. In order to enrich the picture, informants other than the child psychotherapists sometimes were used. The narratives of the psychotherapists were supplemented with, for example, data from questionnaires and analyses of process notes. In some cases, independent judgements and consensus discussions with experienced child psychotherapists were used. Both qualitative and quantitative methods were used in the analysis of data.

Studying important events in psychotherapy research can be viewed as a research paradigm suitable for exploring the nature of change (Elliott, Shapiro, Firth-Cozens, Stiles, Hardy, Llewelyn & Margison, 1994), and has been used for quite a long time in psychotherapy research (Llewelyn & Hardy, 2001; Timulk, 2007). There are studies of "significant events" (Elliott & Shapiro, 1992), "helpful and hindering events" (Llewelyn, 1988) and "good moments" in psychotherapy (Mahrer & Nadler, 1986). However, a search of the literature yielded few empirically grounded studies concerning the nature of change in child psychotherapy. One exception is Terr and co-workers (2005, 2006 a, 2006 b) who described what they call particular "moments" in psychotherapy in short case vignettes.

The project "turning points in child psychotherapy"

The aim of the project was to increase knowledge about processes of change through an analysis of psychotherapists' experiences of "turning points" in child psychotherapy. A relatively broad definition of the concept of turning point was used. The common denominator was that something qualitatively new was identified by the psychotherapist. Three main questions were formulated concerning "the nature of change", "the content of change" and "factors underlying change". In this paper I will mainly concentrate on questions regarding what I call "the nature of change".

The form of psychotherapy studied here may be labelled psychodynamic child psychotherapy. The children were between 3 and 11 years old when the psychotherapies started. The duration of the therapies was generally a year or longer with a frequency of once or twice a week. The psychotherapists were experienced clinicians, a large majority having specialist training in psychodynamic child psychotherapy. Parallel to the therapy, parents met the child psychotherapist or another psychotherapist for parental counselling.

Four studies were conducted. The first study was a pilot study (Carlberg, 1997) in which five turning points were explored intensively, via the analysis of process notes, questionnaires and repeated taped interviews. Secondly, an extensive study was conducted in which time limited "changes" in 102 therapies were analysed via information given by the therapists in a questionnaire. Thirdly, the processes in six therapies were intensively studied over two and a half years with a focus on "negative" and "positive" turning point sessions. Finally, three therapies were intensively studied via interviews with the child therapist, the parental counsellor, parents and other important persons connected to an identified turning point. In the latter study, one turning point could be analysed from five different perspectives. In a broad sense, the goal of the analysis was to uncover common themes and plots in the different narratives.

In total, data were collected from 116 psychotherapies, of which 14 were studied intensively. The project was published as a doctoral thesis (Carlberg, 1999).

In order to illustrate my approach I will present: 1) some findings from the pilot study, 2) main findings from the study of the nature of change, and 3) a case study based on interviews with different informants shedding light on the process of change in a child psychotherapy.

Findings from the pilot study

In the pilot study, five turning points were identified by the child psychotherapists. Choosing data-rich events from psychotherapies, made it possible to explore complex processes, and the psychotherapists involved all became committed participants in the research project (Carlberg, 1997).

In the discussion of the results it was emphasised that the psychotherapists in these cases often identified changes when something unpredictable happened that contrasted to the usually predictable therapeutic frame. In several cases change was connected to planned or unplanned interruptions in therapy. It was as if these interruptions made change more pronounced. It was also emphasised that turning points are often connected to an emotional meeting between the child and the psychotherapist. The concept "intersubjectivity" was important in the analysis of data. "It is the emotional meeting between two subjects, each influencing the other, which prepares the way for change to take place. Phenomena such as turning points need to be viewed in the context of the type of relationship in which they occur." (Carlberg, 1997, p. 345)

The nature of change

Background

Many authors comment on how change can be perceived during psychotherapy and psychoanalysis. Sometimes the idea is presented that change might be associated with an "a-ha" feeling. More often, the idea of change is described as a result of "working through". The "working through" leads to a gradually growing insight of what is going on inside and outside the psychotherapy or psychoanalysis.

Strachey (1934), emphasises the fact that the nature of change in psychoanalysis is often "extremely gradual". Sudden, great changes ought to be met with scepticism. They may be signs of suggestive rather than psychoanalytical processes. Strachey (1934) also says:

> "The gradual nature of the change brought about in psychoanalysis will be explained if, as I am suggesting, those changes are the result of the summation of an immense number of minute steps, each of which corresponds to a mutative interpretation." (p. 144)

Kris (1956) discusses the concept "the good analytic hour", "... an experience which, though not frequent, is familiar to all analysts". The content of such a session can be met with surprise but it often seems as if it has been prepared in advance and outside the realm of awareness. The change may come gradually and is a reaction to preceding analytic work.

Blum (1992) also underlines that real change during psychoanalysis is gradual. Sudden insights, "illuminations", associated with the magic power of the child, cannot be compared with gradual "working through" whereby new connections are found and new meaning is created. This is Blum's comment on the nature of change:

> *Moments of insight, which might have brought Freud to light up a cigar, are today regarded as part of a difficult analytic path which becomes more clearly illuminated and defined as the analysis progresses.* (p. 257)

Klimovsky and co-workers (1994) consider different kinds of change. They distinguish between continuous and discontinuous change. There is a certain tendency among psychoanalytic investigators to use the word "change" in a one-sided way. Klimovsky and co-workers suggest that we usually think in terms of "replacement of one structure by another markedly different" (1994, p. 53). Changes are often seen as "revolutionary", sudden and distinct, but are often a result of a gradual growth-process, the result of many accumulated minor transitions. These kinds of change should rather be called "evolutionary".

An analysis of Klimovsky and co-workers (1994) results in three different types of changes:

- *Continuous change.* Minimal changes which are hard to perceive. A qualitative change due to a change in quantity.
- *Removable discontinuity.* A sudden change constituting a discontinuity. A qualitative jump is identified but the process carries on as if nothing had happened.
- *A jump from one state to another.* A genuine, qualitative change. In this case Klimovsky and co-workers refer to what Bion (1962) calls "catastrophic change" and what Strachey (1934) calls "mutative interpretation".

In conclusion, when psychotherapists and psychoanalysts discuss the process of change it is common to emphasise slow, gradual change processes rather than ones which are sudden and revolutionary.

Main findings and the case of Frida

To illustrate the main findings concerning the nature of change in child psychotherapy, I will use some vignettes from the therapy of a girl named Frida. Frida was eight years old when her parents called the child guidance clinic. An unknown man had sexually molested Frida. Acute help was offered to the family after which Frida could start an individual psychotherapy on a twice a week basis. The parents started to see a parental counsellor. Frida was described as "excessively sensitive, passive and anxious". Diagnostically she was judged as functioning at a high borderline level.

The first turning point session

When the therapist, after two months of therapy, was asked to choose the session that best corresponded to the criteria given for a turning point session, she chose Session 10. The therapist described what was qualitatively new in the following way.

> *Frida arrived at the session without the childish tufts in her hair. Earlier she had been obsessively dependent on them. Her posture was freer. Earlier she had made a remarkably stiff impression. She did not just sit down and wait ... she knew what she wanted to do. She looked straight into my eyes in a frank way. She wanted to know my opinion on what she was doing. I got the chance to meet her and mirror her in a more distinct manner.*

The therapist describes clear signs of change such as "without her childish tufts" and "posture was freer" but, the content of the turning point session also deals with the relationship and the therapist's feeling of a new quality in the contact with Frida. An attachment is established and it seems as if the therapist has a possibility to intervene in a new way. Let us examine this and other turning point sessions in the light of the main findings of the turning point project.

Three main findings can be stressed concerning the nature of change:

- Turning points can often be seen as a part of a process.
- It is possible to describe different kinds of turning points.
- So called "negative" and "positive" changes are related to each other.

Turning points as a part of a process

When psychotherapists are asked to identify turning points, they spontaneously choose a positive change. The change is most often seen as part of a process rather than unexpected events. Turning points in the sense of "sudden, unexpected changes that persist" are not common.

Many therapists describe how the turning point experience was powerful in the meeting with the child but that it had a tendency to change and vaporise when analysed with words. Therapists who are free to select change episodes from ongoing therapies tend to select time-limited episodes, such as a certain session. Often the episodes come from a therapy with a more severely disturbed child. When episodes of change from finished therapies are selected, they more often concern a less disturbed child and the episodes are more often a process extended in time.

Turning points as a part of a process can be illustrated with the help of the therapy with Frida. The therapist gave examples of obvious signs of an ongoing change in the session that preceded the session just referred to. The therapist told me:

> *Frida's own initiative increased in the first session after an interruption around the Easter holiday. This time the tufts in her hair had become a small bun that looked less childish. So, where the turning point actually was you may wonder. It became apparent to me in Session 10.*

In other words the change had showed up before but it became "apparent" during the chosen session. The therapist's reflection: "So, where the turning point actually was you may wonder", is in accord with what many other therapists have told me. On further consideration it can be hard to date a change more precisely.

Different kinds of turning points

From the analysis of the therapists' narratives, I concluded that it is possible to describe a continuum with "turning point" at one end and changes called "the process goes on" at the other. In between these poles exist forms of change that may be designated as "turning point-like changes". No clear borders exist between these forms of change. The difference between more thorough changes and changes characterised as "the process goes on" have also been described by Mahrer and Nadler (1986). Klimovsky et al. (1994), as mentioned earlier, point to the differences between "revolutionary" and "evolutionary" changes.

How identified changes may be categorised depends on several factors. The severity of the child's disorder is one such factor. In a therapy with a severely disturbed child, a sign that the therapeutic alliance is deepening can be seen as "a turning point". The same change in a therapy with a neurotic child might be called "the process goes on". The session just described from the therapy with Frida, might be described as "the process goes on". The session is characterised by a deepening of the therapeutic alliance.

If one follows the change process in an ongoing therapy, it is possible to describe how the content of the turning points change. Psychotherapies often start with the building of the therapeutic alliance. Thereafter the alliance deepens; the therapist notes more of the child's vitality and the child shows more of his/her emotions. Aggression, conflicts and working through will follow. In my data, there are several indications pointing to the fact that conflicts and working through follow after quite a long time of therapy. In many cases the phase of working through becomes visible after six months to a year of therapy.

Frida's therapist described a turning point session at the end of the first year of psychotherapy (Session 57):

> *Frida was able to hold on to aggressive and negative feelings towards me in the transference during the whole session and she left the room with them. In the preceding session aggressive impulses had broken through, so they had been on their way. I noticed more aggression and laughter.*

It was possible to describe a development similar to that seen in Frida's therapy in several other therapies. At the beginning of therapy, the most important changes deal with attachment and the therapeutic alliance. Further into the therapy important changes concern aggression, affects and working through. This pattern is what clinicians may expect to encounter. Data collected in a systematic way through research can serve to validate clinical expertise.

"Negative" and "positive" changes are related to each other

Negative turning points can often be seen as a part of a process leading to a positive change. A crisis starting with something happening in the life of the child, or the fact that the psychotherapist is not psychologically present during a session, might be a break in the therapeutic process that leads to a real change. An important element of psychotherapy is the working through of inner conflicts that are acted out in the therapy room.

In the present study, in which the therapy with Frida was but one, the therapists were asked to choose the most negative turning point session during the first year of therapy. Frida's therapist chose Session 41:

> *The most obvious pattern during this therapy was this: a flow of creative fantasising and emotions. Frida approached negative feelings and*

aggressive impulses. (The threat to her is to be abandoned). Frida drew back.

This session was characterised by an active avoidance of feeling and being. She was sorting, cleaning, wiping – really "doing".

What happened during this session can be interpreted as the awakening of Frida's defences against aggressive impulses. The pattern of Frida approaching important areas and then withdrawing is described as recurrent. Working with this was an important part of the therapy. The earlier quoted positive turning point session in which Frida was "able to hold on to aggressive and negative feelings ... during the whole session" was identified 16sessions later. In that session the pattern had been changed.

There are several examples in the data showing the complex connections between identified negative and positive changes. The phenomena can be viewed as different sides of the same process. An interesting parallel was found in another study by Anderson, Boalt Boëthius, Svirsky & Carlberg, 2006. Child psychotherapists, N = 31, were asked to retrieve emotionally valence therapy episodes by using an autobiographical memory approach with cue words eliciting specific episodes. Results showed that all participants were able to retrieve memories of episodes. Memories derived from positive cue words, were judged to influence the outcome of therapy in a more positive way. Surprisingly, memories of episodes derived from the cue word "irritated" seem to have more positive than negative importance for the outcome. This finding reflects the complex relation between negative and positive episodes for the change process.

The case of Linus

I shall use a case example from one of my studies to further illustrate this approach. The overarching aim of this study was to explore how different informants experienced the course of events in connection to what the child psychotherapist had identified as a turning point. Three cases were studied thoroughly. Results revealed a concordance between the different informants regarding the identification of a change although their opinion on when this change occurred was less clear. The informants' different perspectives influenced the various descriptions of possible factors underlying the change.

In the case of Linus the psychotherapist identified a turning point in the sense of a sudden, unexpected change that persisted. Positive development was also possible to describe from other perspectives than that of the child psychotherapist.

Procedure

Referring to a session identified by the psychotherapist as a turning point, semi-structured interviews were conducted not only with the child psychotherapist, but also with parents and other members of the treatment team, for example, the parental counsellor, the supervisor of the psychotherapist and the special education teacher. The interviews were tape-recorded and transcribed. The child psychotherapist wrote down in as much detail as possible, what had happened during the turning point session and the sessions immediately before and after the turning point session. All informants completed questionnaires providing information about the child and his family in terms of background factors, e.g., reasons for referral, diagnostic considerations and accounts of what happened in and around the family at the time of the turning point session. In this particular case I had access to a total of five narratives shedding light on the period of time encompassing the identified turning point. In a broad sense the goal of the analysis was to uncover the common themes and plots in the different narratives.

Background

Linus was four years old at the time of referral and was described as a boy with a "pervasive developmental disorder". His speech development was notably delayed and he had great difficulty communicating with children and adults. The treatment consisted of psychoanalytic individual psychotherapy twice a week. As a complement to therapy, Linus was also recommended for pre-school group-treatment with four other children and two special education teachers. The parents were offered counselling once a week.

Before the turning point

After about one year the child psychotherapist started to doubt the purpose of the therapy. The content of the sessions was repetitive.

The therapist was cast between sadness, sorrow, hope and doubt. According to the child psychotherapist's supervisor, the therapist was "ambitious", always trying "to be where Linus is". In spite of this it was hard to observe any progress in the therapy. The supervisor used a metaphor to describe how he saw the therapist, i.e. as "being bent almost down to the ground". He also raised the question as to whether it was meaningful to continue the therapy. The supervisor emphasised to the ambitious therapist that it is not possible to have ambitions for somebody else. His advice was: "You have to wait until he contacts you!" and "bide your time!"

The parental counsellor went through a process that she summarised as ranging from "idealising" towards a "more realistic attitude". She also described an equivalent process in the parents: "There has been a development towards greater solemnity and sorrow in Linus' parents as they have begun to perceive his difficulties". Among other things, the parents and their counsellor talked about the problem that Linus' personal assistant, described by the parents as "a treasure", had left and been replaced by another personal assistant who "doesn't like him".

The parents were positive to the treatment Linus received. They also felt very supported by their own counselling. The teacher was taken up with Linus' progress in the treatment group. She described, with great optimism, concrete changes and when they occurred. At the same time she communicated that she had felt "rather distressed" when Linus, during a certain period, was often ill and out of sorts. She was also affected by the fact that Linus' personal assistant had left during this period.

The turning point

The turning point session occurred when therapy had been in progress for 16 months. The therapist's experience during the session was summarised when she said:

> *I arrived at the bottom of the well where he was sitting.*

There was one important sequence where Linus quietly stopped and listened intensely to sounds from the street outside the window. The therapist described "a feeling of a shared peaceful silence".

This tranquillity was very much in contrast to the overactive behaviour normally seen in Linus. The tranquillity was felt as a state of "togetherness". In the analysis, the feeling of tranquillity was connected to the listening, reinforcing the therapist's feeling of "an outside and an inside". "The world outside entered; a differentiation took place". The therapist described the experience as if it happened "in a dreamlike state".

In the analysis it was difficult to distinguish between that which came from Linus and that which came from the therapist. The therapist said: "When dealing with Linus I always have to start from myself—when it is definitely within me—then I presume that it is also within him. It is something within him that generates this within me". That which is unique in this turning point session perhaps lies within the tension of what is merged and what is differentiated?

The analysis of the turning point session in the context of surrounding therapy sessions indicated that during the turning point session, the therapist attained emotional contact with Linus' predicament. She arrived, as she said, at "the bottom of the well". Out of this experience grew hope and a clearer representation of Linus. Obvious signs during the session indicated that Linus related more clearly, for example, he used the therapist's name and engaged in "eye-contact".

The change

Observations made by the therapist, the parental counsellor, the supervisor, the special education teacher and the parents may all be interpreted as signs that Linus had started to construct more adequate boundaries towards others, although the change varied in form in different settings. It looked as if the change became visible at different times to the various informants.

The child therapist's perception of what had changed in connection to the turning point session can be summarised using a few categories. Already, during the turning point session, there existed a feeling that Linus became more distinct and that the relation to the therapist changed. The therapist described the relation as "a vigorous contact" that can be judged "authentic". She also said "...today ... we are two persons in interplay, who have eye contact and are approaching something that could be called play". Linus had started to internalise aspects of the therapist. During periods preceding the turning point session, he penetrated paper and formations of sand with the aim of destroying. The therapist intervened by mending what was destroyed. After the turning point the therapist noticed that Linus not only destroyed – "now he also repairs".

The parents described many evident changes. They could now "take Linus to the shops". He started to postpone his immediate needs. Soft transitional objects became important and were given names by Linus. He was interested in other children for the first time. These changes became obvious to the parents about four weeks after the turning point session. The teacher, on the other hand, described Linus, the day after the turning point session, as sad and in need of being alone. "He looked for narrow spaces and exhibited a more genuine sorrow". The changes the month before and after the turning point session dealt both with cognitive functions and emotional interplay with people around him.

Who had changed?

An evident change can be described in Linus but evident changes could also be noted in all informants. Everybody in the team had, with a certain time delay, gone through a period of varying degrees of pessimism. Around the time of the turning point session, pessimism turned into optimism and doubt into hope, and these feelings had been contained in the treatment team. The child psychotherapist had been "allowed" to go down to the bottom of the well whereas the teacher was able to focus on the concrete progress.

Interactions leading to the change

It is possible to identify important interactions leading to the turning point session. In the beginning of the time-period in question the child psychotherapist felt sad and doubted what was going on in the psychotherapy. Her pessimism was augmented when the supervisor openly expressed his doubt concerning the benefit of the therapy. The reports from the teacher, who met Linus in the group, were optimistic. This created a conflict in the supervision. The child psychotherapist's feeling of incapability increased. After an intervention from the supervisor, the child psychotherapist left her "ambitious" attitude and bided her time waiting for an initiative from Linus. The new strategy was experienced as fruitful.

When the supervisor's intervention was scrutinised, another story emerged. The supervisor had had doubts for quite a long time. He had wondered: "How far down to the ground must the therapist be bent" before the process shows a turn. During an informal discussion with a senior colleague at the clinic his question: "How far down?" was answered: "All the way down!" This became somewhat of a turning point for the supervisor.

During a discussion, the parental counsellor heard the supervisor voice his doubts regarding how the treatment could help Linus to develop. At first the parental counsellor wanted to defend her positive attitude but after reflection she gradually saw Linus' problems in a more realistic way. She also described a parallel process in the parents in which they became more realistic. This process was most probably influenced by the parental counsellor's new view of Linus. It may be suggested that the parents' more serious attitude to Linus also influenced the direct interaction with him.

An interesting reflection is that the person furthest away from Linus was able to say "All the way down". The supervisor, who was closer but without direct treatment responsibility, was able see something other than that perceived by the child psychotherapist who sometimes came too close to Linus. As described earlier in connection with the turning point session, closeness, on the border of merging, can also become a fertile place for differentiation.

Factors underlying the change

Many individuals were engaged in Linus' development. The analysis sometimes gave the impression that Linus was "borne" by their thoughts. The child psychotherapist contributed with her persistence and firm frames, the parental counsellor with her support to the parents, and the teacher by adding structure. Persons like the supervisor had a containing function for those in the front-line. The backdrop is an institution with a therapeutic culture. The senior colleague who talked to the supervisor is a representative of the institution. The parents have contributed to Linus' development by being sensitive to his needs.

How is it that the child psychotherapist identified the change in that specific session? This question is hard to answer. The data exhibits various signs leading up to the turning point. One interesting circumstance is that the turning point session was preceded by a week-long interruption in therapy. In the study mentioned earlier (Carlberg, 1997), changes were also identified by therapists after interruptions in therapy. Perhaps the broken frame, in the form of an interruption, makes the therapist and child stop, thus enabling something new to emerge in contrast to the usually rather predictable therapeutic frame.

A comparison of changes

As mentioned earlier, the psychotherapy with Linus was one of three cases studied in the same way. Two of three therapists identified "turning points". The third was unable to identify a change which he considered to fulfil the turning point criteria. In this case data was nevertheless collected with the focus on how the different informants more generally experienced the change process.

Compared to earlier studies (Carlberg, 1999), some findings were strengthened in the light of this study, e.g., the finding that various processes of change might be described. Linus' therapist experienced a turning point in the sense of "a sudden, unexpected change that persists". This type of change was rather rare. The second of the two turning points detected was identified as one of many "turning point-like" changes. The third therapist did not identify any turning point. He experienced the change process as continuous, more like "the process goes on". These three therapists represent three different ways of looking at the process of change. The way in which this result mirrors the therapists' different attitudes or the differences between the children in therapy is a question which still remains to be explored.

Reflections

Finally, I wish to make some reflections concerning the concept of turning point and the nature of change. In everyday language we often refer to events as "turning points". Philosophers, historians, biographers and others have given thought to the meaning of the concept. It seems as if the search for turning points is an important part of our quest for meaning concerning complex processes. Meaning is created through turning points. We remember in terms of "before" and "after".

If turning points exist, where may they be found? Turning points cannot be studied as if they are concrete objects. The meaning of the term greatly depends upon how it is conceived by the therapist and the way in which the outside observer analyses and interprets the therapist's statements. Much of the term's meaning rests with the therapists who report back from the therapies. Through the analysis of the therapists' narratives, I can conclude that therapists have different ways of organising their experiences of change processes. Some therapists seem to look upon the process as consisting of a chain of turning point-like changes. Other therapists regard psychotherapy as a constantly ongoing process. It may be important to underline that psychotherapy does not just aim at reaching "*The* Turning Point". Rather, most therapists emphasise the gradual change in therapy (Carlberg, 2009; Nahum, 1998; Stern, Sander, Nahum, Harrison, Lyon-Ruth, Morgan, Bruschweiler-Stern & Tronick, 1998). For many psychotherapists thinking of change processes will remind them of "... those steady, plodding cases where nothing new seems to happen yet some gradual change occurs" (Boston, 1998, p. 201).

The aim of psychotherapy is to create meaning, and meaning is created when we tell narratives. Just as we need certain events on which to attach the narrative of our life story, the therapist needs points of reference with which to organise her/his experiences and memories. Just as our life stories are rewritten depending on when we look back on our lives, the narratives about turning points and change processes will be rewritten depending on the prevailing circumstances and on the point of time at which the therapist looks back and reflects.

Evaluation of the approach

In conclusion, focused systematic case studies turned out to be a fruitful approach and one that captured the interest of the psychotherapists. Collected data contained descriptions of episodes from psychotherapy processes which tally closely with experience. In the current studies the psychotherapists and the parents were all very positive about participating in the research project. No negative effects on the therapies were reported. A changed, more positive, attitude towards research could be noticed among the participating psychotherapists.

The numerous complex factors surrounding psychotherapy constitute a serious hindrance to prospective child psychotherapy researchers. The described and exemplified approach presents one alternative. Data from supplementary perspectives encapsulate important aspects of processes of change.

References

Anderson, G., Boalt Boëthius, S., Svirsky, L. & Carlberg, G. (2006). Memories of significant episodes in child psychotherapy: An autobiographical memory approach. *Psychology and Psychotherapy: Theory, Research and Practice, 79*: 229–236.

Bion, W.R. (1962). *Learning from Experience*. London: Heinemann.

Blum, H.P. (1992). Psychic change: The analytic relationship(s) and agents of change. *International Journal of Psychoanalysis, 73*: 255–265.

Boston, M. (1998). Correspondence. Letter to the editors. *Journal of Child Psychotherapy, 24*: 201–202.

Carlberg, G. (1997). Laughter opens the door: turning points in child psychotherapy. *Journal of Child Psychotherapy*, 23: 331–349.

Carlberg, G. (1999). Vändpunkter i barnpsykoterapi. Psykoterapeuters erfarenheter av förändringsprocesser. [Turning points in child psychotherapy. Psychotherapists' experiences of change processes]. Dissertation, Department of Education, University of Stockholm. Stockholm: Ericastiftelsen.

Carlberg, G. (2009). Exploring change processes in psychodynamic child psychotherapy: The therapists' perspective. In: N. Midgley, J. Anderson, E. Grainger, T. Nesic-Vuckovic & C. Urwin (Eds.), *Child Psychotherapy and Research: New Approaches, Emerging Findings*, London: Routledge.

Carlberg, G., Eresund, P. & Boalt Boëthius, S. (2009). *Child and Adolescent Psychotherapy Research. Workshop for Clinicians and Researchers at the Erica Foundation October 2008*. Stockholm: The Erica Foundation.

Elliott, R. & Shapiro, D.A. (1992). Client and therapist as analysts of significant events. In: S.G. Toukmanian & D.L. Rennie (Eds.), *Psychotherapy Process Research. Paradigmatic and Narrative Approaches* (pp. 163–186). London: Sage.

Elliott, R., Shapiro, D.A., Firth-Cozens, J., Stiles, W.B., Hardy, G.E., Llewelyn, S.P. & Margison, F.R. (1994). Comprehensive process analysis of insight events in cognitive-behavioral and psychodynamic-interpersonal psychotherapies. *Journal of Counselling Psychology, 41*: 449–463.

Fonagy, P., Target, M., Cottrell, D., Phillips, J. & Kurtz, Z. (2002). *What Works for Whom? A Critical Review of Treatments for Children and Adolescents*. New York: The Guildford Press.

Fonagy, P. (2003). The research agenda: the vital need for empirical research in child psychotherapy. *Journal of child psychotherapy, 29*: 129–136.

Kazdin, A.E. (2000). *Psychotherapy for children and adolescents. Directions for research and practice.* New York: Oxford University Press.

Kazdin, A.E. (2004). Psychotherapy for children and adolescents. In: M.J. Lambert, A.E. Bergin and Sol.L. Garfield, *Handbook of Psychotherapy and Behavior Change.* Fifth edition. (pp. 543–589). New York: Wiley.

Kennedy, E. (2004). *Child and Adolescent Psychotherapy: A Systematic Review of Psychoanalytic Approaches.* London: North Central London. Strategic Health Authority.

Kennedy, E. & Midgley, N. (2007). *Process and Outcome Research in Child, Adolescent and Parent-infant Psychotherapy: A Thematic Review.* London: North Central London Strategic Health Authority.

Klimovsky, G., Bekman Vainer, S., de Goldberg, D.B., de Kuitca, M.K., de Liberman, J.F. & Siniavsky, M. (1994). Change in psychoanalysis: Epistemological aspects. *International Journal of Psychoanalysis, 75*: 51–58.

Kris, E. (1956). On some vicissitudes of insight in psychoanalysis. *International Journal of Psychoanalysis, 37*: 445–455.

Llewelyn, S.P. (1988). Psychological therapy as viewed by clients and therapists. *British Journal of Clinical Psychology, 27*: 223–237.

Llewelyn, S.P. & Hardy, G. (2001). Process research in understanding and applying psychological therapies. *British Journal of Clinical Psychology, 40*: 1–21.

Mahrer, A.R. & Nadler, W.P. (1986). Good moments in psychotherapy: A preliminary review, a list, and some promising research avenues. *Journal of Consulting and Clinical Psychology, 54*: 10–15.

Midgley, N. (2004). Sailing between Scylla and Charybdis: Incorporating qualitative approaches into child psychotherapy research. *Journal of Child Psychotherapy, 30*: 89–111.

Midgley, N., Anderson, J., Grainger, E. Nesic, T. & Urwin, C. (Eds.) (2009). *Child Psychotherapy and Research: New Approaches, Emerging Findings,* London: Routledge.

Nahum, J.P. (1998). Case illustration: Moving along ... and, is change gradual or sudden? *Infant Mental Health Journal, 19,* [special issue], 315–319.

Safran, J.D., Greenberg, L.S. & Rice, L.N. (1988). Integrating psychotherapy research and practice: Modelling the change process. *Psychotherapy, 25*: 1–17.

Schneider, H., Barwinski, R. & Fäh, M. (1992). Formulating models about change processes by rendering explicit the psychoanalyst's implicit knowledge: A dialogue between science and clinical practice. In: M. Leuzinger-Bohleber, H Schnider & R. Pfeifer (Eds.), *"Two Butterflies on My Head..." Psychoanalysis in the Interdisciplinary Scientific Dialogue* (pp. 309–320). Berlin: Springer-Verlag.

Shirk, S.R. & Karver, M. (2003). Prediction of treatment outcome from relationship variables in child and adolescent therapy: A meta-analytic review. *Journal of Consulting and Clinical Psychology, 71*: 452–464.

Stern, D.N., Sander, L.W., Nahum, J.P., Harrison, A.M., Lyon-Ruth, K., Morgan, A.C., Bruschweiler-Stern, N. & Tronick, E.Z. (1998). Non-interpretive mechanisms in psychoanalytic therapy. The 'something more' than interpretation. *International Journal of Psychoanalysis, 79*: 903–921.

Strachey, J. (1934). The nature of the therapeutic action of psycho-analysis. *International Journal of Psychoanalysis*, 15: 127–159.

Terr, L.C., McDermott, J.F., Benson, R.M., Blos, P. Jr., Deeney, J.M., Rogers, R.R. & Zrull, J.P. (2005). Moments in psychotherapy. *Journal of Academic Child and Adolescent Psychiatry, 44*: 191–1979.

Terr, L.C., Deeney, J.M., Drell, M., Dodson, J.W., Gaensbauer, T.J., Massie, H., Minde, K., Teal, S. & Winters, N.C. (2006 a). Playful 'moments' in psychotherapy. *Journal of Academic Child and Adolescent Psychiatry, 45*: 604–613.

Terr, L.C., Beitchman, J.H., Braslow, K., Fox, G., Metcale, A., Pease, M., Ponton, L., Sack, W. & Wasserman, S. (2006 b). Children's turnarounds in psychotherapy. The doctor's gesture. *Psychoanalytic Study of the Child, 61*: 56–81.

Timulk, L. (2007). Identifying core categories of client-identified impact of helpful events in psychotherapy: A qualitative meta-analysis. *Psychotherapy Research, 17*: 305–314.

Weiss, B., Catron, T., Harris, V. & Phung, T-M. (1999). The effectiveness of traditional child psychotherapy. *Journal of Consulting and Clinical Psychology, 67*: 82–94.

Weisz, J.R., Weiss, B. & Donenberg, G.R. (1992). The lab versus the clinic: Effects of child and adolescent psychotherapy. *American Psychologist, 47*: 1578–1585.

CHAPTER FIVE

The Heidelberg study of psychodynamic psychotherapy for children and adolescents

Klaus-Thomas Kronmüller MD, Annette Stefini, Annette Geiser-Elze, Hildegard Horn, Mechtild Hartmann and Klaus Winkelmann MD

Abstract

The present article gives an overview of the Heidelberg Study on the evaluation of psychodynamic psychotherapy for children and adolescents. The study design is described and instruments for the assessment of structural characteristics and the psychotherapeutic process developed and evaluated in the project are presented. Also, results regarding treatment outcome are reported. The aim of the study was to examine the efficacy of short-term psychodynamic psychotherapy in an RCT-trial as well to assess the effectiveness of long-term psychoanalysis in a naturalistic study design. 71 patients aged 6–18 with internalizing and externalizing disorders were treated with an average of 82 therapy sessions. For several variables, a significant statistical superiority of the therapy group compared to the waiting control group could be shown. Considerably higher effect sizes were found for long-term treatment than for short-term psychotherapy. The results demonstrate that short-term psychodynamic psychotherapy and long-term psychoanalysis are highly effective treatments for children and adolescents with mental disorders.

1 Introduction

Even though there is a large number of psychotherapy outcome studies for children and adolescents, most of them are conducted in order to evaluate short-term psychotherapy and cognitive-behavioural treatments (Fonagy, Target, Cottrell, Phillips & Kurtz, 2002). Whereas in the meantime, numerous studies on CBT exist, psychodynamic therapy for children and adolescents has been rarely studied (Kazdin, 2004). Besides some uncontrolled studies on analytic short-term therapy, so far only a few studies have been carried out examining psychodynamic psychotherapy for children and adolescents using a control group design (Fonagy Target, Cottrell, Phillips & Kurtz, 2002; Windaus, 2005). At the Child Guidance Clinic in London, Moran, Fonagy, Kurtz, Bolton & Brook (1991), studied a sample of children suffering from diabetes mellitus with grossly abnormal blood glucose profiles necessitating repeated admissions to a hospital. Here, the beneficial influence of the psychodynamic treatment on blood glucose profiles could be corroborated. Szapocznik et al. (1989, 1990) studied the efficacy of psychodynamic short-term psychotherapy and structural family therapy in comparison to a control group. The children with aggression problems had 12 to 24 therapy sessions over a period of 6 months. Although no differential effects between the two treatment groups were found, both treatment groups were statistically superior to the control group. In a study by Muratori et al. (2002), 58 children with anxiety disorders and depression were assessed using a controlled study design. Psychodynamic focal therapy over 11 sessions was compared to a control group. Regarding symptomatology and social functioning, the effect size was 0.75). Moreover, in the catamnesis, a further improvement of the treatment group was found as well as a lower utilization of medical care for that group (Muratori, Picchi, Bruni, Patarnello & Romagnoli, 2003). Trowell et al. (2002) compared focal psychodynamic short-term therapy with psycho-educative group therapy in a sample of 71 sexually abused girls. Here, with an effect size of 0.65, the psychodynamic treatment led to a greater reduction of posttraumatic stress symptoms. In a further randomized controlled trial, 72 patients aged 9–15 years with depression were allocated to individual psychodynamic psychotherapy, 16–30 therapy sessions over 9 months, or family therapy (Trowell et al., 2007). Nearly 75% of cases were no longer clinically depressed in both treatment groups. This study shows that focused forms of psychodynamic treatment are effective in the treatment of depression. In contrast to the reported studies with a rather favorable evaluation of the efficacy of psychodynamic treatment in children and adolescents, Smyrnios & Kirkby (1993) could not show the superiority of the treatment group over a minimal contact group. In particular, no superiority of a time unlimited psychodynamic treatment over a psychodynamic short-term therapy was found.

Several meta-analytic reviews suggest that there are a large number of non-responders after short-term psychotherapy (Fonagy Target, Cottrell, Phillips & Kurtz, 2002; Kazdin, 2004). Therefore, it is crucial to examine the efficacy of long-term psychotherapy especially with the necessity of cost minimization in mind. However, although psychodynamic psychotherapies are frequently carried out in this field, the evaluation of its efficacy is still deficient, this even more so the case for long-term psychoanalytic treatment. Three naturalistic retrospective studies (Dührssen, 1964; Fahrig, Kronmüller, Hartmann & Rudolf, 1996; Fonagy & Target, 1994a, b; Target & Fonagy, 1994; Winkelmann et al., 2000) report an 80% treatment success in long-term psychoanalytic psychotherapies for children and adolescents. On the basis of the Berlin study, Dührssen (1964) hypothesized that nearly all patients were treated successfully with long-term psychoanalytic psychotherapy if they did not drop out of treatment. However, all three studies of long-term treatment are retrospective and a control group is missing. Prospective studies for psychoanalytic long-term psychotherapy for children and adolescents are completely missing to date.

The Heidelberg study is one of the first prospective evaluation studies of long term, out-patient psychoanalytic psychotherapy for children and adolescents. The aim of the study was to examine the efficacy of short-term psychodynamic treatment and the effectiveness of long-term psychoanalysis. In addition, the influence of clinical and social variables on treatment outcome was investigated. Another aim was to study the relationship between outcome and the psychotherapeutic process. Also, several instruments for outcome and process research in child and adolescent psychotherapy were developed and evaluated in the project. In the following, the study design of the Heidelberg Study is described with special emphasis on the study instruments. In the third section, the results of the evaluation of the short-term and long-term psychodynamic therapy are reported.

2 Method

Study design

In our study design we attempted to combine the advantages of controlled and naturalistic studies. Thus, in the first part of the study up to the 25th therapy session, we used a waiting-list control panel, whereas for the evaluation of the long-term psychotherapy we used a prospective, naturalistic design. In a third step, follow-up examinations were conducted 3 and 12 months after the end of treatment. Because of the national data collection strategy, a comprehensive cohort design (Olschewski & Scheurlen, 1985; Victor, 1990) was chosen. The controlled trial mainly consisted of patients recruited from the Heidelberg area, whereas patients from other study centers, Stuttgart, Frankfurt, Saarbruecken and Marburg, were examined in the context of the naturalistic continuation of the study. The allocation to the therapy and waiting control group was carried out by quasi-randomization (Kronmüller et al., 2005). Fifty-four patients were allocated randomly to the waiting control and treatment group.

In the trial, the treatment was evaluated by collecting data from all involved persons: symptoms and treatment were assessed from the treated children's and adolescents', their therapists', the parents' and from an independent research experts' point of view. All participants rated symptoms and other variables at four predetermined assessment times: at the beginning and the 25th session and, for the assessment of the therapeutic relationship, at the 3rd and 12th session. Within the context of the naturalistic long-term psychotherapy study, assessments were carried out half-yearly. Follow-up investigations were carried out 3 and 12 months after the end of treatment.

All patients had sought treatment between 1997 and 2002 at the Heidelberg Institute for Psychoanalytic Therapy for Children and Adolescents or in an outpatient analytical children and adolescent psychotherapy setting. All psychodynamic psychotherapies took place in an outpatient-setting. The sample consisted of 71 outpatient children and adolescents with ICD-10 (WHO; Dilling, Mombour, Schmidt & Schulte-Markwort, 1994) mental disorders, aged between 6 and 18 years. The diagnoses were based on the Diagnostic Interview for Mental Disorders in Children and Adolescents (Children-DIPS; Unnewehr, Schneider & Margraf, 1995). Exclusion criteria were psychotic disorders, addiction disorders and serious suicidal tendencies. After a complete description of the study had been given to the patients and the parents, written informed consent was obtained. The study protocol was approved by the local ethics committee and was prepared in accordance with the ethical standards laid down in the Declaration of Helsinki.

Subjects

The sample consisted of 71 outpatient children and adolescents with ICD-10 mental disorders (see Table 1) of whom 28 were male and 43 female. The average age at the beginning of therapy was 11.3 years (SD 3.7, 5–19). Forty-six patients were children, younger than 13 years, and 25 were adolescents. 36 (50.7%) had internalizing mental disorders, 8 (11.3%) had externalizing disorders and 27 (38.0%) had both. The most frequent disorders were emotional disorders of childhood (F93.0) and conduct disorders (F92.0). On average, the therapy lasted 22.9 months (SD = 14.1), with 82.2 therapy sessions (SD = 52.6). 76% of the parents took part in accompanying parents' sessions. Fifty of the patients completed treatment and 21 dropped out. Sixty-four (90.1%) of the patients intended for treatment could be included in the follow-up investigations. Of the 86 patients approached to participate in the study, 15 (17.44%) parents declined. There was no indication of systematic selection bias.

Therapy concept and manual adherence

The therapies were carried out using a manual (Hartmann, Horn, Winkelmann, Geiser-Elze & Kronmüller, 1997). On the basis of psychoanalytical theories such as drive theory, ego psychology, self psychology, object relations theory and attachment theory, a manual was developed that enabled the therapist to use these theories for the therapeutic focus. The therapy focus is the central unconscious conflict (Luborsky, 1995) or the structural constitution of the patient. Initially, a treatment focus is formulated as a focus sentence (Lachauer, 1992) in which the central relationship conflict is formulated. The work on this therapy focus defined at the beginning of treatment, takes place within the therapeutic relationship or by using play or art elements at a level adequate for the child. The interventions used

Table 1. Sociodemographical and clinical characteristics of the sample (n = 71).

	Frequency			
	Absolute	*relative*	*M*	*SD*
Age (years)				
Total	71	100	11.34	3.72
Children	48	67.60		
Adolescents	23	32.40		
Sex				
Female	43	60.56		
Male	28	39.44		
Family Status				
Family of Origin	37	52.11		
Single Parent	20	28.17		
Stepfamily	9	12.68		
Others	5	7.04		
Disorders				
Internalized	36	50.70		
Externalized and Internalized	27	38.03		
Externalized	8	11.27		
Duration of the disorder (years)			2.80	2.13

Note: M: Mean; SD: Standard Deviation; n: sample size.

are related to the therapy focus, expressively interpretative and structure-related. In the manual, concrete therapeutic procedures are described for the three treatment phases "getting to know each other", "working through" and "parting" by using case examples. In the accompanying sessions with the parents, they are presented with the opportunity to understand the child's behavior in the background of its development within the family and, as far as possible, to change interaction patterns that contribute to the genesis and maintenance of the disorder (Horn, 2003). The study therapists were trained in the use of the manual and continually supervised by experienced therapists. For every session, adherence to the manual was assessed using a seven point global rating ranging from 0, no adherence, to 6, very high adherence. Only 5 (1.5%) of the sessions were rated unsatisfactory regarding adherence. On average, adherence was 4.35 (SD = 0.47), which is a high score for adherence in the treatment group. This was also the case for the adherence in the three therapy phases "getting to know each other", "working through" and "parting".

Therapists

Twenty-nine analytical child and adolescent psychotherapists participated in the study. The average age was 48.35 years (SD = 4.68). Twenty-five (86.21%) were women and all had completed their therapeutic training. The average job experience with child psychotherapy was 7.0 years (SD = 6.74). The therapists based their treatment on the manual for psychodynamic psychotherapy for children and adolescents that had been developed within the research project.

Instruments

In the context of the Heidelberg Study, numerous instruments were developed or translated and psychometrically evaluated. This was necessary for several reasons. First of all, disorder specific symptom scales could not be applied to a diagnostically heterogeneous sample. Moreover, only a few instruments for psychodynamic diagnosis or the assessment of the psychotherapeutic process in children and adolescents exist. Quite a few of these instruments were developed in pilot studies and were validated using more than 1000 patients and healthy children and adolescents. We assessed treatment outcome with the 'Psychic and Social-Communicative Findings Report' (PSCR-CA) and the Severity of Impairment Score for Children and Adolescents (SIS-CA). Information about the therapeutic process was gathered with the Therapeutic Alliance Scales for Children (TAS-C; Shirk & Saiz, 1992), the Scales on the Therapeutic Process for Children and Adolescents (STP-CA; Smith-Acuna, Durlak & Kaspar, 1991) and the Work on the Focus Scale for Children and Adolescents (WFS-CA), which assesses the intensity of therapeutic work on the conflict and therapy focus. Expert ratings on the therapeutic process were done using the SASB method (Benjamin, 1974; Hartmann et al., 2000) and the Child Psychotherapy Process Scales (CPPS; Estrada & Russell, 1999). Psychodynamic diagnoses were made using the California Child Q-Sort (CCQ; Block & Block, 1980) and the Operationalized Psychodynamic Diagnostics System for Children and Adolescents (OPD-CA; Bürgin, Resch & Schulte-Markwort, 2007) as well as the Heidelberg Attachment Style Rating for Children and Adolescents (HAR-CA). The development and advancement of such instruments is one of the main research fields in child psychotherapy research and is the basis for an improved assessment of therapy outcome and the psychotherapeutic process. In the following, some of the main instruments used in the Heidelberg Study are described in more detail.

The "Psychic and Social-Communicative Findings Report for Children and Adolescents (PSCR-CA)" (Psychischer und Sozial-Kommunikativer Befund für Kinder und Jugendliche; PSKB-KJ) is an adapted version of the PSKB for adults (Rudolf, 1981). The PSCR-CA allows standardization and quantification of the information gathered by the clinical interview. On the basis of a psychodynamic understanding of symptom genesis, expert ratings in three areas using 104 items are carried out: classical symptoms, interaction patterns and somatic symptoms. This instrument was evaluated using a sample of 300 children and adolescents. By means of factor analysis, 10 dimensions could be detected. These 10 factors explained 44.4% of the overall variance. Moreover, 3 factors of second order were found, which covered psychic, social-communicative and somatic components of mental disorders. The coefficients for the internal consistency of the PSCR-CA-scales were between 0.66 and 0.82 (Cronbachs's alpha). Inter-correlations, Spearman's rho, ranged from 0.01 to 0.55. Most correlations were around 0.30. Coefficients for the inter-rater reliability of the 10 PSCR-CA-Scales were between 0.67 and 0.85, Spearman's rho, in 20studied cases. For the second order and total scores, the inter-rater reliability was between 0.75 and 0.88. The PSCR-CA-Scales show good validity values compared to other instruments.

Therapy outcome was additionally assessed by the "Severity of Impairment Score for Children and Adolescents" (SIS-CA) (Beeinträchtigungsschwerescore für Kinder und Jugendliche; BSS-K), which was developed by Schepank (1995) and our work group. The evaluation of the severity of impairment is made from a psychodynamic background. Ratings are made on six dimensions using a five point scale: mental impairment, physical impairment, difficulties in interaction with parents, brothers and sisters and with friends and impairment in personal achievement. The inter-rater reliability was between 0.73 and 0.84 for the single scales and 0.80 for the overall score (ICC's). The examination of the retest reliability yielded coefficients between 0.73 and 0.86 for the single scales and 0.84 for the overall score (ICC's). Outcome criteria were defined in terms of clinical significance and the reliable change index. The children were defined to be clinically significantly disturbed if above a cut-off-score of 7 (Jacobson & Revenstorf, 1988). With the Reliable Change Index (RC) (Christensen & Mendoza, 1986), we found a change of 4 or more points to be clinically relevant (Fahrig, Kronmüller, Hartmann & Rudolf, 1996).

The Therapeutic Alliance Scales for Children (TAS-C) (Fragebogen zur therapeutischen Beziehung; FTB-KJ) was developed by Shirk & Saiz (1992). The authors used the concept of the therapeutic relationship by Bordin (1979). This concept consists of following components: the affective aspect in the "therapeutic bond" and the cognitive aspect in the two dimensions "agreement on goals" and "agreement on tasks", meaning agreement on goals and tasks in the therapy. The American version includes two scales on the affective reaction of the child in the therapy: "Bond" and "Negativity". A third scale assesses the collaboration regarding therapeutic tasks ("Collaboration on tasks"). The German Version of the FTB-KJ was translated by our working group and psychometrically evaluated in a sample of 80 children and adolescents (Kronmüller et al., 2003). The factor structure of the original version could be replicated and the Cronbachs Alpha scores lying between 0.68 and 0.87 can be regarded as good. Different patterns of the therapeutic relationship in the patient therapist dyads could be differentiated by cluster analysis (Kronmüller et al., 2002).

The Scales on the Therapeutic Process for Children and Adolescents (STP-CA) developed by Smith-Acuna, Durlak & Kaspar (1991) (Skalen zum Therapeutischen Prozess für Kinder und Jugendlichen; STP-KJ) are an adapted version of the "Therapy Session Reports" by Orlinsky & Howard (1975). In order to develop a German version, the original version was first translated into German. The four dimensions with 10 therapist version and 8 patient's version subscales respectively, for the therapeutic alliance are assessed in both versions for patient and therapist. In a sample of 100 children, the STP-KJ showed good internal consistency and validity.

One of our newly developed instruments to measure the psychotherapeutic process is the "Work on the Focus Scale for Children and Adolescents" (WFS-CA) (dt. FBS-KJ; Fokusbearbeitungsskala für Kinder und Jugendliche). In every session, the therapist estimates the intensity of work on the focus using an eight point scale from "problem warded off" to "mastery". The WFS-CA was developed by the Heidelberg Children's Therapy Project based on the "Assimilation of Problematic Experience Scale" (APES, Stiles, Meshot, Anderson & Sloan, 1992) and the "Heidelberg Scale on Therapeutic Restructuring" (Heidelberger Skala zur therapeutischen Umstrukturierung (Grande, Rudolf & Oberbracht, 1997; Grande, Rudolf, Oberbracht & Jakobsen, 2001) in cooperation with the workgroup of Prof. Rudolf. The APES is a rating scale for adults, which aims to assessing systematic changes in the representation of problematic experiences and experience modes in behavior, attitudes, feelings, contents, memories, impulses, wishes, conflicts etc., during the therapeutic process. Other than the "Work on the Focus Scale for Children and Adolescents", the APES is theoretically based on a reflexive, insight-oriented therapy process. This, for psychoanalytically treated adults' typical processes, had to be modified to fit with the cognitive developmental stage of the children. The WFS-CA makes it possible to rate the intensity of the work on each selected problem foci after every therapy session. The assessment can be carried out on three levels: 1. analogical level, work on the focus by scenic play, 2. direct transference, and 3. Environment, reports from family, friends, etc. On all of these levels, intensity in working on the focus can be rated on an eight point scale: problem is warded off, unwanted thoughts, vague awareness, problem statement and clarification, understanding and insight, application and working through, problem solution, and mastery. The psychometric evaluation of the "Work on the Focus Scale for Children and Adolescents" (WFS-CA) yielded good reliability and validity values. The WFS-CA also enables trained raters to reliably assess focus-relevant episodes.

Structure related and psychodynamic variables were assessed with the OPD (Operationalized Psychodynamic Diagnostics System for Children and Adolescents), the CCQ (California Child Q-Sort) and the Heidelberg Attachment Style Rating for Children and Adolescents (HAR-CA). By means of the Operationalized Psychodynamic Diagnostics System for Children and Adolescents (OPD-CA; Bürgin, Resch & Schulte-Markwort, 2007), 7 conflicts were assessed in a standardized manner. OPD Axis III (Conflicts) distinguishes seven mental conflicts and has a category for limited conflict perception: 1. Dependence versus autonomy, 2. Submission versus control, 3. Desire for care vs. autarchy, 4. Conflicts of self-value, 5. Guilt conflicts, 6. Oedipal sexual conflicts, 7. Identity conflicts, 8. Limited perception of conflicts and feelings. Ego-Strength and Ego-Flexibility were rated with the California Child Q-Sort (CCQ) and attachment patterns judged by the newly developed Heidelberg Attachment Style Rating for Children and Adolescents (HAR-CA). Besides showing changes in symptomatology, the aim of the Heidelberg study was to also provide evidence for structural change.

Attachment styles of the Children and Adolescents were examined using the Heidelberg Attachment Rating for Children and Adolescents (HAR-CA). The HAR-CA assesses the four attachment patterns, secure, avoidant, ambivalent, disorganized-disoriented, found by Ainsworth, Blehar, Waters & Wall (1978) and Main & Weston (1981). Further studies by Grossmann, August & Fremmer-Bombik (1989) and Main & Solomon (1986) confirmed these patterns. Attachment assessment was based on semi-structured interviews conducted by trained experts and on observed interaction behavior patterns with parents. The interview situation included a separation and reunion with the parents. The rating manual allows for the assessment of attachment characteristics for children aged 6–12 years, 13–15 years and 16–18 years. Different attachment styles are illustrated with examples for every age group. In addition to the assessment of attachment styles in the four categories described above, the intensity of attachment ratings is assessed on a ten point scale ranging from 1, not typical, to 10, very typical. This dimensional rating takes into account the fact that attachment styles depend on the person to whom the attachment is measured and that a person can have more than one attachment style. Reliability of the HAR-CA was measured in a sample of 16 children and adolescents and two raters. Inter-rater reliability for the rating of the four main attachment patterns was good, with a Cohen's kappa of 0.64. For the classification of secure and insecure attachment, kappa was 0.76. Validation of the dimensional HAR-CA rating was measured in a sample of 23 adolescents. Correlations (test) with the German version of the Inventory of Parent and Peer-Attachment (IPPA) (Armsden & Greenberg, 1987), revealed a significant positive relation of attachment to mother (IPPA) and secure attachment (HAR-CA) where $r = 0.43$, $p = 0.04$. The correlation between attachment to mother and disorganized-disoriented attachment showed a negative significant relation ($r = -0.41$, $p = 0.05$). The IPPA-Scale Alienation also revealed significant correlations with secure attachment ($r = -0.51$, $p = 0.02$) and disorganized-disoriented attachment ($r = 0.69$, $p = 0.001$). The HAR-CA is an economic instrument for the assessment of attachment styles in children and adolescents by means of clinical ratings.

Statistical analysis

Data were subjected to a repeated measures Analysis of Variance (ANOVA) assessing the main and interaction effects of the within-subjects factor time, and the between factor group. Contrasts were performed using the Tukey test. Effect sizes for pre to post-test data were calculated (Cohen, 1988; Hartmann & Herzog, 1995). Results were considered statistically significant if at, or below 5% probability level (two-tailed). Analyses were performed with SAS Version 9.12 (SAS Institute, Cary, N.C.).

3 Results

As a first step, we examined the outcome of the short-term psychodynamic treatment for children and adolescents. Outcome criterion were the pre- and post-test scores (25th therapy session) of the Psychic and Social-Communicative Findings Report for Children and Adolescent (PSCR-CA). Analyses were calculated as a two-factorial Analyses of Variance with repeated measures. Compared to the patients in the waiting control group, patients of the treatment group showed a significantly higher reduction in the PSCR-CA total score (see Table 2). Thus, for the PSCR-CA total score, a highly significant interaction effect could be found ($F = 8.28$; $p = 0.007$). Also,

Table 2. Comparison of waiting control and treatment group in the Psychic and Social-Communicative Findings Report for Children and Adolescents (PSCR-CA).

	Treatment Group (n = 27)				*Waiting Control Group (n = 27)*							
	T1		*T4*		*T0*		*T1*					
PSCR-CA -Scales	*M*	*SD*	*M*	*SD*	*M*	*SD*	*M*	*SD*	*ES*		*F*	*p*
PSCR-DP	0.91	0.46	0.69	0.42	0.96	0.42	1.02	0.40		G	1.63	0.21
Depressive Powerlessness									0.73	T	1.75	0.20
										GxT	5.32	0.03*
PSCR-AS	0.89	0.80	0.74	0.75	0.88	0.65	0.79	0.63		G	0.04	0.84
Anxiety Symptoms									0.07	T	5.32	0.03*
										GxT	1.11	0.30
PSCR-PL	0.98	0.96	0.67	0.88	0.50	0.58	0.61	0.66		G	1.08	0.31
Personal Loss									0.07	T	1.80	0.19
										GxT	7.08	0.01**
PSCR-ED	0.71	0.49	0.55	0.53	0.98	0.53	0.84	0.47		G	2.62	0.12
Emotional Detachment									0.58	T	5.41	0.03*
										GxT	0.04	0.85

(Continued)

Table 2. *Continued.*

	Treatment Group (n = 27)				*Waiting Control Group (n = 27)*							
	T1		*T4*		*T0*		*T1*					
PSCR-CA -Scales	*M*	*SD*	*M*	*SD*	*M*	*SD*	*M*	*SD*	*ES*		*F*	*p*
PSCR-SP	0.60	0.39	0.44	0.41	0.99	0.48	1.02	0.47		G	10.17	0.003**
Self-Esteem Problems									1.36	T	2.75	0.11
										GxT	5.67	0.02*
PSCR-NR	0.41	0.25	0.38	0.41	0.80	0.31	0.77	0.27		G	12.33	0.001***
Narcisstic-schizoid									1.41	T	0.41	0.53
Relationship										GxT	0.01	0.93
PSCR-AP	0.75	0.55	0.67	0.55	1.31	0.59	1.29	0.56		G	9.06	0.005**
Achievement Problems									1.09	T	0.89	0.35
										GxT	0.20	0.66
PSCR-CS	0.75	0.48	0.65	0.40	1.15	0.91	1.22	0.85		G	4.20	0.05*
Conflict with Siblings									0.83	T	0.48	0.49
										GxT	3.38	0.08
PSCR-ES	0.63	0.39	0.40	0.34	0.39	0.24	0.43	0.34		G	1.32	0.26
Effort for Siblings									0.08	T	1.95	0.17
										GxT	4.83	0.04*

PSCR-S	0.46	0.43	0.38	0.48	0.51	0.32	0.51	0.24		G	0.50	0.49
Suicidality									0.35	T	0.60	0.45
										GxT	0.60	0.45
PSCR-PA	0.78	0.39	0.60	0.42	0.86	0.25	0.86	0.27		G	1.72	0.20
Psychic Aspects									0.73	T	7.10	0.01**
										GxT	6.46	0.02*
PSCR-SCA	0.57	0.21	0.49	0.30	0.83	0.31	0.84	0.32		G	9.94	0.004**
Social-Comm. Aspects									1.41	T	1.18	0.29
										GxT	2.14	0.15
PSCR-SA	0.25	0.29	0.15	0.13	0.23	0.12	0.24	0.12		G	0.41	0.53
Somatic Aspects									0.36	T	0.96	0.33
										GxT	1.45	0.24
PSCR	0.53	0.20	0.42	0.23	0.64	0.16	0.65	0.16		G	6.21	0.02*
Total Score									1.26	T	6.60	0.02*
										GxT	8.28	0.007**

Note: M: Mean, SD: Standard Deviation, ES: Effect Sizes, T: Time, G: Group, T1: Beginning of Therapy; T4: End of Therapy.

for the PSCR-CA subscales, differential effects for the waiting control group and the treatment group were detected (see Table 2). A significant interaction effect with more prominent changes for the treatment group was found for the PSCR-CA secondary scale "Psychic Aspects" but not for the social-communicative or somatic aspects. This pattern of significant interaction effects was found on the PSCR-CA scale level for the dimensions "depressive powerlessness", "personal loss", "self-esteem problems" and "effort for siblings". No significant interaction effects were found for the variables anxiety symptoms, emotional detachment, relationship disorder, achievement problems or suicidality.

As a second step, changes from the beginning to the end of treatment, comprising 88 therapy sessions on average, were investigated for the whole sample of 71 patients. Applying Analysis of Variance with repeated measures, significant changes were found for all the PSCR-CA scales (see Table 3). Effect sizes ranged from 0.66 to 1.41 for the primary scales of the PSCR-CA. For the secondary scales, effect sizes ranged from 0.84 to 1.37. The PSCR-CA total score had an effect size of 1.41. Thus, effect sizes for long-term treatment were considerably higher than for short-term treatment. Looking at the effect sizes on the secondary scale level, the most prominent changes occurred for "Psychic Aspects" followed by "Social-Communicative Aspects", whereas somatic symptoms achieved the lowest effect size.

4 Discussion

The aim of this study was to evaluate the outcome of short-term and long-term psychoanalytic psychotherapy for children and adolescents. The results of the present study on the PSCR-CA show that the treatment group is superior to the waiting control group according to expert ratings. For the global symptom ratings, moderate to high effect sizes could be found. In contrast to the waiting control group, the treatment group improved significantly in the PSCR-CA total score. An effect size at the 25th therapy session of 0.47, is comparable to effect sizes reported in previous meta-analyses of short-term psychotherapies (Fonagy, Target, Cottrell, Phillips & Kurtz, 2002). The effect size of 1.41 found for the long-term psychotherapy evidences superior effectiveness in comparison to effect sizes reported by other studies of between 0.54 and 0.71 (Weisz, Weiss,

Table 3. PSCR-CA scales for therapy beginning, 25th session and end of long-term therapy (n = 71).

Psychic and Social-Communicative Findings Report for Children and Adolescents (PSCR-CA)	*Beginning of Treatment*		*25. Session*		*End of Treatment*		*Beginning until 25. Session*			*Beginning until End of Treatment*		
	M	*SD*	*M*	*SD*	*M*	*SD*	*ES*	*F*	*p*	*ES*	*F*	*P*
Depressive Powerlessness	1.12	0.57	0.85	0.48	0.44	0.37	0.53	29.12	0.0001	1.41	93.95	0.0001
Anxiety Symptoms	0.99	0.72	0.67	0.66	0.35	0.54	0.46	31.81	0.0001	1.01	69.46	0.0001
Personal Loss	0.78	0.83	0.58	0.79	0.27	0.62	0.26	3.31	0.07	0.70	22.71	0.0001
Emotional Detachment	0.81	0.51	0.62	0.51	0.33	0.39	0.36	18.37	0.0001	1.04	60.12	0.0001
Self-Esteem Problems	0.45	0.40	0.35	0.38	0.22	0.31	0.27	9.14	0.004	0.62	25.20	0.0001
Narcisstic-Schizoid Relationship	0.49	0.38	0.41	0.37	0.19	0.26	0.20	5.97	0.02	0.91	44.31	0.0001
Achievement Problems	0.67	0.47	0.56	0.51	0.35	0.46	0.22	5.22	0.03	0.67	24.66	0.0001
Conflict with Siblings	0.66	0.55	0.63	0.55	0.36	0.40	0.06	0.80	0.37	0.63	15.29	0.0002
Effort for Siblings	0.54	0.39	0.39	0.35	0.20	0.25	0.41	12.53	0.0008	1.03	46.74	0.0001
Suicidality	0.39	0.38	0.31	0.36	0.15	0.33	0.21	4.99	0.03	0.66	33.00	0.0001
Psychic Aspects	0.79	0.33	0.59	0.37	0.32	0.35	0.55	37.01	0.0001	1.37	116.62	0.0001
Social-Comm. Aspects	0.52	0.29	0.45	0.30	0.25	0.27	0.26	7.22	0.009	1.00	54.49	0.0001
Somatic Aspects	0.25	0.23	0.20	0.19	0.09	0.14	0.24	5.24	0.03	0.84	41.94	0.0001
Total Score	0.52	0.22	0.41	0.24	0.22	0.21	0.47	28.87	0.0001	1.41	112.75	0.0001

Note: M: Mean, SD: Standard Deviation, ES: Effect Sizes.

Han, Granger & Morton, 1995). Different effect sizes were found for different components of a disorder specifically in that changes in psychic aspects were achieved by this treatment. Changes in other aspects like social-communicative and somatic impairments were less pronounced. The study demonstrated that short-term and long-term psychoanalytical treatment is highly effective for a wide range of mental disorders in children and adolescents.

In the context of the Heidelberg study, analyses for disorder specific subsamples were carried out. Besides anxiety disorders, depressive disorders and behavioral disorders were analyzed separately. Comparing these, anxiety disorders appeared to be more effectively treated with short-term therapy. Psychodynamic short-term psychotherapy yielded an effect size of 1.5 for anxiety disorders (Kronmüller et al., 2005), compared to a lower effect size for depressive disorders (Horn et al., 2005) and behavioral disorders (Winkelmann et al., 2005). Accordingly, it can be assumed that different disorders do not respond similarly well to short-term psychodynamic therapy.

Comparing the results to those of studies on cognitive behavioral therapies, some similarities exist. The majority of cognitive behavioral anxiety treatments reach effect sizes of between 0.8 and 2.3. However, these indirect comparisons are valid only to a limited extent and, to date, a study directly comparing psychodynamic and cognitive behavioral treatment does not exist. In comparison to meta-analytic studies such as that of Weisz, Weiss, Han, Granger & Morton (1995) or of Beelmann & Schneider (2003), who found effect sizes between 0.4 and 0.7 for psychodynamic approaches, the effect sizes found in the present study are considerably higher. Following Cohen (1988), the effect sizes of psychodynamic treatment for children and adolescents can be classified as high and are comparable to those found for cognitive behavioral therapy.

However, some children and adolescents could not be treated successfully with psychodynamic therapy. This raises the question of therapy improvement. It can either be assumed that these patients have not been treated long enough because they dropped-out, or that they would have benefited more from an alternative treatment. To what extent a more disorder-specific treatment strategy would have improved the effectiveness of the treatment, cannot be answered by the data but represents an important question for future evaluation research.

Numerous instruments have been developed or adapted in the context of the Heidelberg Study of Psychodynamic Treatment for Children and Adolescents. Here, emphasis was placed on the assessment of structure-related characteristics and on instruments for the investigation of the psychotherapeutic process. These developments are an important basis for further empirical psychotherapy studies and are a prerequisite for the identification of therapeutic factors or constellations leading to less successful therapies and drop out. Instruments like the "Work on the Focus Scale for Children and Adolescents" (WFS-CA) make it possible to test therapy-theoretical assumptions, advance them and thus close the gap between psychotherapy research and clinical practice.

Several limitations of the study require to be mentioned. First of all, this evaluation has been carried out using a relatively small sample. Also, for ethical reasons, the long-term study was conducted without a control design. Only up to the first four months, 25 sessions, was there a waiting group as control. Another limitation is that the sample includes heterogeneous ICD-10 diagnoses. In further studies, psychoanalytic therapy for specific diagnosis should be evaluated. To what extent the results can be generalized to different mental disorders has to be explored by further studies. However, it can be stated that compared to samples of other studies, the Heidelberg Study included patients with severe disorders thus the sample has high clinical representativeness. Although the therapies were carried out according to a manual, adherence was only globally examined. In further studies, a differentiated examination of adherence is necessary.

Despite the methodological shortcomings, the results show that psychodynamic short-term and long-term psychotherapy represents an effective treatment approach for children and adolescents with mental disorders. In future studies, which children and adolescents benefit from short-term psychodynamic psychotherapy should be investigated, which mechanisms and processes characterize successful therapies and which patients need longer or different psycho-therapeutical treatment. The results can not only contribute to closing the gap between psychotherapy research and clinical practice, but also facilitate empirical testing of theoretical therapy assumptions and thus help to improve psychotherapeutic treatment of children and adolescents.

Acknowledgements

The authors wish to express their thanks to the patients and their parents who kindly participated in this study. The study was funded by the Research Commission of the Medical Faculty of the University of Heidelberg (grant No. 6/98), the Institute for Analytic Child- and Adolescent-Psychotherapy Heidelberg, der Vereinigung Analytischer Kinder- und Jugendlichen-Psychotherapeuten in Deutschland e.V. (VAKJP) and the Fischer-Stiftung

References

Ainsworth, M., Blehar, M.C., Waters, E. & Wall, S. (1978). *Patterns of Attachment: A Psychological Study of the Strange Situation*. Hillsdale, NJ: Lawrence Erlbaum.

Armsden, G.C. & Greenberg, M.T. (1987). The inventory of parent and peer attachment: individual differences and their relationship to psychological well-being in adolescence. *Journal of Youth and Adolescence, 16*: 427–454.

Beelmann, A. & Schneider, N. (2003). Wirksamkeit von Psychotherapie bei Kindern und Jugendlichen. Eine Übersicht und Meta-Analyse zum Bestand und zu Ergebnissen der deutschsprachigen Effektivitätsforschung. *Zeitschrift für Klinische Psychologie und Psychotherapie, 32*: 129–143.

Benjamin, L.S. (1974). Structural analysis of social behaviour. *Psychological Review, 81*: 392–425.

Block, J.H. & Block, J. (1980). The role of ego-control and ego-resiliency in the organization of behavior. In: W.A. Collins (Ed.), *Development of Cognition, Affect, and Social Relations: The Minnesota Symposia on Child Psychology, Volume 13*:39–101. Hillsdale, NJ: Lawrence Erlbaum.

Bordin, E.S. (1979). The generalizability of the psychoanalytic concept of the working alliance. *Psychology and Psychotherapy: Theory, Research and Practice, 16*: 252–260.

Bürgin, D., Resch, F. & Schulte-Markwort, M. (2007). *Operationalisierte Psychodynamische Diagnostik für die Kinder- und Jugendpsychiatrie OPD-KJ*. Bern: Huber.

Christensen, L. & Mendoza, L.J. (1986). A method of assessing change in a single subject: an alteration of the RC Index. *Behavior Therapy, 17*: 305–308.

Cohen, J. (1988). *Statistical Power Analysis for the Behavioral Sciences*. New York: Academic Press.

Dilling, H., Mombour, W., Schmidt, M.H. & Schulte-Markwort, E. (Eds.) (1994). *Internationale Klassifikation psychischer Störungen. ICD-10, Kapitel V (F). Forschungskriterien.* Bern: Huber.

Dührssen, A. (1964). Katamnestische Untersuchung bei 150 Kindern und Jugendlichen nach analytischer Psychotherapie. *Praxis der Kinderpsychologie und Kinderpsychiatrie, 7*: 241–255.

Estrada, A. U. & Russell, R.L. (1999). The development of the Child Psychotherapy Process Scales (CPPS). *Psychotherapy Research, 9*: 154–166.

Fahrig, H., Kronmüller, K.-T., Hartmann, M. & Rudolf, G. (1996). Therapieerfolg analytischer Psychotherapie bei Kindern und Jugendlichen. *Zeitschrift für Psychosomatische Medizin und Psychoanalyse, 42*: 375–395.

Fonagy, P., Target, M., Cottrell, D., Phillips, J. & Kurtz, Z. (2002). *What Works for Whom. A Critical Review of Treatments for Children and Adolescents.* London: Guilford Press.

Fonagy, P. & Target, M. (1994 a). The efficacy of psychoanalysis for children with disruptive disorders. *Journal of the American Academy of Child and Adolescent Psychiatry, 33*: 45–55.

Fonagy, P. & Target, M. (1994 b). Predictors of outcome in child psychoanalysis: A retrospective study of 763 cases at the Anna Freud centre. *Journal of the American Psychoanalytic Association, 44*: 27–77.

Grande, T., Rudolf, G. & Oberbracht, C. (1997). Die Praxisstudie Analytische Langzeitpsychotherapie. Ein Projekt zur prospektiven Untersuchungen struktureller Veränderungen in Psychoanalysen. In: M. Leuzinger-Bohleber & U. Stuhr (Eds.), *Psychoanalysen im Rückblick. Methoden, Ergebnisse und Perspektiven der neueren Katamneseforschung.* Gießen: Psychosozial Verlag.

Grande, T., Rudolf, G., Oberbracht, C. & Jakobsen, T. (2001). Therapeutische Veränderungen jenseits der Symptomatik – Wirkungen stationärer Psychotherapie im Licht der Heidelberger Umstrukturierungsskala. *Zeitschrift für Psychosomatische Medizin und Psychotherapie, 47*: 213–233.

Grossmann, K.E., August, P. & Fremmer-Bombik, E. (1989). Die Bindungstheorie: Modell und entwicklungspsychologische Forschung. In: H. Keller (Ed.), *Handbuch der Kleinkindforschung* (pp. 31–55). Berlin: Springer.

Hartmann, A. & Herzog, T. (1995). Varianten der Effektstärkenberechnung in Meta-Analysen: Kommt es zu variablen Ergebnissen? *Zeitschrift für Klinische Psychologie, 24*: 337–343.

Hartmann, M., Kronmüller, K.-T., Horn, H., Reck, C., Backenstraß, M., Neumann, K., Victor, D. & Winkelmann, K. (2000). Wirkfaktoren in der Kurzzeittherapie bei Kindern und Jugendlichen. *Zeitschrift für Theorie und Praxis der analytischen Kinder- und Jugendlichen-Psychoanalyse, 106*: 123–152.

Hartmann, M., Horn, H., Winkelmann, K., Geiser-Elze, A. & Kronmüller, K.-T. (1997). *Therapieleitfaden der Heidelberg Studie zur Evaluation Analytischer Psychotherapie bei Kindern und Jugendlichen*. Unpublished manuscript.

Horn, H. (2003). Involving parents in child psychoanalytic psychotherapy. *Praxis der Kinderpsychologie und Kinderpsychiatrie, 52*: 766–776.

Horn, H., Geiser-Elze, A., Reck, C., Hartmann, M., Stefini, A., Winkelmann, K. & Kronmüller, K.-T. (2005). Efficacy of psychodynamic short-term psychotherapy for children and adolescents with depression. *Praxis der Kinderpsychologie und Kinderpsychiatrie, 54*: 578–597.

Jacobson, N.S. & Revenstorf, D. (1988). Statistics for assessing the clinical significance of psychotherapy techniques: issues, problems, and new developments. *Behavioral Assessment, 10*: 133–145.

Kazdin, A.E. (2004). Psychotherapy for children and adolescents. In: A.E., Bergin & S.L. Garfield (Eds.), *Handbook of Psychotherapy and Behavior Change* (pp. 543–589). New York: Wiley.

Kronmüller, K.-T., Hartmann, M., Postelnicu, I., Stefini, A., Geiser-Elze, A., Gerhold, M., Horn, H. & Winkelmann, K. (2005). Efficacy of psychodynamic short-term psychotherapy for children and adolescents with anxiety disorders. *Praxis der Kinderpsychologie und Kinderpsychiatrie, 54*: 559–577.

Kronmüller, K.-T., Hartmann, M., Reck, C., Victor, D., Horn, H. & Winkelmann, K. (2003). Therapeutic alliance in child and adolescent psychotherapy: evaluation of a German version of the Therapeutic Alliance Scales for Children. *Zeitschrift für Klinische Psychologie und Psychotherapie, 32*: 14–23.

Kronmüller, K.-T., Victor, D., Horn, H., Winkelmann, K., Reck, C., Geiser-Elze, A. & Hartmann, M. (2002). Muster der therapeutischen Beziehung in der Kinder- und Jugendlichen-Psychotherapie. *Zeitschrift für Klinische Psychologie, Psychiatrie und Psychotherapie, 50*: 267–280.

Lachauer, R. (1992). *Der Fokus in der Psychotherapie: Fokalsätze und ihre Anwendung in Kurztherapie*. München: Pfeiffer.

Luborsky, L. (1995). *Einführung in die Analytische Psychotherapie*. Göttingen: Vandenhoeck & Ruprecht.

Main, M. & Solomon, J. (1986). Discovery of an insecure-disorganized/disoriented attachment pattern: procedures, findings and implications for the classification of behavior. In: T.B. Brazelton & M. Yogman (Eds.), *Affective Development in Infancy* (pp. 95–124). Norwood, NJ: Ablex.

Main, M. & Weston, D.R. (1981). The quality of the toddler`s relationship to mother and to father: related to conflict behavior and the readiness to establish new relationships. *Child Development, 52*: 932–940.

Moran, G., Fonagy, P., Kurtz, A., Bolton, A. & Brook, C. (1991). A controlled study of psychoanalytic treatment of brittle diabetes. *Journal of the American Academy of Child and Adolescent Psychiatry, 30*: 926–935.

Muratori, F., Picchi, L., Casella, C., Tancredi, R., Milone, A. & Patarnello, M.G. (2002). Efficacy of brief dynamic psychotherapy for children with emotional disorders. *Psychotherapy and Psychosomatics, 71*: 28–38.

Muratori, F., Picchi, L., Bruni, G., Patarnello, M. & Romagnoli, G. (2003). A two-year follow-up of psychodynamic psychotherapy for internalizing disorders in children. *Journal of the American Academy of Child and Adolescent Psychiatry, 42*: 331–339.

Olschewski, M. & Scheurlen, H. (1985). Comprehensive cohort study: an alternative to randomized consent design in a breast preservation trial. *Methods of Information in Medicine, 24*: 131–134.

Orlinsky, D.E. & Howard, K.I. (1975). The psychological interior of psychotherapy: explorations with therapy session reports. In: L.S. Greenberg & W.M. Pinsof (Eds.), *The Psychotherapeutic Process: A Research Handbook* (pp. 477–501). New York: Guilford Press.

Rudolf, G. (1981). *Untersuchung und Befund bei Neurosen und psychosomatischen Erkrankungen. Materialien zum psychischen und sozialkommunikativen Befund PSKB*. Weinheim: Beltz.

SAS System for Windows, Version 9.1. (2002–2003). Cary, NC: SAS Institute.

Schepank, H. (1995). *Der Beeinträchtigungsschwere-Score (BSS). Ein Instrument zur Bestimmung einer Psychogenen Erkrankung*. Göttingen: Beltz.

Shirk, S.R. & Saiz, C.C. (1992). Clinical, empirical, and developmental perspectives on the therapeutic relationship in child psychotherapy. Special issue: Developmental approaches to prevention and intervention. *Development and Psychopathology, 4*: 713–728.

Smith-Acuna, S., Durlak, J.A. & Kaspar, C.J. (1991). Development of child psychotherapy process measures. *Journal of Clinical Child Psychology, 20*: 126–131.

Smyrnios, K.S. & Kirkby, R.J. (1993). Long-term comparison of brief versus unlimited psychodynamic treatments with children and their parents. *Journal of Consulting and Clinical Psychology, 61*: 1020–1027.

Stiles, W.B., Meshot, C.M., Anderson, T.M. & Sloan, W.W. (1992). Assimilation of problematic experience. The case of John Jones. *Psychotherapy Research, 2*: 81–101.

Szapocznik, J., Kurtines, M.W., Santisteban, W. & Rio, A. (1990). Interplay of advances between theory, and application in treatment interventions aimed at behavior problem children and adolescents. *Journal of Consulting and Clinical Psychology, 58*: 696–703.

Szapocznik, J., Rio, A., Murray, E., Cohen, R., Scopetta, M., Rivas-Vazquez, A., Hervis, O., Posada, V. & Kurtines, W. (1989). Structural family versus psychodynamic child therapy for problematic hispanic boys. *Journal of Consulting and Clinical Psychology, 57*: 571–578.

Target, M. & Fonagy, P. (1994). The efficacy of psychoanalysis for children with emotional disorders. *Journal of the American Academy of Child and Adolescent Psychiatry, 33*: 361–370.

Trowell, J., Joffe, I., Campbell, J., Clemente, C., Almqvist, F., Soininen, M., Koskenranta-Aalto, U., Weintraub, S., Kolaitis, G., Tomaras, V., Anastasopoulos, D., Grayson, K., Barnes, J. & Tsiantis, J. (2007). Childhood depression: a place for psychotherapy. An outcome study comparing individual psychodynamic psychotherapy and family therapy. *European Child and Adolescent Psychiatry, 16*: 157–167.

Trowell, J., Kolvin, I., Weeramanthri, T., Sadowski, H., Berelowitz, M., Glasser, D. & Leitch, I. (2002). Psychotherapy for sexually abused girls: psychopathological outcome findings and patterns of change. *British Journal of Psychiatry, 180*: 234–247.

Unnewehr, S., Schneider, S. & Margraf, J. (Eds.) (1995). *Diagnostisches Interview bei psychischen Störungen im Kindes- und Jugendalter (Kinder-DIPS)*. Heidelberg: Springer.

Victor, N. (1990). Methodische Fragen. In: *Materialien zur Gesundheitsforschung. Klinische Studien in der Psychiatrie*. Bonn: Schriftenreihe zum Programm der Bundesregierung: Forschung und Entwicklung im Dienste der Gesundheit.

Weisz, J.R., Weiss, B., Han, S.S., Granger, D.A. & Morton, T. (1995). Effects of psychotherapy with children and adolescents revisited: a meta-analysis of treatment outcome studies. *Psychological Bulletin, 117*: 450–468.

Windaus, E. (2005). Efficacy studies in the field of psychotherapy – psychoanalytical and psychodynamic psychology—for children and adolescents: a survey. *Praxis der Kinderpsychologie und Kinderpsychiatrie, 54*: 530–58.

Winkelmann, K., Hartmann, M., Neumann, K., Hennch, C., Reck, C., Victor, D., Horn, H., Uebel, T. & Kronmüller, K.-T. (2000). Stability of outcome in children and adolescent psychoanalysis at 5 year follow-up. *Praxis der Kinderpsychologie und Kinderpsychiatrie, 49*: 315–328.

Winkelmann, K., Stefini, A., Hatmann, M., Geiser-Elze, A., Kronmüller, A., Horn, H. & Kronmüller, K.-T. (2005). Efficacy of psychodynamic short-term psychotherapy for children and adolescents with behavioral disorders. *Praxis der Kinderpsychologie und Kinderpsychiatrie, 54*: 598–614.

CHAPTER SIX

Attention-Deficit-Hyperactivity Disorder (AD/HD): A field for contemporary psychoanalysis?: Some clinical, conceptual and neurobiological considerations based on the Frankfurt Prevention Study[1]

Marianne Leuzinger-Bohleber and Tamara Fischmann

1 Introductory remarks

It seems surprising that psychoanalysts have only started to engage more intensely in the ongoing controversial discussions on

---

[1]The Frankfurt Prevention Study was performed by a large group of researchers and therapists. Chairs: Marianne Leuzinger-Bohleber, Gerald Hüther and Angelika Wolff. Responsible for methodological questions and design: Tamara Fischmann, Yvonne Brandl, Stephan Hau, and Bernhard Rüger. Psychologists and educational scientists: Lars Aulbach, Betty Caruso, Katrin-Marleen Einert, Oliver Glindemann, Gerlinde Göppel, Paula Hermann, Pawel Hesse, Jantje Heumann, Gamze Karaca, Julia König, Jochen Lendle, Alex Schwenk, Adelheid Staufenberg, Sibylle Steuber, Christiane Uhl, Judith Vogel, Christina Waldung, Lisa Wolff. Also many of our colleagues from the Institute for Psychoanalytic Child- and Adolecent Psychotherapy (IAKJP) engaged in the study as therapists or supervisors. We thank all of them for their engagement and professional support of the study. Since writing this chapter we have worked on another publication with a similar topic. Therefore some theoretical considerations and clinical materials of this chapter are also found in: Leuzinger-Bohleber, M., Canestri, J., Target, M: (in press): Controversies on different approaches in psychoanalytic research on early development and ADHD. Chapter One in: Leuzinger-Bohleber, M., Canestri, J., Target, M.(eds): Early Development and its Disturbances. Clinical, Conceptual and Empirical Research on ADHD and other Psychopathologies and its Epistemological Reflections. Will be published 2010, in London: Karnac.

'Attention-Deficit/Hyperactivity-Disorder' (AD/HD) during the past few years, e.g. casebook on learning disabilities by Rothstein and Glenn, 1999; special volume of Psychoanalytic Inquiry, 22, 2002; panel on AD/HD and trauma at the IPA Congress in Rio, 2005, reported by Sugarman (2006). Carney (2002) writes in his prologue to this volume: "Not so long ago, some practitioners both inside and outside psychoanalysis discouraged the use of psychodynamic treatment for patients with AD/HD" (p. 301). Salomonsson (2004) agrees by writing: "Psychoanalysis is an often-neglected treatment method for children with neuropsychiatric disorders" (p. 132).

There may be many reasons for the increasing interest in this topic during the past few years. We want to mention just three possible ones, which for us had been essential in becoming involved in this topic:

a. The dialogue between psychoanalysis and contemporary neurobiology/brain research opens a fascinating window for a new understanding of an old problem in European culture: the mind-body-problem. This exchange also promises to enlarge the understanding for psychic problems probably connected with some neurobiologically founded pathologies as postulated for AD/HD.
b. New developments in psychoanalytic theory based on findings from empirical infant, attachment, and memory research, offer alternative conceptualizations and therapeutic techniques for treating early disturbances of affect regulations, of the development of symbolization and mentalization, all central dysfunctions in AD/HD.
c. The growing competition with other therapeutic disciplines and treatment possibilities, e.g. medication with Ritalin, Cognitive Behavioral Therapies, etc., and some political realities due to a modern 'Zeitgeist' in Western countries, probably motivates many self-critical psychoanalysts to engage intensely in relevant public and professional debates as the one on AD/HD, which is considered as one of the most controversial debates child psychiatry has ever gone through (Riedesser, 2006).

Within the limits of this paper we would like to focus on discussing conceptualizations, results and some considerations based on a fruitful dialogue between psychoanalysis and neurobiology within the framework of a large, prospective, randomized, controlled study: the so-called Frankfurt Prevention Study. This study was conceptualized, planned and performed by an interdisciplinary research team of psychoanalysts, neurobiologists, medical doctors and social psychologists. We begin with some remarks on the afore mentioned ongoing public and professional debates which had been the backdrop to the motivation to perform the Frankfurt Prevention Study (2.). In the following section, we would like to compare a psychoanalytic conceptualization of AD/HD with a so-called 'multimodal treatment of AD/HD', that is cognitive-behavioral treatment in combination with medication, and their implications for diagnoses and therapy (3a, b). Then we will discuss that the richness of psychoanalytic concepts, explaining the possible biographical and psychodynamic as well as genetic and biological roots of AD/HD, seems to be in excellent concordance with contemporary neurobiological memory research (3c). This interdisciplinary point of view was the base for conceptualizing the Frankfurt Prevention Study (FPS) (4). We can only summarize this study here (4a), elaborating on some of the most important empirical and clinically relevant findings. (4b).[2]

2 *The dramatic increase of treating ADHS by medication, e.g. Ritalin: An indicator for the danger of medicalizing contemporary social problems?*

In 2001 the German Ministry of Health published an official statement expressing the concern that prescriptions of Ritalin® for AD/HD children had increased 270% from 1997 to 2000 (Amft et al., 2004; Mattner, 2006). Mattner (2006), Amft (2006), and Gerspach (2006) give a short overview of the historical and societal context in which this increase of Ritalin and other psychopharmacological

---

[2] Gilmore (2000) begins her excellent overview on historical and contemporary literature on Attention-Deficit/Hyperactivity-Disorder with the following statement: "It (AD/HD, L-B.) has a highly prevalent disorder in clinical populations, and has been estimated to involve as many as fifty percent of child psychiatry patients. Despite the burgeoning interest in and research on this disorder, and the literature emanating from a range of child related disciplines, there continues to be skepticism among psychoanalytic clinicians as to the validity of the syndrome as a meaningful discrete diagnostic entity"(p. 1258). In the section 4b of our paper we will discuss some findings of the Frankfurt Prevention Study supporting this skepticism.

medication for children could be understood while Mattner (2006) discusses the idea that the search for neurophysiological reasons for explaining socially deviant behavior has a long tradition in European countries, particularly in Germany.[3]

Similar findings are reported by Gilmore (2000), summarizing the history of this diagnosis in child psychiatry in the USA. Still (1902) first observed a group of children in his practice "...who showed a pattern of aggressiveness, resistance to discipline, excessive emotionality, little 'inhibitory volition', 'lawlessness', spitefulness, and cruelty: these children were also notable for their impaired attention, over-activity, and a defect in motor control. This syndrome was attributed to an underlying neurological deficiency, and, consistent with the then current view of behavioral disorders, the influence of environment was largely ignored" (Gilmore, 2000, p. 1266/67). The interest in this disorder grew after the encephalitis outbreak of 1917–18, when many children, after recovering from this illness, showed impairments in attention, regulation of activity, and impulse control, the now so-called 'post-encephalitic behavior disorder'. Laufer and Denhoff (1957) characterized a subgroup of these children as 'hyperkinetic impulse disorder'. It was attributed to a postulated brain mechanism, namely 'poor filtering of stimuli'. These children were often treated with antipsychotic drugs. Later the term 'minimal brain damage' continued to be fashionable. In the 1960s, the more modest term 'minimal brain dysfunction' was more widely used. Gilmore (2000) agrees with Mattner (2006) that both these diagnostic terms ultimately,

> "...yielded to scientific objections, as it became clear that many children and many syndromes were being lumped together without heuristic or prescriptive benefit under the umbrella of a pseudoscientific classification. As part of the growing trend towards descriptive, rather than etiological, classifications, the

[3] In the 1980s the "Minimal Cerebral Dysfunction" (MCD) was widely spread (see Mattner, 2006). It was seen in close connection with the oppositional defiant disorder. This connection could already be observed in the 1950s. At that time German authors discussed Encephalopathische Psychopathie (Enke, 1953), hirnorganisch-psychisches Achsensyndrom (Göllnitz, 1954), and frühkindliches exogenes Psychosyndrom (Lempp, 1970). In Switzerland one used the term frühkindliches psycho-organisches Syndrom (POS) (Ruf-Bächtinger, 1987). Berger (1977) talked about "Teilleistungsstörungen" or "Teilleistungsschwächen".

diagnostic wastebasket was broken down into observable and verifiable deficits" (Barkley, 1990, p. 10)

The specific 'hyperactive child syndrome' (Laufer and Denhoff 1957), or 'hyperactive reaction of childhood' (DSM-II), reappeared as the official nomenclature for children with features of impulsive and aggressive behavior and poor attention span. While demonstrable brain damage could produce this syndrome, the majority of children so diagnosed were without known injury. Nonetheless, brain mechanisms responsible for these behavioral 'lags' were postulated, and prognosis was felt to be good on the basis of developmental maturation; that is, puberty was viewed as a watershed, after which there was good likelihood of resolution. Environmental factors were deemphasized. (Gilmore, 2000). According to Gilmore, the research in particular carried out by Virginia Douglas and her group at McGill, led to the development of a paradigm which renamed the syndrome as 'Attention Deficit Disorder' (ADD) by the time DSM-III was published in 1980. In the following years environmental toxicity, food additives or technical overstimulationwas also seen as relevant for ADD and the learning disabilities of these children. Learning disabilities were formally recognized by the government with the Public Law 94–142 in 1975. To children diagnosed with ADD, as one form of learning disabilities, a multimodal treatment approach which included medication, special classroom programs, dietary management, and parent counseling were offered. In the 1980s, according to newer studies, in DSM-III-R the classification of ADD without hyperactivity was dropped and renamed as the syndrome Attention-Deficit/Hyperactivity Disorder (AD/HD), linking it with the Oppositional Defiant Disorder and Conduct Disorder under the Disruptive Disorders in Childhood. As such it has been retained in DSM-IV.[4]

Gilmore (2000) mentions that in the past few decades AD/HD has achieved validity as a discrete diagnostic entity through

---

[4] Rothstein (2002) summarizes the diagnostical criteria as follows: "According to DSM-IV criteria 'Attention Deficit/Hyperactivity Disorder'(AD/HD) is diagnosed if *four* conditions are met. One is either *a persistent pattern of inattention or hyperactivity-impulsivity* more frequent than is typical for the patient's age. A second is that *some of the symptoms must have been present before the age of seven*. Third the *symptoms must be observed in at least two settings*, such as at home and at school or work. Finally, clear evidence is required of *compromised social, academic, or occupational functioning....*" (p. 392).

epidemiological characterization, in that it shows strong hereditary patterns and clusters with other specific psychiatric disorders, and through increasingly promising neuro-anatomical studies that further differentiate subpopulations (Cantwell, 1996). Research in neurotransmitters has also burgeoned, although this has so far failed to yield the anticipated solution. In a recent ten-year-review of the disorder for the Journal of the American Academy of Child and Adolescent Psychiatry, Cantwell (1996) emphasizes that AD/HD is "one of the most important disorders that child and adolescent psychiatrists treat". It is a robust disorder, with a high prevalence and a serious lifetime morbidity that responds best to a multimodal intervention. He asserts unequivocally that "psychosocial factors are not thought to play a primary etiological role" (Cantwell, 1996, p. 979) although, presumably, secondary, negative, mother-child interactions are commonly observed. (Gilmore, 2000, p. 1269).

Mattner (2006) questions these conclusions. He reflects on historical and societal factors for such, as he calls it, "biological explanations for psychosocial problems of AD/HD children". He quotes Crary (1999) who showed in detail that only during the beginning of the 19th century, the 'industrial century', that it became necessary for children as well as adults to develop the capability to 'show attention in a disciplined way', 'to concentrate' and to submit to a joint process of production, without destructive and aggressive conflicts. Only since then, 'attention', 'concentration' and the capability to 'sit still during hours in learning situations in school or at work' have become socially required virtues. Mattner therefore concludes: "Probably the epidemic increase of psychopathologies in children with AD/HD indicates in a seismographic way the sufferings and problems of children in our postmodern times, which escape in our analyses from a purely neurobiological perspective" (2006, p. 18, translation M.L-B.). In a similar vein, Amft (2006) has emphasized that Ritalin or other medicines, without any doubt, can be of help for some children suffering from AD/HD, particularly taking into account certain social situations at school contributing to a first de-escalation of conduct problems of AD/HD children. At the same time, he warns against the neglect of family, social and environmental factors.

> "Without any doubt the application of Ritalin and other psychopharmacological medication has a highly seductive character

> because they are very efficient, fast in their effects, not very costly and can adapt 'difficult children' to the everyday requirements of schools in our Western societies.... According to this argumentation it seems even unethical not to hand out these medicines to children with AD/HD.... Such a radically biological explanation of social problems of children does not consider the influence of factors of the so called 'changed childhood' ('veränderte Kindheit') in our Western societies with its well known features of broken families, early emotional neglect of children, the 'clash of civilizations and values', the influence of media as well as the complex realities of growing up in a globalized multicultural world etc." (p. 119ff., translation M.L-B. Further to this topic see also Garlichs and Leuzinger-Bohleber, 1999).

Therefore, Amft, Gerspach & Mattner, (2004) plea for critical and differentiated analyses of multiples fields of problems that children in post-industrial societies grow up with (Sennett, 1998). In talking about AD/HD, and here we do agree with these authors, societal and cultural factors should thus be taken as seriously as findings from modern neurobiology and brain research.

To analyze the symptoms of a child as the products of complex unconscious and conscious factors due to the idiographic biographical factors on the one hand, and specific genetic, biological, and neurobiological determinants on the other, has always been at the core of psychoanalytic conceptualizations. Therefore, we agree with many contemporary authors that psychoanalysis, as a theory as well as a treatment method, has a lot to offer for understanding children with ADD and could even be seen as "the" method of choice in treating them (Carney, 2002; Rothstein, 2002; Gilmore 2002, 2002; Sugarman, 2006; Zabarenko, 2002). This view will further be elaborated in the following sections of our paper as it was also the base for planning and conceptualizing the Frankfurt Prevention Study.

Some remarks on psychoanalytic concepts concerning the genesis, the psychodynamics, prevention and therapeutic possibilities of children suffering from AD/HD

In contrast to the opinions held in behavioural therapy and psychiatry, which are outlined above, it is emphasized in psychoanalytic publications that attention deficit and hyperactivity are symptoms which may at most be summed up into syndromes, but which cannot be considered a full-blown clinical picture even if it turns out that a genetic disposition actually exists. There are no clear borders between a 'normal' and 'pathological' form of hyperactivity and attention deficit. As generally known, children with AD/HD are capable of addressing certain tasks full of attention and concentration if they are really interested in them. Therefore, it is not the 'objective measurement and evaluation' of the symptoms of hyperactivity and attention deficit which is characteristic for a psychoanalytic approach, but the attempt to understand the various personality structures underlying these symptoms as well as to grasp something of the dynamics of the emotional relationships in the families and educational institutions which might contribute to trigger AD/HD. We have observed different structural levels in so-called AD/HD children and a wide range of divergent object relations which is the reason why a monocausal aetiology cannot be assumed. As is generally known, many genetic researchers have continuously pointed out that even a genetic disposition does not 'linearly' generate a phenotype of behaviour but that it takes certain environmental conditions and specific situations, in our case usually very complex early experiences in relationships, to trigger certain gene constellations and thus to activate them (Stassen et al., 2004a, 2004b). In the meantime, there have been many empirical clues that a baby's temperament plays an important role in the aetiology of AD/HD, especially if there is a clash of temperaments with the primary attachment figure, usually the mother (Emde and Fonagy, 1997; Stern, 1995; Beebe and Lachman, 2002). It may be a risk factor if a bubbly baby has a quieter mother, above all because this mother will probably have difficulty in adequately empathizing with her child and regulating his affects. However, it has turned out to be empirically very difficult to capture differences in temperament in an unequivocal way.

We know from psychoanalytic retrospective studies that the tolerance of the primary attachment figure for the baby's eruptions as well as her ability to soothe, to hold and to 'contain' them, play a central role in the genesis of AD/HD (Bürgin, 2005; Dammasch, 2006; Leuzinger-Bohleber et al., 2006). It has been shown that the complex early interactions between mothers and children with AD/HD have often been characterized by over- or under-stimulation and intrusive or neglecting motherly behaviour (Beebe and Lachmann, 2002, Green, 2005). Often, the babies seemed to have no other choice but to motivate their mothers to deliver the most basic care by showing hyperactive and overstimulated behaviour, a pattern which is probably generalized later on.

As is generally known, modern psychoanalysis offers via its pluralism of theories (inter alia Bürgin, 2005; Leuzinger-Bohleber, Dreher and Canestri, 2003), a chance to look at complex phenomena such as AD/HD from different theoretical perspectives. Just a few examples:

Ego psychological authors suggest that the primary attachment figures in "AD/HD families" do not provide the child with sufficiently stable supporting ego functions. However, the child needs reliable and continuing support in order to regulate its behaviour, i.e. to modulate and control its physiological, sensory, motor and affective processes. If the parents cannot provide this support, the child is hardly able to develop adequate primary regulation of drive impulses and affects. The development of attention also depends on such regulatory processes. According to ego psychology, attention is an ego function searching for potential situations offering drive satisfaction in the outer reality. Neurophysiologically, it is connected with the search system (inter alia Panksepp, 2001, Schore, 2005/6). According to most psychoanalytic authors, a basal regulatory weakness or disorder is therefore at the bottom of both hyperactivity and attention deficit and also influences the regulation of fine and gross motor activities. This may be the reason why AD/HD is 4 to 10 times more frequent in boys than in girls. A genetically based dimorphism in muscular activity is likely to exist (inter alia Bürgin, 2005).

Connected to these processes is the development of one's ability to symbolize. A basal frustration tolerance for apparently unbearable affects and impulses may only be developed in a trusting relationship with a 'Meaningful Other'. If a child receives, as just mentioned, not enough stable supporting ego functions and shows a lack of object consistency, a transitional space according to Winnicott, generally known as a precondition for symbolization and creativity, cannot develop adequately.

Authors committed to the psychoanalytic object relations theory have also tried to conceptualize these early regulatory processes (inter alia Kernberg, 2001). Psychoanalytic object relations theory focuses on the internalization of important relationships in early childhood which are considered as vital for the formation of psychic structures and also of drive requirements and personality traits. More recent clinical and empirical studies have shown the importance of differentiating between two affective states in the baby: states with relatively low affect activation and states of vehement, intense affect activation, the so-called 'peak affects'. In the first 'mild' affective state, 'normal' internalization of our experiences in contact with other people take place, resulting in the development of normal ego functions. These experiences are connected with pleasant, realistic bodily sensations which are kept in memory and are finally connected with images and verbalizations. These experiences are in sharp contrast to experiences of the so-called 'peak affects', i.e. intense positive and negative affects which overstrain a baby's capacity for stimulus processing. In such extreme affective states of joy, euphoria, happiness in the presence of another on the one hand, and fear, terror, rage or pain on the other hand, result in the development of psychically problematic, but extremely effective, embodied memories: images of idealized relationships similar to the happy moments of a child at its mother's breast and reflected in the desire for fusion with the love object, unity and absolute affiliation. The extremely negative affects produce, in an analogous way, extreme images of a hateful being, helplessly exposed to intense aggression from the outside. The more intense frustrations and painful experiences are, e.g. in traumatic experiences, the more intense the aggressive impulses provoked which the infantile ego is unable to endure or to attribute to its own self: therefore it immediately projects these aggressive impulses onto the Other and thus experiences itself as threatened and persecuted by the outside. The result is that memories of negative and, for the self and the object, dangerous experiences with relationships are condensed as 'psychic truths'. Thus, in moments of discharge of peak affects or traumatic situations, a psychic tendency develops to categorize experiences in absolutely good or absolutely bad extremes: relationships are split into an idealized and into a persecuting part. Moreover, traumatic experiences imply that the extreme bodily experiences cannot be connected with visualizations or language.[5]

Under normal, non-traumatic or, as Winnicott puts it, 'good enough' conditions, an increasing tolerance towards such extreme situations develops so that the archaically primitive experience of the split between 'good' and 'bad' can eventually be integrated psychically. Melanie Klein characterized the early psychic state of splitting which can only be overcome by projective mechanisms known generally as the 'paranoid-schizoid position'. The process of remembering a first integrated mental experience of ambivalence reveals the fact that the object possesses both 'good' and 'bad' parts, known as the 'depressive position'. Psychoanalytic object relations theory has stressed that the outer object, by means of empathy for the baby's condition of helplessness, has to contribute to the process of softening peak affects 'reliably' and predictably time and again, thus enabling the baby to develop basic confidence in a good object. Simultaneously, the 'emerging self' experiences itself as psychically able to contribute its own part to disappearance of extreme feelings of frustration, rage and hate. Thus, it defines itself as a basically active, potent and not simply passively, exposed being. In the words of psychoanalytic self psychology, the self is therefore successively able to abandon archaic primitive defense mechanisms like the phantasy of the grandiose self or the omnipotent parent imago, and to develop a supporting, secure, coherent sense of a core self instead.

In therapy and biographies of AD/HD children we often find deficiencies in these early developmental processes. An example of 'not good enough' primary objects are severely depressed mothers. In the early interaction with a severely depressed mother, it is possible for the baby to develop the afore mentioned basic knowledge of a 'good enough' object that is reliably capable of softening the baby's peak affects and to communicate mild, pleasant and positive experiences as the psychically dominant ones. In microanalyses of

---

[5] A current interesting debate between psychoanalysts and brain researchers deals with these aspects, e.g van der Kolk's hypothesis that traumatic experiences are differently stored in memory than 'normal' ones (in the amygdala or the limbic system) and cannot be connected with neocortical processes (see inter alia Bohlber, 2006; Fischer and Riedesser, 1999; Leuzinger-Bohleber, 2006; Leuzinger-Bohleber, Roth an Buchheim, 2008.

videotaped interaction sequences between depressed mothers and their babies, Stern (1995) has shown in an impressive way that a certain type of child tries to revive the depressed mother by demonstrating hyperactive behaviour; an early interactive pattern which is probably generalized, as already mentioned above, and might result in hyperactive behaviour in the future. Moreover, these babies do not have enough outer and inner space in order to be able to use the perception of their own impulses and feelings as indicators of an 'emerging self' due to the experiences of self-agency, self-coherence and self-affectivity delivering a basic feeling for one's self-history, this being one of the main preconditions for constituting a core self and thus the base for developing a secure sense of one´s identity. These might be possible reasons for the development of a 'false self' which is often clinically observed in AD/HD children (Dammasch, 2006; Leuzinger-Bohleber, Brandl, Hüther, 2006). The child can only pass through these early phases of self-development in a 'good enough' way if he has the secure and continuing experience so that his drive manifestations, impulses and affects are correctly understood and interpreted by his primary attachment figure. A depressed or otherwise emotionally neglecting mother is not capable of delivering these experiences well enough as she lacks empathy for the child's inner state.

To summarize, despite their theoretical differences all contemporary psychoanalytic schools share the basic belief that stable psychic structures can only develop in good enough and empathic early object relations that include a well functioning regulation of drive impulses and affects as well as secure inner borders between the self and object representations. Moreover, more recent psychoanalytic publications stress, apart from a sensitive and empathic mother, the relevance of the early relationship with the father, in the sense of early triangulation, (Bürgin, 1998; Klitzing, 2002) for the child as well as the father's function as the 'third party' and his emotional support for the mother (inter alia Herzog, 2001; Metzger, 2000; Dammasch, 2000). AD/HD children seem to have experienced only insufficient, unstable primary relationships. They were only able to develop insufficient secure inner structures and the ability for self-regulation (Dammasch, 2006; Leuzinger et al., 2006). Furthermore, they did not have good enough compensatory relational experiences which could have become a factor fostering development in the sense of an 'interactive repair' (see Klitzing, 2002, p. 883; Häußler and Hopf, 2002; Heinz, 2002; Lüpke, 2004, Green 2005/6).

Authors committed to the empirical attachment theory have presented analogous findings and concepts. There has been evidence in many studies that maternal sensitivity is the most important factor for the formation of attachment type in the first year of life. According to Grossmann et al. (1989), sensitivity consists of the following traits:

a. perception of the baby's behavioural patterns,
b. appropriate interpretation of his expressions,
c. prompt reaction to them, and
d. adequate reaction.

Ainsworth et al. (1978) have shown in their empirical studies that mothers reacting sensitively to their child's signals during its first year of life, i.e. promptly and adequately, have children who show safe attachment behaviour in the Strange Situation (a standardized situation to investigate attachment behaviour); "Those who sometimes react adequately but sometimes also rejecting or overprotecting tend to have anxious-preoccupied children and a third group of mothers reacting to the grief and needs for consolation rather rejecting usually have dismissive-avoidant children" (Dornes, 1999, p. 165).

Some studies have already revealed that fewer children with secure attachment behaviour develop AD/HD during their years at elementary school (Lüpke, 2006).

Let us just briefly mention that Fonagy and Target (2002), authors who did much research in the field of attachment theory, consider 'the ability to focus attention as needed' and 'the ability to behave as appropriate' as characteristic problems of AD/HD children, functions which both have very important meaning for the development of reflective capacities. "Incapability's in these self-regulatory skills lie at the heart of a specific, genetically linked neurological syndrome AD/HD" (Carney, 2002, p. 300). Understanding such deficits and trying to modify them is a joint goal in the psychoanalytic treatments of children suffering from AD/HD shared by psychoanalysts of different psychoanalytic schools.

Prevention and early intervention: some psychoanalytic and neurobiological considerations on psychosocial disintegration

The afore mentioned psychoanalytic concepts constituting the explanation and treatment of AD/HD, formed the theoretical basis of the Frankfurt Prevention Study. These psychoanalytic concepts about the aetiology of AD/HD as well as the enormous significance of prevention and intervention in the first years of life, have gained interdisciplinary support through some of the more recent neurobiological findings. In various psychiatric and psychoanalytic papers, recent neuroscientific research is summarized, and seems to be relevant for the understanding of AD/HD (Barkley, 1997; Levin, 1997; Gilmore, 2000; Rothstein, 2002; Salomonsson, 2004). Zabarenko (2002) mentions three research areas which are immediately relevant for AD/HD: a) research on attention and executive control, b) learning and neural plasticity, and c) memory (p. 415ff.).

For our own approach in the Frankfurt Prevention Study a contemporary understanding of 'embodied memory and problem solving' was essential for supporting our thesis that an intense psychoanalytic treatment of AD/HD children has many advantages compared with an exclusively medical treatment (Leuzinger-Bohleber & Pfeifer, 2002, 2006, Pfeifer & Scheier, 1999; Pfeifer & Bongard, 2007). In the field of 'Embodied Cognitive Science', results of biologically oriented memory research have been taken into account as they suggest that the computer metaphor that still forms the basis of many theories on memory is fundamentally wrong e.g. when we talk about 'storage' contained in long-term memory and from which knowledge is transferred to short-term memory, or a 'defect' in the neurotransmitter system which has to be 'restored' by psycho-stimulants. Living systems are forced to adapt constantly to a continuously changing environment. In this process, knowledge from earlier situations is used but has to be 're-written' again and again and to be adapted to the new situation. Therefore, memory is nowadays understood as an active, creative process of the whole organism based upon sensory-affective coordination processes and associated 'automatic', constantly adapting re-categorizing processes. Thus, memory does not predominantly imply cognitive processes but is always 'embodied'.

Thus, it can be assumed that even if certain genetic dispositions exist, specific early 'embodied' interaction experiences in object relations must have taken place which 'trigger' the development of attention deficit and hyperactivity. These early, pathological experiences may in turn only be modified or corrected permanently in the sense of a self-regulation of the infantile organism by means of new 'embodied' experiences and not by medication proposed to adjust a particular malfunction in the brain. In other words, neurobiologically and psychically failed developments may largely be corrected or at least softened by suitable, adequate, 'corrective' experiences with one's objects and the environment. Although we agree that more research is still needed, we assume that such corrective chances are not, by and large, utilised productively by means of the medical treatment of AD/HD children.

Panksepp (1998), one of the leading neurobiologists and brain researchers on emotional development, adds some more perspectives from a similar position when dealing with AD/HD children.

To briefly summarize some of his arguments: Recent brain-imaging data have revealed that the major difference in the brains of individuals with AD/HD is in the frontal areas. "At a gross structural level, brains of children diagnosed with ADHD exhibit a 5% reduction of overall size.... There are also some neuro-chemical differences (Solanto, 1998), but none of them is sufficiently large to permit us to conclude that the differences constitute a medically significant abnormality" (Panksepp, 1998, p. 93).

The neural differences in ADHD children have recently been formulated by Barkley (1997), summarized in Figure 1.

"According to this view, the fundamental problem in ADHD is not a deficit in attention, but an abnormally low level of behavioural inhibition, a global function that allows better reflection, imagination, empathy, and creativity. These abilities promote behavioural flexibility, better foresight, and a more mature regulation of behavior. If we accept the existence of a frontal lobe contribution to ADHD, we still must consider whether there are environmental or physical ways to improve such frontal lobe functions permanently". (Panksepp, 1998, p. 93).

Medical treatment seems one of the 'physical' possibilities. Without any doubt short-term behavioural improvements certainly

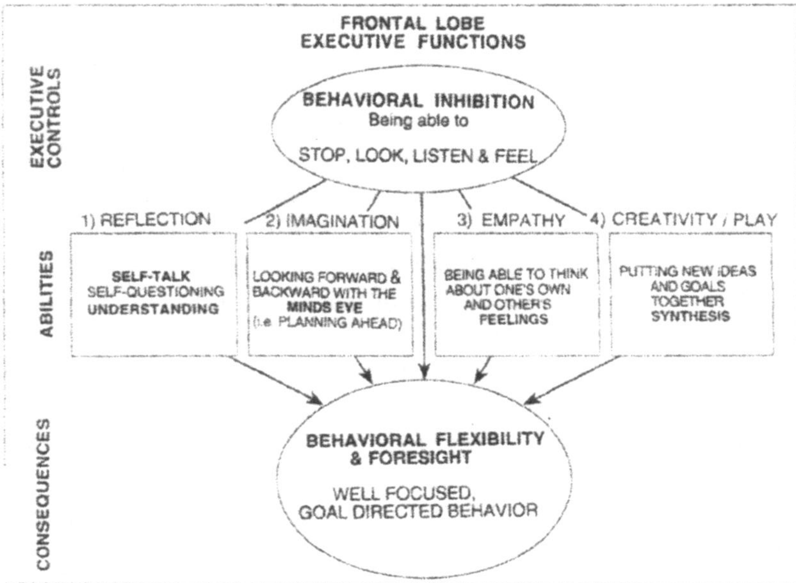

Figure 1. A synoptic interpretation of the frontal lobe functions that may be deficient in attention deficit hyperactivity disorder (adapted from Barkley, 1997).

occur with psycho-stimulants. The problem is, as many studies have shown in the meantime, that "...long-term effects have rarely been evident. When medication is terminated, ADHD symptoms typically return, suggesting the children are not learning to manage their lives any better. Evidence for long-term improvements of cognitive functions and other abilities remains practically nonexistent (for a summary of such work, see Barkley, 1997)..." (Panksepp, 1998, p. 93). Panksepp then argues that short-term benefits of treatment with psycho-stimulants would be acceptable if psycho-stimulants did not have any negative bodily consequences, i.e., small decrease in physical growth, relatively rare incidences of seizures, tics, mania and delusional tendencies, and the potential for more difficulties when these children grow up such as drug abuse, which is a controversial finding.

Due to methodological issues, the long-term effects of treatment with psycho-stimulants cannot be studied in human beings, therefore,

Panksepp (1998) quotes animal studies. There is some evidence from these studies that psycho-stimulants decrease instead of increase, neural plasticity. "In general, dopaminergic arousal, as can be achieved with psycho-stimulants, tends to reduce glutamatemediated neural plasticity" (p. 95). Panksepp thus pleads for a different strategy in the treatment of AD/HD children in our societies; to create more possibilities for young children to develop the frontal lobe executive functions by playing, particularly by playing so-called rough-and-tumble games. "The urge to indulge in rough-and-tumble play is a birthright of the mammalian brain.... Social play may be an *experience-expectant*, or preparatory, process that helps program higher brain areas that will be required later in life. Indeed 'youth' may have evolved to give complex organisms time to play and thereby to exercise those natural skills they will need as adults. We already know that as the frontal lobes mature, frequency of play goes down.... Might access to rough-and-tumble play promote frontal lobe maturation?" (p. 95/96).

To sum up, like many contemporary brain researchers, Panksepp (1998) postulates a user-dependent emergence of brain organic changes in hyperactivity and attention deficit. Particularly for children born with a probably genetically determined impulsive temper and character, the opportunity to engage in active exploration of their environment and in 'rough- and tumble-play' seems to be essential in order to develop their frontal lobe executive functions. If, for several reasons, children do not have enough of these opportunities due to their early object relations, traumatic experiences or simply environmental factors such as missing playground for small children, they might develop AD/HD. Medication probably does not help them to compensate this deficit in the frontal lobe executive functions. Organic brain, just as psychic changes, can only take place 'user-dependently', i.e. in new playful and explorative situations and are particularly effective if combined with intense, positive emotional relationship experiences (Damasio, 1994, 2003; Passolt, 2004; Hüther, 2006; Dawirs et al, 1992; Moll et al, 2000).

These theoretical and interdisciplinary considerations are the background of the Frankfurt Prevention Study. Instead of treating possible neurobiological or psychic deficits solely with medication, we have been trying to give the respective child, or his brain, the chance to correct problematic experiences with their objects by means of new, more adequate experiences gained in psychoanalytic therapy and pedagogic, playful approaches, which influence the development of the self and the identity of the child positively.

3 The Frankfurt Prevention Study: Psychoanalysis and neurobiology in dialogue

Short summary

The representative, randomized, controlled and prospective Frankfurt Prevention Study[6] ran from September 2003 to August 2006. In order to be able to draw a representative sample of roughly 500 children in the prevention/intervention group and a control-comparison group of another 500 children, we had to perform a basic assessment in all public kindergartens in Frankfurt, 114 kindergartens with around 4500 children. The main hypothesis of the study was that a two- year- psychoanalytic, non-psychopharmacological prevention and intervention program will result in a statistically significant decrease in the number of children suffering from psychosocial disturbances, particularly from AD/HD, in their first year in school compared to the control group.

In order to define AD/HD we used the following instruments:

- Child Behaviour Checklist (CBCL4–18)
- Questionnaire on Hyperactivity (Döpfner et al. 2003)
- Conner's Teacher's Rating Form (CTRF)
- Conner's Parent's Ratings Form (CPRF)
- BADO (modified basic documentation)

From spring 2004 to summer 2006, we offered the prevention and intervention program in 14 randomly chosen kindergartens. The psychoanalytic prevention and intervention program consisted of several components based on a psychoanalytic understanding of AD/HD:

---

[6] The study financally supported mainly by the Zinnkan Foundation, but also by the Research Advisory Board of (RAB) the International Psychoanalytical Association, the Hertie Foundation and the Polytechnische Gesellschaft, Frankfurt.

- intense psychoanalytic supervision of the kindergarten teams focusing on the psychodynamic and psychosocial understanding of individual children and their families,
- a weekly, psychoanalytically oriented, educational program for individual children or the children's groups by members of the research team, including a violence prevention program called FAUSTLOS, 'FISTLESS', developed by Cierpka and his group (Cierpka and Schick, 2006),
- parental talks and parent counseling, in groups or individually,
- psychoanalytic individual therapies, always including the parents, offered to children with severe psychopathologies, e.g. ADHS in the kindergartens,[7] and
- cooperation with medical doctors, child psychiatrists, Mental Health Institutions, Welfare Institutions and potential schools, if necessary.

It took almost one year until the project was fully accepted by the teams and parents in the different institutions. The best 'proof' of this acceptance was that nearly all teams expressed their wish to continue the supervisions and some other elements of our prevention program after the project officially ended in August 2006.

In the meantime, we have obtained statistical results supporting our main hypothesis. We will publish them in detail in another paper (Leuzinger-Bohleber et al., in press). Within the limits of this paper we only want to report some of the most important.

Some empirical results on the effects of the prevention programme

We achieved excellent response rates (see Table 1).

---

[7] It has been an open question if we will be able to offer psychoanalytic therapies to children of low and problematic social groups, children who would never find their ways into private practices of our psychoanalytic colleagues. Until now we were able to offer such therapies to 17 children. For 10 other children we saw an indication for psychoanalytic treatments but the parents were not willing to accept treatments. We are evaluating therapy outcome of these 17 children (with F90 diagnosis) and other children from the outpatient clinic service of the institute for Psychoanalytic Child and Adolescence Therapy in Frankfurt in another study (Leuzinger-Bohleber, et al. in press).

Table 1. Response rates t1: Begin of study; t4: end of study (after two years).

t1	$N_{absolut}$	$N_{return\ rate}$	$N_{in\%}$
prevention group	480	412	86%
comparison group	493	450	91%
Total	**973**	**862**	**89%**

t4	N_{t1}	N_{t1+t4}	$N_{in\%}$
prevention group	412	227	55%
comparison group	450	217	48%
Total	**862**	**444**	**52%**

Some results comparing children of the prevention with those of the control group before and after the prevention programme (+ two years)

I Hyperactivity

In both groups we had a statistically significant decrease of hyperactivity after two years. The difference between the prevention and the control group is not significant (see Fig. 2)

N/Prevention = 178; N/Control group = 184
Factor time: F = 71.95; p = .00**
Factor group: F = 1.31; p = .25 (n.s.)

In order to interpret these findings, we have to bear in mind that the subscale 2: Hyperactivity of the VBV, contains questions concerning the impulsivity of the children on the one hand, as e.g. question 34: '...he is constantly moving and only stays sitting on a chair briefly'. On the other hand, questions concerning the capability to concentrate are included, e.g. question 19: 'can only concentrate in a game or activity shortly'. It is well known that motoric impulsivity and activity decreases in children from age 3 to age 6. Therefore the above mentioned results seem plausible; hyperactivity decreases significantly in the prevention as well as in the control group. It will be interesting to observe if we find a significant difference between

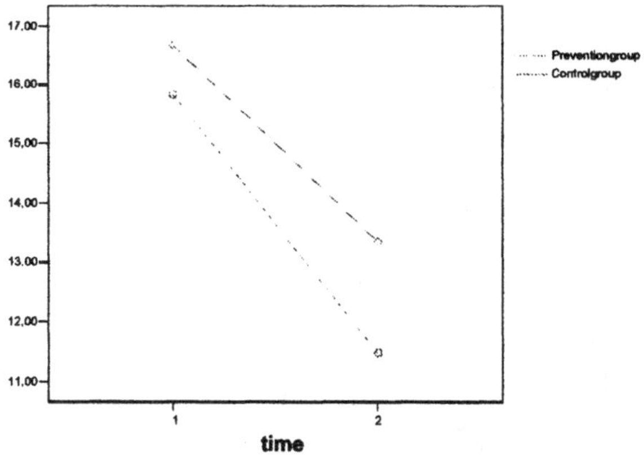

Figure 2. Hyperactivity: comparison of the prevention and control group.

the prevention and the control group concerning the capability to concentrate after the first year of school, a capacity which becomes highly relevant in school but not as yet in Kindergarten.[8]

Another interesting result is that girls seem to change more than boys in the prevention group compared to the control group. Taking only the ratings of the girls, we find a statistically significant decrease in hyperactivity (see Fig. 3) (Leuzinger-Bohleber, Staufenberg und Fischmann, in press).

N/Prevention = 70; N/Controlgroup = 62
Factor time: $F = 32.41$; $p = .00^{**}$
Factor group: $F = 7.74$; $p < .01^{**}$

II Aggression

We found a statistically significant decrease in aggression after two years. (See Fig. 4)

N/Prevention = 177; N/Control group = 185
Factor group: $F = 5.90$; $p < .02^{*}$

[8] We also would like to mention that none of the 412 children in our prevention group had taken Ritalin or other Amphetamines which means that medical doctors in Frankfurt are acting according to German law which does not allow prescription of these medications to children younger than 6 years.

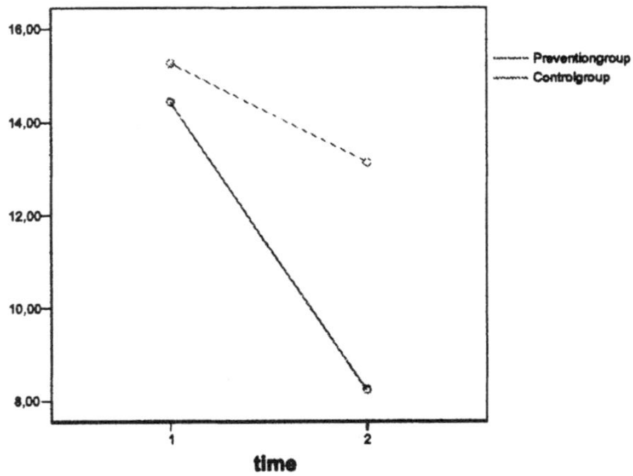

Figure 3. Hyperactivity of girls: comparison of the prevention and control group.

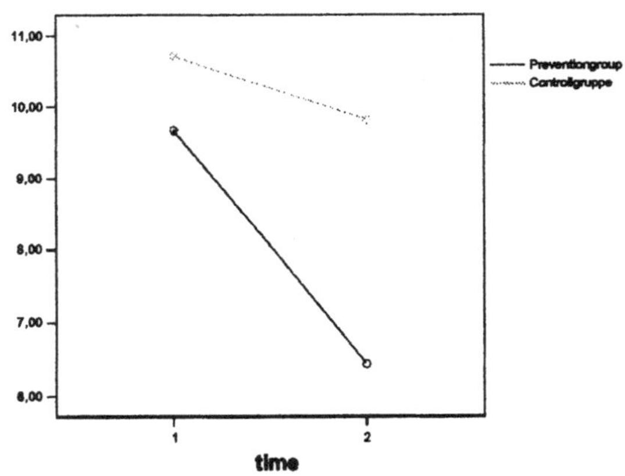

Figure 4. Comparison of the prevention and control group concerning aggression.

III Anxiety

We found a statistically significant decrease of anxiety after two years. (See Fig. 5)

N/Prevention = 177; N/Control group = 184
Factor group: $F = 4.96$; $p < .03$*

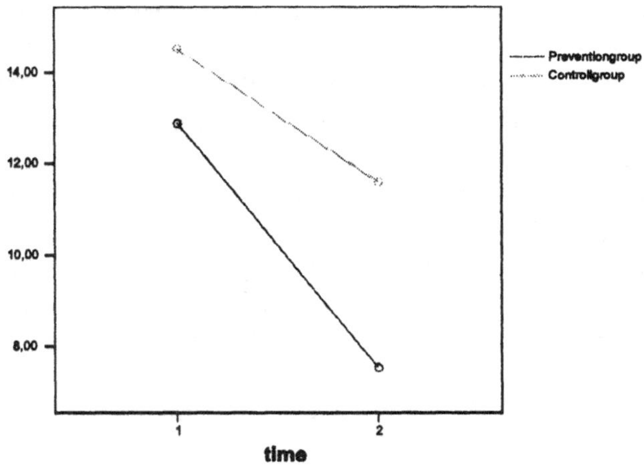

Figure 5. Comparison of the prevention and control group concerning anxiety.

Short interpretation

To find a statistically significant decrease in aggression and anxiety is a surprisingly clear indication that the psychoanalytically oriented prevention and intervention programmes had a positive effect on the social behaviour of Kindergarten children. We had not expected such a clear result in this 'field' study combining experimental and naturalistic investigation methods. Therefore our results are a strong indication that our psychoanalytically oriented, preventions program has proved to be successful in the sense that the aggressive and anxious behaviour of children decreases.

AD/HD is not AD/HD: Some observations concerning different psychodynamic subgroups of AD/HD in the frankfurt prevention study

Another aim of our study was to contribute to a differentiation of the AD/HD diagnosis by examining it from a psychoanalytic point of view. As briefly discussed above, AD/HD seems to have become a 'fashionable or waste bucket diagnosis' for all kinds of different problems lying behind the manifestation of hyperactive and non attentive behaviour.

We have been able to gather numerous and extensive single case observations as well as statistical data from the original sample of the 500 children of our prevention/intervention group. Discussing our observations, we have found different subgroups of children who had been diagnosed with AD/HD according to the above mentioned criteria of the Döpfner and the Conner Scales, both instruments are based on DSM IV criteria. In other words, on a descriptive level, all the following children suffered, according to DSM-IV, from AD/HD which of course, does not include co-morbidities. Nevertheless, it does not seem very helpful for a more thorough understanding of these children, to stick to a "meaningful discrete diagnostic entity" (Gilmore, 2000, p. 1258). From a psychoanalytic perspective, a more dynamic, precise perception of each child´s idiosyncratic psychic and psychosocial situation offers, in our view, a better base for adequate treatment of the relevant child.

In the frame of this paper we only want to mention these divergences subsumed under the syndrome AD/HD by defining different subgroups. We have discussed them elsewhere in detail (Leuzinger-Bohleber, Goeppel, Hau in press).

I. Children with a brain organic problem.
II. Children with an early emotional neglect.
III. AD/HD and trauma.
IV. AD/HD and culture.
V. AD/HD and extraordinarily talented children.
VI. AD/HD and mourning or depression.
VII. AD/HD—a compensation for growing up with a 'dead mother' (André Green, 1986; Daniel Stern, 1995).

In Chapter 3b, we summarized the psychoanalytic conceptualization that AD/HD may be determined by coping with a 'dead mother' (Green, 1986) the infant trying to bring her to life by showing hyperactive behavior. Leuzinger-Bohleber has reported extensively on such a case, a girl whom she had in psychoanalysis with four sessions a week for 3 years (Leuzinger-Bohleber, 1984). As just one example of the afore mentioned 7 different subtypes of children receiving a diagnosis of ADHD, we summarize some of the major findings concerning the connection between 'growing up with a depressed primary object' and AD/HD.

Nora was brought to the analyst when she was 10 years old because her parents, both professors of ethnology, did not know "how to cope with her anymore...". They had tried a variety of different therapies and educational programs without success. Nora, because of her total failure in school, would now be sent to a special school for children with low intelligence. Nora also suffered from adipositas, severe sleeping disorders, skin problems, total social withdrawal and isolation, self-destructive behavior in that sometimes she cut herself with a knife and sudden aggressive outbursts against her younger brother.

Fron psychological testing, we found that Nora was highly intelligent with an IQ of 132 according to the Kramer Intelligence Test, and vivid, but she revealed very threatening fantasies in the projective tests. We were also surprised to find all the characteristics present indicative of a 'Minimal Brain Dysfunction' according to the Göttinger Formreproduktionstest. Her score was 46.6%, which means that 46.6% with a diagnosed brain organic problem achieved the same score as Nora while 63.4% of this sample achieved better.

What did we find concerning the biographical roots of Nora's AD/HD?

The mother decided to give birth to her first child, Nora, in the same clinic where she had been working as a researcher studying birth rituals before. "It was terrible—I had a 24 hour- delivery which was so complicated that finally we had to make a Caesarean section. I felt so disappointed or even humiliated that I was not able to give birth in a normal way like thousands of other women—and all this happened before the very eyes of my former colleagues...", Mrs B. said during the initial interview. Two days after her baby Nora was born, her father died, which was a traumatic loss for her and another reason why she became severely depressed. "I felt horrible during these first months—I was not able to breast feed without reading a criminal story at the same time...and Nora was never ever satisfied. She seemed to be hungry all the time, cried a lot and after 4 months had already problems with her weight...". When she was 8 months old, her father held her on his arm at the window on the third floor. "Nora suddenly moved and fell out of the window", he reports during the interview when being told that Nora had "abnormally high scores in the Göttinger Formreproduktionstest". "Maybe this is one reason for her problems—I had such heavy guilt feelings" he commented. Nora had to be in hospital for several weeks and continued to have severe sleeping and eating problems. "She was such an hyperactive toddler, too, always moving ... and terribly jealous toward her 1 1/2 year younger brother ... she suffered from hardly bearable temper tantrums..." (Mrs B.). In Nora´s third year of life the family moved to an African country where both parents worked in a research project. "This was the best time for all of us. Nora was such a vivid and happy little girl, being outside the whole day playing with the children of the little village, socially very well integrated ... she just loved it.... And I finally overcame my depression because I could combine my professional life with my motherhood excellently. I had a warm- hearted nanny for my children, worked in the project and was available for the children whenever they wanted to see me...". But then another catastrophe happened: the father was diagnosed with cancer and had to go back to Germany to undergo surgery. Although he recovered fairly well, the family lived under the constant threat that the cancer could reappear.

When Nora was 6 years old, the parents decided to go back to Germany because they wanted to give Nora a good education. "But now the problems started- Nora felt kicked out of the infantile paradise- she hated German children and school in particular- and rebelled against school all the time. And myself, I became depressed again because I could not work as a assistant professor anymore and had to stay home being a house wife." (Mrs B.). Nora failed completely in school and repeated several classes without success. Several short therapies and educational special trainings failed; Nora became severely depressed, pseudo-debilitated and psychosomatically ill.

Fortunately, Nora opened a door to her disastrous inner state for me as her analyst. She was a wonderful ***drawer*** and told me about her terrifying fantasies being unconsciously convinced that she was a murderous human being, responsible for her mother's severe depression which she was not even able to cure by developing hyperactive behaviour (a 'sunshine') as a baby and toddler. She was also suffering from the unconscious 'truth' that she wanted to kill her little brother and was responsible for the deadly illness of her oedipal father. Her psychosomatic illnesses as well as her pseudo-debility were due to a mixture of self-punishments due to archaic guilt feelings, revenge fantasies and a deep hatred towards her primary objects. It also became very clear that she had not been able to develop a basic stable self-regulation of her affects and drive impulses. When her aggressive impulses manifest themselves in the transference, she did not talk with me for three months. I felt desperate and helpless and was often convinced that this psychoanalysis would end without any positive results. Fortunately we were finally able to make the connection to her own inner despair and murderous fantasies. It seemed to be essential for Nora that I, as a 'good enough object' and psychoanalyis survived her fantasized attacks. In the following summer break she was writing up a 'criminal story' of a detective who was saving a psychologist from several murder attempts by a gang of Mafiosi.... At the same time her first menstruation appeared. Puberty, with its tremendous dynamics fortunately took Nora into a progressive development partially overcoming her infantile fixations. She started to be good at school, developed a wonderful sense of somewhat black humour and finally found some very good friends. After three years of psychoanalysis, she decided to terminate her treatment. She did not show up to the last session. Of course, I was disappointed and a bit anxious. Nora then wrote me a postcard: "I am sorry I have forgotten my last session with you but a very good friend of mine just came to visit me- and then I forgot the session. It was more important to talk with him—I am sure that you will understand this...."

Last year, 31 years after the termination of this treatment, Nora wrote me an e-mail. She had found my address by coincidence and wanted to contact me. We arranged a telephone call. It was remarkable to hear from her that she had found her way. She had been a teacher for handicapped children for 15 years and now started to study psychology. She had made a good professional career, had many friends but still seemed to have problems with her weight. "This is one reason why I did not get married and have children..." she said sadly. She also told me emotionally about the death of her father and the many intense talks she had had with him during his last months of life. She remembered very few details of her therapy, only "that it has been very important for me. I could leave this very dark and sad childhood behind me", she said.

This short summary of an intense psychoanalytic process may illustrate the complex interaction of different factors determining the development of AD/HD symptoms. Even though the traumatic early interaction with a depressed primary object might be considered to be the main source of the pathogenic development of Nora, it turned out that organic factors, minimal brain damage due to her accident in her first year of life, and other traumatic life events played an important role. Psychoanalysis offers one way of trying to understand and modify such a variety of conscious and unconscious forces lying behind one specific syndrome like AD/HD. Therefore, we agree with Rothstein (2002) who writes: "Psychoanalysts are in a unique position to grasp these complex relationships" (p. 393).

4 *Summary and Conclusion*

In this paper, we first discussed some possible reasons for the enormous worldwide increase of children diagnosed with AD/HD, treated with Ritalin or other amphetamines. Some authors for example, Amft, Gerspach & Mattner, 2004) talk about the danger of a "medicalization of social problems" because medication sometimes seems to be a seductive way to get rid of difficult children and to adapt them, in a very efficient and socially acceptable way, to the requirements of the modern schools and kindergartens in our Western societies. Without any doubt, medication is sometimes an optimal way to de-escalate an unbearable social situation. Thus, it is a necessary prevention measure not to exclude AD/HD children from their peer group at school or other group situations. Nevertheless, in our perspective, medication does often not solve the problems of these children completely, who, as illustrated by our case examples, often struggle with very difficult internalized conflicts and/or current problems in their external realities. These determinants of their AD/HD should be understood in detail in order to realistically help them to cope productively with their life and learning situations. Therefore, we plead for critical and differentiated analyses of multiple fields of problems concerning the raising of children in post-industrial and globalized societies. When talking about AD/HD, societal and cultural factors should thus be taken as seriously as the research results from modern neurobiology and brain research.

We also discussed some differences between the cognitive behavioral and psychoanalytical understanding of AD/HD, mentioning the current danger that a combination of medical treatment with CBT could exclude psychoanalytical treatment of hyperactive children, at least in Germany. In contrast to the definition of AD/H, according to a 'medical model', 'defects in the brain' or maladaptation in social learning etc., we share the view of many psychoanalytic colleagues, such as Bürgin (2005), that attention deficit and hyperactivity are symptoms that can build a syndrome but never an illness, even if an underlying, common genetic base is postulated. Furthermore, no internationally accepted cut-off points exist defining quantitatively either attention deficit or hyperactivity. By summarizing different psychoanalytic conceptualizations of AD/HD, observations and data from the Frankfurt Preventions Study as well as from some psychoanalytic treatments with hyperactive children, we wanted to illustrate the following: a psychoanalytic perspective on AD/HD focuses on the different underlying structures of the personality due to the idiosyncratic life history of the child with his early object relations, traumatizations, ego- and self developments and his specific deficiencies as well as the forms of relational and emotional exchanges in the child's current family situation. Our diagnostic and clinical experiences reveal a wide range of structural and object-relational levels in such children: there is no monocausal etiology. Often AD/HD may constitute a genetically based, over-reactivity and hypersensitivity to various stimuli in infants, which was misunderstood by the caretakers. The consequent failure to regulate drive impulses and affects result in a disruption of what Bürgin (2005) called the 'narrative function', depleting the ego of secondary-process functions. We believe children of one subgroup of AD/HD are sharing such early 'mis-matched' object relations or overstimulation combined with missing security of attachment which would help to prevent being overloaded with stimuli and stress (Hüther, 2006). These early experiences in their object relations have also left deficiencies concerning attention, seen as a highly complex ego function that develops in a specific relational context, influenced by genetic factors, early emotional exchanges, temperament and micro traumata.

> "Children diagnosed with AD/HD often demonstrate normal attention and activity when doing something they like, but experience difficulty in doing so when the demand comes from the external world. Thus attention deficit is thought to reflect an early dysfunction of the ego brought about by the primary object's failure to contain and focus (center) attention, and to

> construct trust in a co-established temporality. A number of ego dysfunctions arise out of this failure in holding. One of the most serious is the failure to learn to use verbal symbolizations in order to express emotion, thus leaving imperative action as a prominent mode of avoiding being overwhelmed by unbearable feelings" (Sugarman, 2006, p. 238).

As we have tried to demonstrate, other subgroups of AD/HD children might have quite different biographical roots, e.g. a history of early neglect, traumatization, undigested dramatic life events or even a current mis-match between their specific personality traits, cultural differences, and the educational system they are currently in. Therefore, we have formulated a plea for a differentiated diagnostic view, taking into account idiosyncratic biographical factors, current family and institutional situations as well as neurobiological and genetic determinants of AD/HD such as contemporary, pluralistic psychoanalysis has to offer.

We briefly mentioned that Embodied Cognitive Science and neurobiological research performed by Huether et al., Panksepp, and many other contemporary researchers, as e.g Damasio, 1994, Edelman, 1992, Kandel, 2005 offer an understanding of AD/HD, which seems in excellent concordance with psychoanalytic conceptualizations. Understanding the brain as a self-regulating system in constant interaction with the environment, with astonishing possibilities to correct maladaptions and 'inadequate sensory motor co-ordinations' in new relational experiences, offers fascinating new possibilities to help children with AD/HD overcome their difficulties with professional new object relations (Leuzinger-Bohleber & Pfeifer, 2002). We have summarized some of these therapeutic experiences in our case examples. To develop such new self-regulation in the realm of affects and behaviors, first in therapeutic and afterwards in social situations, seems to be a unique therapeutic chance for these children. This chance is missed if offered an exclusively medical treatment, often experienced as the unconscious truth by the child that "there is something wrong in my brain. It has some kind of a 'defect'. I am not a normal kid. Without medication I am a human being, which is not bearable for my parents, siblings, peers, and teachers... I am a wild animal which cannot tame itself...".

We have tried to discuss that AD/HD, seen from a psychoanalytic perspective, always has to be understood as a product of complex interactions of mostly unconscious, idiosyncratic, biographical, relational, institutional, societal as well as neurobiological, neurophysiological, and genetic factors. This is one reason why we think that psychoanalysis with its unique conceptualizations to understand psychic realities as products of such complex intertwining of unconscious and reality factors, while taking into account biological as well as societal roots of human behavior, could be regarded as the best available approach nowadays which is capable of deal theoretically and therapeutically with children suffering from AD/HD. We fully agree with Gilmore (2000) when she writes: "However, I believe that the analytic process, especially in the form that is familiar to child analysts, offers the best opportunity to treat the underlying disturbance of AD/HD in children and adults" (p. 1291).

It was beyond the limits of this paper to describe the textbook which a group of experienced child analysts in Frankfurt has written describing the specific technique for the psychoanalytic treatment of children with AD/HD (Staufenberg et al., 2006). This textbook was the common ground for all the 17 treatments, which were offered to children suffering from AD/HD within the framework of the Frankfurt Prevention Study. We have not been able to summarize our clinical experiences in detail here. Nevertheless, we hope to have communicated that our clinical observations as well as our empirical findings have supported our view that contemporary psychoanalysis, due to its richness of conceptualizations and clinical experiences, taking into account neurobiological as well as societal factors at the same time, should be considered as attractive field for understanding and treating children with AD/HD.

References

Ainsworth, M., Blehar, M., Waters, E. & Wall, S. (1978). *Patterns of Attachment: A Psychological Study of the Strange Situation*. Hillsdale: Erlbaum.

Amft, H., Gerspach, M. & Mattner, D. (2004). *Kinder mit gestörter Aufmerksamkeit. ADS als Herausforderung für Pädagogik und Therapie*. 2. Auflage. Stuttgart: Kohlhammer.

Amft, H. (2006). ADHS: Hirnstoffwechselstörungen und/oder Symptom einer kranken Gesellschaft? Psychopharmaka als Mittel einer gelingenden Naturbeherrschung am Menschen. In: M. Leuzinger-Bohleber,Y. Brandl & G. Hüther, (Eds.), *ADHS – Frühprävention statt Medikalisierung. Theorie, Forschung, Kontroversen* (pp. 70–90). Göttingen: Vandenhoeck & Ruprecht.

Barkley, R. (1990). *Attention Deficit Hyperactivity Disorder: A Handbook for Diagnosis and Treatment*. New York: Guilford Press.

Barkley, R. (1997). *ADHD and the Nature of Self-control*. New York: Guilford Press.

Beebe, B. & Lachman, F.M. (2002). *Infant Research and Adult Treatment: Co-constructing Interactions*. Hillsdale/London: The Analytic Press.

Berger, E. (Ed.) (1977). *Teilleistungsschwächen bei Kindern*. Bern.

BMGS (Bundesministerium für Gesundheit und soziale Sicherung) (2002). Pressemitteilung vom 27.12.2002. Available from: http://www.bmgs.bund.de/archiv/presse_bmgs/presse2002/m/213.htm.

Bürgin, D. (1998). *Triangulierung. Der Übergang zur Elternschaft*. Stuttgart: Schattauer.

Bürgin, D. (2005). Presentation, Panel Attention deficit hyperactivity disorder and trauma , 44th Congress of the IPA, Rio de Janeiro, Brazil, 28 July 2005.

Busch de Ahumada, L.C. (2005). Presentation, Panel Attention deficit hyperactivity disorder and trauma , 44th Congress of the IPA, Rio de Janeiro, Brazil, 28 July 2005.

Cantwell, D. (1996). Attention deficit disorder: A review of the past ten years. *Journal of the American Academy of Child and Adolescent Psychiatry, 35*: 978–987.

Carney, J.K. (2002). Prologue. *Psychoanalytic Inquiry, 22*: 299–307.

Cierpka, M. & Schick, A. (2006). Das Fördern von emotionalen Kompetenzen mit FAUSTLOS bei Kindern. In: M. Leuzinger-Bohleber, Y. Brandl & G. Hüther (Eds.), *ADHS – Frühprävention statt Medikalisierung. Theorie, Forschung, Kontroversen* (pp. 286–301). Göttingen: Vandenhoeck & Ruprecht.

Crary, J. (1999). *Suspension of Perception*. Cambridge: MIT Press.

Damasio, A.R. (1994). *Descartes' Error*. New York: Putnam.

Damasio, A.R. (2003). Feelings of emotion and the self. *Annals of the New York Academy of Sciences, 1001*: 253–261.

Dammasch, F. (2000). *Die innere Erlebniswelt von Kindern alleinerziehender Mütter. Eine Studie über Vaterlosigkeit anhand einer psychoanalytischen Interpretation zweier Erstinterviews*. Frankfurt a.M.: Brandes & Apsel.

Dammasch, F. (2006). ADHS endlich hat das Kind einen Namen. Psychoanalytische Gedanken zur Bewegung des ruhelosen Kindes und zur Bedeutung von Ritalin®. In: M. Leuzinger-Bohleber,Y. Brandl & G. Hüther, (Eds.), *ADHS – Frühprävention statt Medikalisierung. Theorie, Forschung, Kontroversen* (pp. 189–221). Göttingen: Vandenhoeck & Ruprecht.

Dawirs, R.R., Teuchert-Noodt, G. & Kacza, J. (1992). Naturally occurring degrading events in axon terminals of the dentate gyrus and stratum lucidum in the spiny mouse (Acomys cahirinus) during maturation, adulthood and aging. *Developmental Neuroscience, 14*: 210–220.

Dornes, M. (1999). Bindungstheorie und Bindungsforschung eine Herausforderung für die Schule? In: A. Garlichs & M. Leuzinger-Bohleber, (Eds.), *Identität und Bindung. Die Entwicklung von Beziehungen in Familie, Schule und Gesellschaft* (pp. 161–173). Weinheim/München: Juventa Verlag.

Edelman, G. (1992). *Bright Air, Brilliant Fire. On the Matter of the Mind.* New York: Basic Books.

Emde, R.N. & Fonagy, P. (1997). An emerging culture for psychoanalytic research? *International Journal of Psychoanalysis, 78*: 643–651.

Enke, W. (1953). Ätiologie und Therapie bei Schwererziehbarkeit. *Medizinische Klinik, 48*: 231–235.

Fischer, G. & Riedesser, P. (1998). *Lehrbuch der Psychotraumatologie.* München/Basel: Reinhardt.

Fonagy, P. & Target, M. (2002). Neubewertung der Entwicklung der Affektregulation vor dem Hintergrund von Winnicotts Konzept des "falschen Selbst". *Psyche – Z Psychoanalysis, 56*: 839–862.

Fonagy, P. (2006): Der Interpersonale Interpretationsmechanismus (IIM). In: V. Green, (Ed.), *Emotionale Entwicklung in Psychoanalyse, Bindungstheorie und Neuowissenschaften* (pp. 141–165). Gießen: Psychosozial Verlag.

Garlichs, A. & Leuzinger-Bohleber, M. (1999). *Identität und Bindung. Die Entwicklung von Beziehungen in Familie, Schule und Gesellschaft.* Weinheim/München: Juventa Verlag.

Gerspach, M. (2006). Zum Verstehen von Kindern mit Aufmerksamkeitsstörungen. In: M. Leuzinger-Bohleber,Y. Brandl & G. Hüther, (Eds.), *ADHS – Frühprävention statt Medikalisierung. Theorie, Forschung, Kontroversen* (pp. 91–110). Göttingen: Vandenhoeck & Ruprecht.

Gilmore, K. (2000). A psychoanalytic perspective on attention-deficit/hyperactivity disorder. *Journal of the American Psychoanalytic Association, 48*: 1258–1293.

Gilmore, K. (2002). Diagnosis, dynamics, and development: Considerations in the psychoanalytic assessment of children with AD/HD. *Psychoanalytic Inquiry, 22*: 372–391.

Göllnitz, G. (1954). *Die Bedeutung der frühkindlichen Hirnschädigung für die Kinderpsychiatrie.* Leipzig: Thieme.

Göppel, G. (in press). *Children in urban areas of social conflict—prevention and intervention of behaviour disorders in kindergartens.*

Green, A. (1986). The dead mother. In: A. Green, (Ed.), *On private madness* (pp. 222–253). London: The Hogarth Press.

Green, V. (2005). *Emotional Development in Psychoanalysis: Attachment Theory and Neuroscience. Creating Connections.* London: Brunner-Routledge.

Grossmann, K.E., August, E.P., Fremmer-Bombik, E., Friedl, A., Grossmann, K., Scheuerer-Englisch, H., Spangler, G., Stephan, C. & Suess, G.J. (1989). Die Bindungstheorie: Modell und entwicklungspsychologische Forschung. In: H. Keller, (Ed.), *Handbuch der Kleinkindforschung* (pp. 31–35). Berlin: Springer.

Hagner, M. (2004). *Geniale Gehirne. Zur Geschichte der Elitegehirnforschung.* Göttingen: Wallstein.

Hauser, S.T., Allen, J.-P. & Golden, E. (2006). *Out of the Woods: Tales of Resilient Teens.* London: Harvard University Press.

Häußler, G. & Hopf, H. (2002). Psychoanalytische Theorien. In: G. Bovensiepen, H. Hopf & G. Molitor, (Eds.), *Unruhige und unaufmerksame Kinder. Psychoanalyse des hyperkinetischen Syndroms* (pp. 20–42). Frankfurt a.M.: Brandes & Apsel.

Heinz, J. (2002). Nervosität der Moderne. In: G. Bovensiepen, H. Hopf & G. Molitor, (Eds.), *Unruhige und unaufmerksame Kinder. Psychoanalyse des hyperkinetischen Syndroms* (pp. 315–340). Frankfurt a.M.: Brandes & Apsel.

Herzog, J.M. (2001). *Father Hunger: Explorations with Adults and Children.* Hillsdale/London: The Analytic Press.

Hüther, G. (2006). Die nutzungsabhängige Herausbildung hirnorganischer Veränderungen bei Hyperaktivität und Aurmerksamkeitsstörungen. Einfluss präventiver Maßnahmen und therapeutischer Internventionen. In: M. Leuzinger-Bohleber, Y. Brandl & G. Hüther, (Eds.), *ADHS – Frühprävention statt Medikalisierung. Theorie, Forschung, Kontroversen* (pp. 222–237). Göttingen: Vandenhoeck & Ruprecht.

Kandel, E.R. (1999). Biology and the future of psychoanalysis: A new intellectual framework for psychiatry revisited. *Am. J. Psychiat., 156*: 505–524.

Kandel, E.R. (2005). *Psychiatry, Psychoanalysis, and the New Biology of Mind.* Washington/London: American Psychiatric Publishing.

Kernberg, O.F. (2001). Object relations, affects, and drives. *Psychoanalytic Inquiry, 21*: 604–619.

Klitzing, K. V. (2002). Früher Entwicklung im Längsschnitt: Von der Beziehungswelt der Eltern zur Vorstellungswelt des Kindes. *Psyche – Z Psychoanalysis, 56*: 863–887.

Koukkou, M., Leuzinger-Bohleber, M. & Mertens, W. (Eds.) (1998). *Erinnerung von Wirklichkeiten. Psychoanalyse und Neurowissenschaften im Dialog*. Bd. 1: *Bestandsaufnahme*. Stuttgart: Verlag Internationale Psychoanalyse.

Laufer, M. & Dehnhoff, E. (1957). Hyperkinetic behaviour syndrome in children. *Journal of Pediatrics, 50*: 463–474.

Lehmkuhl, G. & Döpfner, M. (2006). Die Bedeutung multimodaler Therapieansätze bei Kindern mit Aufmerksamkeitsdefizit-/Hyperkativitätsstörungen. In: M. Leuzinger-Bohleber, Y. Brandl & G. Hüther, (Eds.), *ADHS – Frühprävention statt Medikalisierung. Theorie, Forschung, Kontroversen* (pp. 118–133). Göttingen: Vandenhoeck & Ruprecht.

Leuzinger-Bohleber, M. (1984). Nora. Die Analyse einer Zwölfjährigen. *Arbeitshefte Kinderanalyse, Nr. 4*: 29–90.

Leuzinger-Bohleber, M. (2006). Einleitung. In: M. Leuzinger-Bohleber, Y. Brandl & G. Hüther, (Eds.), *ADHS – Frühprävention statt Medikalisierung. Theorie, Forschung, Kontroversen* (pp. 9–50). Göttingen: Vandenhoeck & Ruprecht.

Leuzinger-Bohleber, M. & Pfeifer, R. (2002). Remembering a depressive primary object? Psychoanalysis and Embodied Cognitive Science: A dialogue on memory. *International Journal of Psychoanalysis, 83*: 3–33.

Leuzinger-Bohleber, M. & Pfeifer, R. (2006). Recollecting the past in the present. Memory in the dialogue between psychoanalysis and cognitive science. In: M. Mancia, (Ed.), *Psychoanalyis and Neuroscience*. Milano: Springer.

Leuzinger-Bohleber, M., Brandl, Y. & Hüther, G. (Eds.) (2006). *ADHS – Frühprävention statt Medikalisierung. Theorie, Forschung, Kontroversen*. Göttingen: Vandenhoeck & Ruprecht.

Leuzinger-Bohleber, M., Mertens, W. & Koukkou, M. (Eds.) (1998). *Erinnerung von Wirklichkeiten. Psychoanalyse und Neurowissenschaften im Dialog*. Bd. 2: *Folgerungen für die psychoanalytische Praxis*. Stuttgart: Verlag Internationale Psychoanalyse.

Leuzinger-Bohleber, M., Brandl, Y., Hau, S., Aulbach, L., Caruso, B., Einert, K.-M., Glindemann, O., Göppel, G., Hermann, P., Hesse, P., Heumann, J., Karaca, G., König, J., Lendle, J., Rüger, B., Schwenk, A., Staufenberg, A., Steuber, S., Uhl, Ch., Vogel, J., Waldung, Ch., Wolff, L. & Hüther, G. (2006). Die Frankfurter Präventionsstudie. Zur psychischen und psychosozialen Integration von verhaltensauffälligen Kindern (insbesondere ADHS) im Kindergartenalter—ein Arbeitsbericht. In: M. Leuzinger-Bohleber, Y. Brandl & G. Hüther, (Eds.), *ADHS – Frühprävention statt Medikalisierung. Theorie, Forschung, Kontroversen* (pp. 238–269). Göttingen: Vandenhoeck & Ruprecht.

Leuzinger-Bohleber, M., Dreher, A.U. & Canestri, J. (Eds.). (2003). *Pluralism and Unity? Methods of Research in Psychoanalysis*. London: IPA.

Leuzinger-Bohleber, M. (in press). *The Frankfurt Prevention Study*. Preliminary Results.

Levin, F.M. (1997). Discussion of Mark Solms' "Why consciousnes?" *Journal of the American Psychoanalytic Association*, 45: 732–739.

Lüpke, H.v. (2004). Hyperaktivität zwischen Stoffwechselstörung" und Psychodynamik. In: M. Passolt, (Ed.), *Hyperaktivität zwischen Psychoanalyse, Neurobiologie und Systemtheorie* (pp. 99–116). 2. Auflage. München/Basel: Reinhardt.

Lüpke, H.v. (2006). Der Dialog in Bewegung und der entgleiste Dialog. Beiträge aus Säuglingsforschung und Neurobiologie. In: M. Leuzinger-Bohleber, Y. Brandl & G. Hüther, (Eds.), *ADHS – Frühprävention statt Medikalisierung. Theorie, Forschung, Kontroversen* (pp. 169–188). Göttingen: Vandenhoeck & Ruprecht.

Mattner, D. (2006). ADS die Biologisierung abweichenden Verhaltens. In: M. Leuzinger-Bohleber, Y. Brandl & G. Hüther, (Eds.), *ADHS – Frühprävention statt Medikalisierung. Theorie, Forschung, Kontroversen* (pp. 51–69). Göttingen: Vandenhoeck & Ruprecht.

Metzger, H.-G. (2000). *Zwischen Dyade und Triade. Psychoanalytische Familienbeobachtungen zur Bedeutung des Vaters im Triangulierungsprozeß*. Tübingen: Edition diskord.

Moll, G.H., Mehnert, C., Wicker, M., Bock, N., Rothenberger, A., Rüther, E. & Hüther, G. (2000). Age-associated changes in the densities of pre-synaptic monoamine transporters in different regions of the rat brain from juvenile life to adulthood. *Developmental Brain Research*, *119*: 251–257.

Panksepp, J. (1998). Attention deficit Hyperactivity Disorders, psychostimulants, and intolerance of childhood playfulness: A tragedy in the making? *Current Directions in PsychologicalScience*, 7(3), 91–98.

Panksepp, J. (2001). The long-term psychobiological consequences of infant emotions. *Neuro-Psychoanalysis*, *3*: 149–179.

Passolt, M. (Ed.) (2004). *Hyperaktivität zwischen Psychoanalyse, Neurobiologie und Systemtheorie*. 2. Aufl. München/Basel: Reinhardt.

Pfeifer, R. & Bongard, J. (2007). *How the Body Shapes the Way We Think: A New View of Intelligence*. Cambridge: MIT Press.

Pfeifer, R. & Scheier, C. (1999). *Understanding Intelligence*. Cambridge: MIT Press.

Riedesser, P. (2006). Einige Argumente zur ADHS-Kontroverse in der Kinder- und Jugendpsychiatrie. In:M. Leuzinger-Bohleber, Y. Brandl & G. Hüther, (Eds.), *ADHS – Frühprävention statt Medikalisierung. Theorie, Forschung, Kontroversen* (pp. 111–117). Göttingen: Vandenhoeck & Ruprecht.

Rothstein, A. (2002). Plea for a balanced conception of AD/HD and its diagnosis and treatment. *Psychoanalytic Inquiry, 22*: 391–412.

Rothstein, A. & Glenn, J. (1999). *Learning Disabilities and Psychic Conflict: A Psychoanalytic Casebook.* Madison: International Universities Press.

Ruf-Bächtiger, L. (1987). *Das frühkindliche psychoorganische Syndrom.* Stuttgart: Thieme.

Salomonsson, B. (2004). Some psychoanalytic viewpoints on neuropsychiatric disorders in children. *International Journal of Psychoanalysis, 85*: 117–136.

Schore, A.N. (2006): Das menschliche Unbewußte: die Entwicklung des rechten Gehirns und seine Bedeutung für das frühe Gefühlsleben. In: V. Green,(Ed.), *Emotionale Entwicklung in Psychoanalyse, Bindungstheorie und Neuowissenschaften* (pp. 35–69). Gießen: Psychosozial Verlag.

Seeman, P., Machias, B.K. (1998). Anti-hyperactivity medication. Methylphenidate and amphetamine. *Molecular Psychiatry, 3*: 386–396.

Sennett, R. (1998). *The Corrosion of Character: The Personal Consequences of Work in the New Capitalism.* New York: Norton.

Solanto, M.V. (1998). Neuropsychopharmacological mechanisms of stimulant drug action in attention-deficit hyperactivity disorder. A review and integration. *Behavioural Brain Research, 94*: 127–152.

Solms, M. (2006). Sigmund Freud heute. Eine neurowissenschaftliche Perspektive auf die Psychoanalyse. *Psyche – Z Psychoanalysis, 60*: 829–859.

Stassen, H., Begleiter, H., Beirut, L., Culverhouse, R., Hinrichs, T., Porjesz, B., Rice, J., Scharfetter, C. & Reich, T. (2004a). Oligogenic approaches to the predisposition of alcohol dependence. A genome-wide search on 255 families. *Neurology, Psychiatry and Brain Research, 11*: 13–22.

Stassen, H.H., Bridler, R., Hell, D., Weisbrod, M. & Scharfetter, C. (2004b). Ethnicity-independent genetic basis of functional psychoses. A Genotype-to-phenotype approach. *American Journal of Medical Genetics, 124*: 101–112.

Staufenberg, A. *et al.* (2006). Manual zur psychoanalytisch-psychotherapeutischen Behandlung psychosozialer Integrationsproblemen bei Kinder. Die Fraunkfurter Präventionsstudie). Unpublished.

Stern, D. (1995). *The Motherhood Constellation: A Unified View of Parent-infant Psychotherapy.* New York: Basic Books.

Still, G.F. (1902). Some abnormal psychical conditions in children. *Lancet, 1*: 1008–1012, 1077–1082, 1163–1168.

Sugarman, A. (Reporter) (2006). Attention deficit hyperactivity disorder and trauma. *International Journal of Psychoanalysis, 87*: 237–241.

Waldung, C., Göppel, G. & Wolff, L. (2006). Ein Fallbeispiel (Die Frankfurter Präventionsstudie). In: M. Leuzinger-Bohleber, Y. Brandl &

G. Hüther, (Eds.), *ADHS – Frühprävention statt Medikalisierung. Theorie, Forschung, Kontroversen* (pp. 256–262). Göttingen: Vandenhoeck & Ruprecht.

Zabarenko, L.M. (2002). AD/HD, Psychoanalysis and neuroscience: A survey of recent findings and their applications. *Psychoanalytic Inquiry*, 22: 412–432.

CHAPTER SEVEN

Research on therapeutic processes: In psychodynamic psychotherapy with children and adolescents

Stephen R. Shirk and Rebecca A. Burwell

Contemporary psychodynamic child and adolescent therapy is informed by a rich history of descriptive analyses of therapeutic processes dating from Freud's account of his treatment of "Little Hans" (Freud, 1909). Numerous case studies involving narrative portrayals of the therapeutic process have contributed to the evolution of psychodynamic theory and treatment. Yet, unlike its adult counterpart, therapeutic processes in child and adolescent psychodynamic therapy have received minimal systematic, empirical attention. This state of affairs may not be surprising. First, research on therapeutic processes with children is markedly limited relative to the substantial body of process research on adults (Shirk & Russell, 1998). Second, empirical research on the outcome of psychodynamic child treatment has lagged behind research on other therapeutic approaches with children (Target, Slade, Cottrell, Fuggle & Fonagy, 2005). A recent multi-site, controlled outcome study on psychodynamic therapy for child depression (Tsiantis, Kolvin, Anastasopoulos, Trowell, Tomaras, Miles, Papadopoulos, Soininen, Bostrom & Almqvist, 2005) indicates that the latter is changing. Of equal importance, this study demonstrates that empirical methods can be applied effectively to the investigation of child psychodynamic treatment outcomes. In the spirit of this important advance, we focus this chapter on the potential usefulness of empirical research on therapeutic processes in child psychodynamic therapy. Many within the tradition have been skeptical about the measurement of meaningful outcomes in a treatment that is as idiographic as dynamic therapy and it is likely that this skepticism will be magnified when it comes to measuring critical therapy processes. Mindful of this skepticism, we review what has been done thus far, but also consider what might be accomplished to advance our understanding of child psychodynamic therapy. Because of the nascent state of the empirical literature, we also draw upon process research with adults to guide us in our task.

What are the core assumptions of psychodynamic child therapy?

As Fonagy (1999) has observed, psychodynamic psychotherapy with children is not easily defined as a unitary practice. Important theoretical and technical differences separate various types of dynamic therapy. But, relative to other prominent treatment approaches such as behavioral, family systems, and cognitive-behavioral therapies, a number of core assumptions distinguish the psychodynamic approach and inform its therapeutic methods. These assumptions, enumerated by Fonagy (1999), are summarized here.

First, and perhaps foremost, is the assumption of unconscious mental processes. Although other approaches acknowledge processes that operate outside of awareness, e.g., information processing patterns, at the heart of the psychodynamic approach is the tenet that complex unconscious processes influence emotional experience and overt behavior. Second, internal conflict among incompatible wishes, emotions and ideas are pathogenic and can undermine the process of development. For example, problematic early relationships might engender conflicting needs and emotions, ambivalence toward the caregiver, which could increase the risk of separation difficulties. Third, unacceptable feelings, wishes or ideas are managed by unconscious mental processes or defenses. Although other approaches consider emotional regulation strategies, their focus often is on conscious, effortful behaviors. The psychodynamic approach is unique in its emphasis on unconscious, automatic processes that regulate internal states. Fourth, over the course of development, but especially in early development, individuals form relatively enduring representations of self in relation to significant others. These representations structure expectations about others and influence ideas and feelings about the self. Further, these representations influence social behavior, including behavior and emotions in the therapeutic relationship. Finally, behavior signifies meaning. The child's actions, including verbal behaviors, reflect both conscious intentions and unconscious layers of meaning. Understanding behavior then, cannot be reduced to the situation that prompted it, but must be understood in terms of its communicative function. Though it is likely that psychodynamic therapists vary in their adherence to specific assumptions, these core tenets clearly distinguish psychodynamic therapy from the other major approaches to child treatment.

What are the core change processes in psychodynamic child therapy?

Given these core assumptions, what are the implications for the therapeutic process? Again, it would be folly to assume a unitary model of therapeutic action in psychodynamic child therapy. This approach has been shaped by a number of theories including, but not limited to, those of Anna Freud (1946), Melanie Klein (1932), and David Winnicott (1958). Further, it is not evident that there is a close correspondence between psychoanalytic theory and treatment techniques (Fonagy & Target, 2000). Although theory and practice have been reciprocally informative, they have developed at very difference rates (Fonagy & Target, 2000). Finally, psychodynamic child therapy has continued to evolve over the last half century, thus, it is important to recognize both early and more recent conceptualizations of the therapeutic process.

Early psychodynamic child therapy emphasized the importance of verbal interpretation of the child's behavior, verbalizations, or play for symptom reduction and improved functioning (Target et al., 2005). Anna Freud (1965) maintained that interpretation is indispensable for the treatment of patients of all ages, including children, and that "distress and arrests are counteracted when anxieties are clarified and interpreted...." (p. 226). This view was later echoed by Kennedy (1971) who proposed that the primary function of child therapy is to provide "a conceptual framework to the child whereby he can understand his present experiences and dilemmas" (p. 400). In brief, according to this early view, emotional and behavioral change is mediated by reorganization in the child's understanding of his or her experiences. From this perspective, a 'good"' therapeutic process would involve the expression of symbolic material through play, verbalizations, or behavior by the child, and the complementary facilitation and interpretation of such expressions by the therapist. Of course, 'good' process entails far more, including the timing and titration of interpretations, as well as the establishment of a stable relational context for these therapeutic activities. But as one facet of psychodynamic child therapy, the child's expression of material and the therapist's facilitation and interpretation of expressed material, represent salient targets for process research.

Recent views on the curative factors in psychodynamic child therapy have de-emphasized the role of interpretation as the primary change mechanism and have re-conceptualized symbolic process in terms of mentalizing functions (Target, Slade, Cottrell, Fuggle & Fonagy, 2005). Mentalization or what has been called reflective function (Fonagy & Target, 1997; Baron-Cohen, Tager-Flusberg & Cohen, 1993), involves the capacity to interpret one's own behavior and the behavior of others' in terms of internal mental states. It is proposed that behavior becomes both meaningful and predictable through inferences involving mental states (Fonagy & Target, 1997). An emerging body of evidence indicates that impaired mentalizing or reflective function is associated with problematic early relationships between caregiver and child, and subsequently with various forms of child psychopathology (Fonagy & Target, 1997).

Based on this reformulation, the central change process in psychodynamic therapy involves "enhancing the child's symbolic, imaginative, and mentalizing capacities" (Target et al., 2005). With children, this involves broadening self-experience by increasing the range, depth, and emotional richness of play in the safety of an accepting therapeutic relationship (Rogers, 1995). With older children and adolescents, this process can take place through talk, but the aim remains the enhancement of mentalizing or reflective function through broadening and deepening self-experiences.

As Target et al. (2005) note, at its core, psychodynamic child therapy essentially involves two people playing together, whether with toys or other symbolic representations, i.e. language). The task of the therapist then, is less about interpreting the meaning of symbolic expressions, although interpretation remains a part of the therapy process, and more about helping the child play. In connection with this, the therapist's job may involve facilitating a coherent narrative, supporting inferences about the inner life of imagined characters, or finding solutions to intensely depicted emotional scenarios (Target et al., 2005). It is noteworthy that this perspective is consistent with a large body of developmental research on the adaptive function of children's play (Russ, 2004). Furthermore, this view suggests that changes in children's capacity to play as well as the therapist's capacity to facilitate play represent important targets for psychodynamic process research.

It has long been recognized that therapeutic 'work' in psychodynamic therapy hinges on the development of a stable, secure relationship (Shirk & Russell, 1996). Anna Freud (1946) observed that an 'affectionate attachment' between child and therapist is a 'prerequisite for all later work' in child therapy (p. 31). The same can be said about therapeutic play. The child's capacity to play in a rich symbolic manner depends on experiencing the therapist as both accepting and containing (Target et al., 2005). Similarly, adolescents' willingness to disclose, share or reflect upon important feelings, wishes, and experiences is closely tied to the quality of the therapeutic relationship. As has been proposed and empirically investigated in the adult literature (Horvath & Luborsky, 1993), the therapeutic alliance represents a central construct in psychodynamic therapy. It is not clear if associations between alliance and treatment outcome are primarily mediated through patient involvement in therapeutic tasks, e.g., the expression of symbolic material, or if the alliance directly affects outcome through other mechanisms e.g., corrective emotional experience. Nevertheless, the quality of the relationship between child and therapist is central to psychodynamic child therapy and a significant target for process research.

Toward a researchable model of change processes in psychodynamic child therapy

The core assumptions and corresponding views on change processes provide a framework for reviewing extant process studies and other research relevant to psychodynamic child therapy. Three sets of process targets have been identified; interpretive interventions, facilitation of mentalization or reflective function, and the therapeutic alliance. In terms of process research, a number of basic psychodynamic hypotheses can be generated. It should be noted that our approach to hypothesis generation is grounded on a pragmatic and potentially controversial assumption, namely that process research serves outcome research (Shirk & Karver, 2005). That is, process research aims at increasing our understanding of change mechanisms so that treatment outcomes might be enhanced.

The first hypothesis, based on an early model of therapeutic action, is that outcome in child psychodynamic therapy should be associated with the interpretive activity of the therapist. To the degree that interpretations facilitate insight and the expansion of self-awareness, meaningful interpretations should be related to symptom change or improved functioning over the course of therapy. Although it is unlikely that the mere frequency of interpretations will predict better outcomes, interpretations may be more strongly associated with outcomes than other therapist verbalizations e.g., requests for information. Second, changes in the range and depth of children's symbolic play in therapy should predict better outcomes. To the degree that increased symbolic play capacity leads to gains in mentalizing, improvement in play should predict better outcomes. A corollary of this hypothesis is that therapist's interventions that facilitate symbolic play or expressions should relate to treatment outcome through improved mentalization. One related hypothesis is that mentalization in play will lead to the development of structures for regulating emotion (Target et al., 2005). Thus, increased mentalization over the course of therapy should be associated with improved emotion regulation capacity. Third, the quality of the therapeutic alliance should be associated with the child's engagement in symbolic play or production of symbolic materials e.g., narrative accounts of personal experiences. In turn, the alliance should be associated with treatment progress, either directly or indirectly, through the child's involvement in symbolic play or other expressions of symbolic material such as personal narratives.

Inherent in these hypotheses is an important distinction in the child psychotherapy process literature. Two types of processes are considered; the first involves specific treatment processes or procedures e.g., therapist facilitation of symbolic play, and the second involves specific treatment targets or the postulated pathogenic process that accounts for the development, maintenance, or desistence of the overt problems. Most research in the child literature has focused on the latter. For example, research on mechanisms of change in cognitive-behavioral child treatment has examined changes in cognitive distortions and the association between change in distortions and symptom improvement. Fewer studies have addressed the association between specific therapeutic processes, therapist's interpretations, and change in underlying pathogenic processes, maladaptive defenses.

Therapy process research often involves an examination of mediated relationships among constructs. For example, we might find a significant, predictive association between the therapeutic alliance and changes in symptoms or functioning, but from a process perspective, we typically are interested in the mechanisms that account for this association. Thus, inclusion of both the therapeutic process construct, the alliance, as well as the pathogenic mechanism that might account for its association with outcome, increased mentalization, increases our understanding of how treatment works. In reality, most models are more complex. Figure 1 depicts a slightly more complex model linking the therapeutic alliance to the child's involvement in symbolic play to increased mentalization to

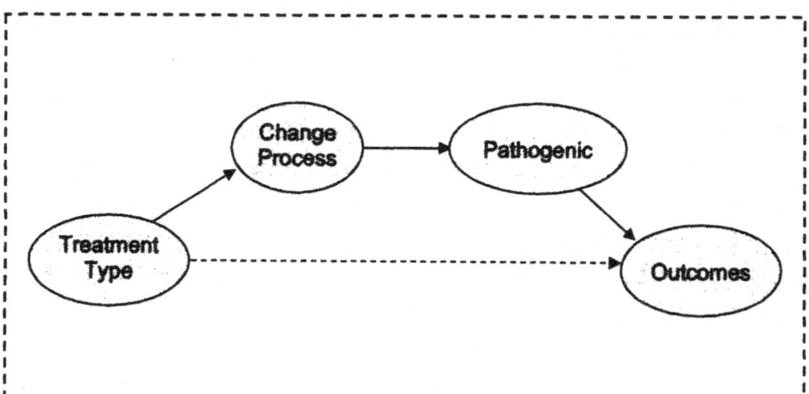

Figure 1. Mediation model linking treatment to outcome through pathogenic mechanisms and change processes.

improvement in symptoms or functioning. This model could also be elaborated to include therapist interventions that facilitate symbolic play. Although the model is essentially linear, it is possible to include reciprocal associations, especially with time-lag data.

Of course, the evaluation of models of therapy processes depends on the reliable and valid measurement of core constructs. Psychodynamic therapy process introduces additional challenges in this respect given the centrality of unconscious processes, nuanced interactions, and the idiographic nature of individual case material. For some, these challenges render psychodynamic therapy inaccessible to empirical investigation. (Fonagy & Target, 2000). We propose that these challenges must be taken seriously, and may demand more than process research 'as usual'. Our review of the emerging literature suggests some potentially effective ways to bridge these barriers.

Relationship processes in psychodynamic child therapy

Given the fundamental importance of the therapeutic relationship in psychodynamic therapy (A. Freud, 1946; Target et al., 2005), we begin our review of the existing literature by examining research on the relationship in child therapy. As Target et al. (2005) observed, "...the child's capacity to establish a relationship with the therapist (and conversely, the therapist's capacity to establish a relationship with the child) is central to the treatment" (p. 342). In line with this observation, relationship processes have received more, albeit limited, attention than most process variables in child therapy.

A substantial body of evidence has shown that the therapeutic alliance is one of the most consistent predictors of treatment outcome with adults across multiple forms of therapy including psychodynamic therapy (Martin, Graske & Davis, 2000). Recently, Shirk and Karver (2003) demonstrated similar results through their meta-analysis of 23 studies of child and adolescent therapy. Like results from the adult literature, there was a modest association between measures of therapy relationship and treatment outcome across varied forms of therapy. Of specific interest, 5 studies were identified that included psychodynamic child therapy although treatment fidelity was not assessed in any of these studies. On average, measures of the therapeutic relationship were associated with measures of treatment outcomes (r = .29), or slightly but not reliably above the mean for the full sample of studies (r = .25). While the strength of this association is comparable to alliance-outcome associations with adults, it should be noted that measures of relationship and outcomes varied widely, and not all studies measured alliance prior to treatment outcome. Therefore, the predictive association between therapy relationship and outcome cannot be established by these studies. In the adult literature, there has been considerable controversy regarding the causal direction of associations between alliance and outcomes with some evidence suggesting that early change in therapy predicts alliance (Feeley, DeRubeis & Gelfand, 1999), whereas others show that alliance predicts future benefits even after controlling for early gains (Barber, Connolly, Crits-Christoph, Gladis & Siqueland, 2000). Results from the multi-national European controlled trial of psychodynamic therapy for child depression could shed light on this issue in child treatment as both alliance and depressive symptoms were measured at multiple points in time (Tsiantis et al., 2005).

Two studies were identified that examined the hypothesis that the alliance between child and therapist is related to the degree to which child patients engage in the 'work' of psychodynamic therapy. In a study of 62 inpatient children with diverse forms of psychopathology, Shirk and Saiz (1992) illustrated that the quality of the emotional bond between child and therapist was associated with the child's active participation in therapy. Participation was operationalized as the child's disclosure and expression of feelings as well as their willingness to talk about personal material. A major limitation of this study involved the assessment of alliance the emotional bond, and participation at the same point in time, thereby obscuring the direction of effects. Furthermore, associations between bond and participation were obtained within but not across, child and therapist perspectives, thus raising concerns that shared source variance might be inflating these effects. This concern is magnified by results from a study by Estrada and Russell (1999) who did not find a significant association between observed ratings of the therapeutic relationship and the child's level of therapeutic work in psychodynamic therapy. Again, within ratings of child behavior, relationship and work were modestly correlated. Despite these mixed results, the study by Estrada and Russell (1999) is particularly noteworthy insofar as it provided an observational measure of both the therapy relationship and therapeutic work based on recorded sessions. A factor analysis of coded items revealed that child therapeutic work was defined by high item loadings on ratings of exploration, productivity, feelings expression, and understanding. Child therapeutic relationship was characterized by high positive loadings on openness, synchrony, trust, cooperation, and negative loadings for lack of interest, negative reactions, and noncompliance. The advantage of this method is that it avoids the potential biases of the child and therapist report, and provides a window on aspects of interaction that may not be salient to participants, i.e., to the therapist and child.

The extremely limited body of research on associations between relationship variables and either treatment outcomes or treatment involvement, provides a relatively weak foundation for core assumptions about treatment processes. Based on current results, one might reasonably conclude that the therapy relationship plays only a modest role in influencing outcomes, and that the bond between child and therapist has less to do with facilitating children's active participation in therapy than we might have expected. In fact, a reasonable rival hypothesis might be that bond, participation, and outcomes in psychodynamic child therapy have less to do with in-session processes, and much more to do with the pre-treatment characteristics of child patients. That is, variation in treatment response observed in uncontrolled studies of psychodynamic child treatment might be predicted from variations in child characteristics rather than variations in the therapy process. Such a view would be consistent with the notion that certain prerequisites are critical in order to benefit from psychodynamic therapy including good verbal skills, a supportive environment, motivation for treatment, and the capacity to form relationships. In fact, it may be important to evaluate this rival hypothesis in the context of evaluating associations between process variables and treatment outcomes. One might discover that what we have termed 'alliance' is nothing more than a marker for the capacity to form relationships that children bring to therapy. While this would be an important finding, that capacity for relationship is a predictor of treatment benefit and necessary for positive treatment results, it would suggest that outcomes may be more a function of patient selection than subtleties of within-session, alliance formation processes.

However, it would be terribly premature to abandon the core hypothesis that within session relationship processes are essential for both active involvement in therapy and treatment progress. In fact, one could easily conclude that existing empirical research provides only a crude estimate of these associations. How, then, might research be improved to address these core process issues in psychodynamic child therapy?

The first question is how best to conceptualize and assess the quality of the therapeutic relationship? Clearly, Freud (1912; 1913) distinguished two core facets of the therapeutic relationship, the alliance and transference. Freud acknowledged that the analyst's sympathetic understanding would connect with the healthy, reality-oriented side of the patient's self to form a working relationship. But one of Freud's most enduring insights involved recognition of transferred images, affects, and relational patterns into the therapeutic relationship. Research on psychodynamic therapy with adults has distinguished between these two facets (Horvath & Luborsky, 1993) and as such, process research with children and adolescents is likely to benefit from this distinction.

With regard to the alliance, a large body of empirical evidence indicates that the alliance is one of the most consistent predictors of outcome across types of therapies and types of problems among adults (Martin, Graske & Davis, 2000). A variety of approaches to conceptualizing and measuring the alliance have emerged from this literature. Early work focused on the patient's experience of the therapist and the working relationship. Both rating scales and patient reports were developed to assess this aspect of the alliance (Alexander & Luborsky, 1986). Subsequent scales have been developed to assess a range of dimensions including therapist behaviors and attitudes that might facilitate or impede progress (Suh, Strupp & O'Malley, 1986), affective aspects of the alliance (Marziali, Marmar & Krupnick, 1984), patient capacity for and commitment to therapy (Marmar, Gaston et al., 1989), and emotional bond between patient and therapist (Saunders, Howard & Orlinsky. 1989). One model that has attained a significant foothold in the adult literature is Bordin's (1979) conceptualization of the alliance as multidimensional. From this perspective, the alliance involves the emotional bond between patient and therapist, level of collaboration on specific treatment tasks, and degree of agreement on methods and goals of therapy.

This framework strongly shaped the original development of the *Therapeutic Alliance Scales for Children (TASC;* Shirk & Saiz, 1992).

Based on a factor analysis of child and therapist reports, Shirk and Saiz (1992) identified two primary components of the alliance in dynamic child therapy. These two inter-related components involved emotional bond and task collaboration. In turn, a twelve item scale was developed for child and therapist reports. Although significant relations were found between emotional bond perspectives, child and therapist tended to diverge in their perspectives on task collaboration. A number of studies have supported the reliability and predictive validity of the *TASC* as a measure of therapy alliance, including a recent study showing predictive associations between child reported alliance and treatment progress in community based therapy for youths (Hawley & Weisz, 2005). In a recent study, the adolescent version of the *TASC*, the *Therapeutic Alliance Scale for Adolescents (TASA)* was shown to predict changes in depressive symptoms in a school-based clinical trial for adolescent depression.

Given the importance of emotional bond in both child and adult models of alliance, it seems reasonable to ask, "How should therapeutic bond be conceptualized and assessed?" Does the bond refer to something more than 'liking' or 'feeling comfortable' with the therapist? Perhaps we need to take Anna Freud's (1946) view of the therapy relationship as an 'affectionate attachment' quite seriously in our efforts to assess process. Indeed, the notion of the therapeutic relationship as an attachment relationship is not new. In his later writings, Bowlby (1988; p. 138) observed that the "therapist has a number of tasks ... first, and above all, to provide the patient with a secure base from which to explore both himself and also his relations with all those with whom he has made or might make, an affectional bond". From this perspective, the emotional bond between child and therapist is an attachment bond, a relationship optimally infused with stability, safety, and security. Furthermore, this secure relationship provides the base for exploration of experience and involvement in therapy. Bowlby (1988) goes so far as to say that without this felt security, "therapy cannot begin" (p. 140). In relation to this it is interesting to note that Main, Kaplan, and Cassidy (1985) demonstrated a relationship between attachment security and openness and ease of disclosure in child interviews.

When the therapy relationship is viewed as an attachment relationship, a number of issues come to the foreground. First, what constitutes the experience of felt security? If we draw on attachment theory and research (Ainsworth, Blehar, Waters & Wall, 1978), felt security in the therapeutic relationship should be linked to the experience of the therapist as responsive and reliable; that is, as a figure who is attuned to emotional signals, especially signals of distress, who responds in a way that allows the child to experience and manage emotions without distortion, and who does so on a consistent basis. At its core, felt security should engender an experience of the therapist as caring and the self as worthy of care (Bowlby, 1988).

A related question, then, is how best to measure felt security in the therapy relationship? As the child's experience of the therapist it would seem follow that the child should be the source of the data. Certainly one could imagine constructing self-report measures of emotional bonds that explicitly include attachment relevant dimensions, for example, ratings of therapist as dependable, emotionally responsive, in touch with the child's feelings, and caring. In fact, Shirk (2003) included these types of ratings in the adolescent version of his therapeutic alliance scale *(TASA)*. But a major question, and one that finds a parallel in the social development literature, is whether attachment experiences are accessible to self-report, and if accessible, are subject to defensive modification when reported. Recent research on adult and adolescent attachment has distinguished two types of relational views (Furman, Simon, Shaffer & Bouchey, 2002), working models that contain implicit representations of the self in relation to attachment figures, and relational styles that involve explicit interpersonal expectations and self attitudes. Interestingly, both approaches to attachment assessment have demonstrated patterns of associations with psychiatric symptoms and relationship problems, despite limited association between the two types of assessment (Crowell, Fraley & Shaver, 1999). To the degree that child psychodynamic therapy stresses the importance of unconscious working models, the measurement of therapeutic security will require alternatives to self-reports. It is possible, at least with adolescents, that the attachment interview devised by Mary Main and colleagues (1985), or other narrative based assessment tools, could be adapted to examine representations of self in relation to therapist. Such an approach would represent a significant advance over the field's reliance on self-report measures of alliance, and is likely to come closer to the heart of the psychodynamic conception of the therapeutic relationship.

It is intriguing to consider the distinction between working models and self-reported representations of the therapist as a potential way of separating the constructs of transference and alliance. If alliance represents the perspective of the healthy, reality-oriented self as Freud (1912) suggested, but transference involves unconscious representations and expectations, then alliance might be reasonably assessed via self-report whereas transference would require an alternative method akin to the assessment of working models (Westen, 1991). In the adult literature, Luborsky and Crits-Christoph (1998) developed a method of narrative analysis that involves the examination of core relationship themes and their transformation over the course of therapy. Virtually no work of this type has appeared in the child therapy literature despite its relevance to treatment models that emphasize the importance of interpersonal representations for adaptive functioning. Adolescent narratives of relationship experiences or children's thematic play could be rich sources of data for investigating change in interpersonal representations and their association with improved functioning.

Play and interpretive processes in psychodynamic child therapy

An enduring contribution of the psychodynamic approach to child treatment has been the recognition of play as a critical communicative medium for children (Target et al., 2005). Thus, play has been viewed as a form of symbolic representation of the concerns, conflicts, fears, and urges that underlie children's emotional and behavioral difficulties. Thematic material that exceeds the child's capacity for verbal representation or results in sufficient anxiety to necessitate indirect expression through play constitutes the content of psychodynamic child therapy. One of the therapists' principal roles then, is to facilitate the expression of thematic material through play, and to assist the child in understanding the meaning and relevance of play productions for everyday emotional life (Shirk, 1988). As Erikson (1964) noted, "Those children who transfer … the unsolvability of their problems into the play situation and onto the person of the observer need to be induced by systematic interpretation to reconsider, on a more verbal level, the constellations that have overwhelmed them…." (p. 265). From this perspective, progress hinges on the therapist's interpretive activities.

More recently, the function of play in psychodynamic child therapy has been re-conceptualized. According to this revised account, play itself is the agent of change. As Target et al. (2005) observe, "… what is thought to be curative is enhancing the child's symbolic, imaginative, and mentalizing capacities by increasing the range, depth, and emotional richness of his play" (p. 341). In essence, the focus shifts from play content to play process. Rather than interpreting the specific meaning of children's play, the therapist facilitates play processes by helping the child with the basics of narrative organization, by promoting the imagination of an inner life among play characters, and by facilitating the expression of intense emotions in the safety of play (Target et al., 2005). The play process then, leads to increased mentalization and the development of structures for regulating emotion and understanding oneself and others (Fonagy & Target, 1996).

Both perspectives accord a central role to play in psychodynamic treatment process. However, what evidence is there for an association between play and outcome in child therapy? Unfortunately, most evidence on this process-outcome issue is indirect. A recent meta-analysis of play therapy outcomes based on 93 studies revealed that play methods yielded a substantial effect (d = .80) across a variety of childhood emotional and behavioral problems (Bratton, Ray, Rhine & Jones, 2005). This result is likely to be surprising to clinicians familiar with recent meta-analytic findings on child and adolescent therapy. The conclusion of two broad meta-analyses conducted by Weisz and colleagues (Weisz, Weiss, Han, Granger & Morton, 1995; Weisz, Weiss, Alicke & Klotz, 1987), showed that behavioral treatments produced significantly larger effects than non-behavioral treatments, including play therapy, across age groups and childhood problems. One notable difference in these sets of meta-analyses is the sheer number of non-behavioral treatment studies included; the play therapy evaluation included 67 non-behavioral play treatments alone. Nevertheless, despite pointing to the potential efficacy of play as a therapeutic process, like many meta-analyses, the play evaluation has a number of limitations. First, as the authors noted, most studies failed to describe the specific play interventions used in the study, nor were play protocols provided by most, thus making it difficult to know much about specific play processes. Second, and of particular relevance, the vast majority of the studies in the sample were humanistic treatments, and no results were reported for psychodynamic play therapy per se. Therefore, while the study suggests that play-based therapies may produce significant change, specific links between play processes and treatment outcomes remain unexamined.

A similar pattern is found for insight-oriented, psychodynamic child therapy, but here, current evidence from controlled trials suggests less substantial treatment effects. For example, Weisz and colleagues (1995) identified nine controlled outcome studies of psychodynamic child therapy and reported an average effect size of .30, a statistically significant but relatively small effect. Emerging findings based on controlled trials for well-defined problems (Muratori, Picchi, Bruni, Patarnello & Romagnoli, 2003; Tsiantis et al., 2005) should provide a better index of treatment effectiveness. But like research on play therapy, existing research on insight-oriented treatment, while essential for demonstrating efficacy, provides little 'insight' into the role of specific treatment processes such as interpretation.

Although interpretation has received substantial attention in the clinical literature and in the adult psychotherapy research literature, empirical research on the relationship between interpretation and outcome in child therapy is virtually non-existent. Although types of interpretations have been distinguished (Kernberg, 1995), links between interpretation and outcomes have not been investigated. In the adult process literature, for example, a review of associations between transference interpretations and outcomes has yielded mixed outcomes (Hoglend, 2004). It is worth noting that research indicates that interpretations can be operationalized and reliably counted, but most studies have relied on a simple dose-response model. That is, it is assumed that the frequency of interpretations will be predictive of outcomes. Such an approach ignores important issues such as the timing, relational context, and perhaps most critically, the accuracy of interpretations.

How then, might process research be improved in the area of play and interpretation in psychodynamic child therapy? Let us first consider play. A large body of developmental research indicates that play is critical for children's social and cognitive development (Russ, 2004). As Russ concludes, the empirical literature has shown that pretend play relates to, or facilitates: (1) problem-solving that requires insight, (2) flexibility in problem-solving, (3) the ability to generate alternative coping strategies, (4) the experience of positive emotion, and (5) the ability to understand the emotions of others. Thus, play, especially pretend play, not only serves as a communicative medium, play itself facilitates the development of capacities that support adaptive functioning.

Given the importance of play, it would seem that the first task involves specification of play processes and the development of a system for measuring children's play activity in therapy. One dimension that emerges from recent psychodynamic theory (Fonagy & Target, 1996), in addition to emerging evidence on the role of play in development is the importance of pretend play, or play that is representational. As Target et al. (2005) have noted, not all play in therapy is equal and some forms of play like repetitive board games may lack the representational quality of thematic play. Thus, it would appear that process research would be advanced by the development of a play typology and research on its observational reliability.

Several systems have been developed that might provide a foundation for research in this area. For example, Kernberg, Chazan, and Normandin (1998), developed and evaluated the *Children's Play Therapy Instrument* that distinguished four structural components, affective, cognitive, dynamic and developmental as well as the quality of the relationship within the play activity. Of specific relevance to psychodynamic models, emphasizing the link between play and mentalization is the cognitive component. This component involves the assessment of the child's social representations and the degree to which "the child is capable of creating narrative structures to represent different affect-laden relationships" (p. 199). A reasonable hypothesis, then, would be that positive changes on this dimension would be associated with better treatment outcomes.

From a clinical perspective, it would be useful for process studies to address therapist actions that facilitate and maintain the child's engagement in pretend or representational play. Important questions pertaining to the degree to which the therapist structures play activities, joins the child in play, or comments on the meaning of play, have yet to be addressed. For example, if an initial goal is to help the child with the rudiments of narrative (Target et al., 2005), should the therapist guide this process by asking questions about setting, temporal ordering and character development as the child's play unfolds? Does this facilitate the child's narrative capacity or are there other therapist interventions, e.g., merely reflecting on the story line, more conducive of change? Research on parental scaffolding of children's storytelling might provide some important insight into this core process (Russell & van den Broek, 1988).

With regard to the role of interpretation in psychodynamic child therapy, alternatives to the frequency approach, that is, simply measuring the dose of interpretations, need to be developed. Research on adult psychodynamic therapy has revealed associations between the accuracy of interpretations and treatment progress (Crits-Christoph, Cooper & Luborsky, 1988). Of course, assessing the accuracy of interpretations depends on a reliable method for defining the conflicts or interpersonal themes that are central to the child's functioning. In the adult literature, central relationship themes are derived from patient narratives (Crits-Christoph et al., 1988). It is not clear if a similar method could be used with children who typically do not provide rich interpersonal narratives at the start of therapy. Alternatively, Weiss and colleagues (1986) have proposed that interpersonal and emotional problems originate in pathogenic beliefs derived from recurrent interactions with significant others. For example, in a child who has grown up with a mother debilitated by chronic illness, one might find the unconscious belief, 'my needs are a burden to others'. In turn, the child might be characterized by strong denial of desires and wishes, and present interpersonally in a self-sacrificing manner. Identification of idiographic beliefs is based on family and developmental history in conjunction with the patient's presenting problems and interpersonal patterns (Weiss et al., 1986). The approach provides a method for evaluating the goodness-of-fit of therapist interventions while preserving the uniqueness of individual cases. Higher rates of interpretations that are on target would be expected to be related to greater improvement over the course of therapy.

One exemplary study of process in child psychodynamic therapy merits comment in this connection. Moran and Fonagy (1987) successfully operationalized and measured core dynamic themes in the analysis of an adolescent with brittle diabetes. Using time series analysis, these investigators were able to show that the emergence and interpretation of conflict themes predicted subsequent improvements in diabetic control. Two aspects of this study deserve attention. First, the study demonstrates that it is possible to reliably identify core dynamic themes that can be used in statistical analyses of process. Second, the study highlights the importance of examining change processes in relation to proximal outcomes, in this case, diabetic control. With regard to this, research on play or interpretive processes in child therapy will be enhanced by examining change processes in relation to child capacities or functions that are expected to contribute to more distal outcomes. For example, studies of play process might include measures of reflective function, cognitive flexibility, or emotional reactivity as a more proximal measure of change than symptom reduction.

In sum, progress in the developmental play literature and in adult psychodynamic process research provides new directions for child therapy research. As the foregoing examples suggest, research in this area need not be confined to methods that merely count the frequency of child or therapist behaviors. Instead, emerging approaches to process highlight the importance of both qualities of play and the contextual meaning of interpretation. Utilization of these ideas in process research should permit investigators to remain faithful to the nature of psychodynamic child therapy.

Emotion processes in psychodynamic child therapy

In the psychodynamic tradition, accessing and gaining awareness of unconscious and conflicting desires, wishes, and emotions is an important goal of treatment. Addressing defenses such as denial, distortion, and displacement that block access is central to this process (A. Freud, 1965). Such defenses serve to "distort or transform the appearance of more candid but less acceptable thoughts and feelings" (Chandler, Paget & Koch, 1978, p. 197). The goal of treatment then, is not only to process conscious emotions, but also to gain access to non-conscious feelings and emotions, which have different biological causes and behavioral outcomes relative to conscious emotions (Fonagy & Target, 2000; Westen,1999). As Fonagy and Target (1997, p. 416) state, "to the extent that unconscious as well as conscious factors have a role to play, then abnormalities in unconscious functioning, as postulated by psychoanalysis, will remain highly significant."

Therapists' use of self and observation facilitates access to unconscious emotions, at which point they may be interpreted and reflected upon, whether directly or indirectly. "The repetition of patterns of emotional arousal in association with the interpretive process elaborates and strengthens structures of meaning and emotional response" (Fonagy, 2003, p. 74). However, as Westen notes,

> "Making the unconscious conscious is more complex than it may once have appeared, because it entails not only helping people to see what they have been afraid to see, but also helping them to see patterns of functioning—ways of dealing with emotions, of interacting with other people, of viewing themselves—that they could not have seen if they wanted to" (Westen, 2002, p. 371).

Fonagy (2004) has highlighted a number of core processes in child psychotherapy. Among these include the examination of past experiences to gain insight into the child's reactions and coping abilities; interpretations of non-conscious processes that affect current emotion regulation, including emotional experience and coping strategies; and awareness of defensive processes and behaviors developed to distort threatening emotions. The therapist attempts to integrate, elaborate and clarify conscious or non-conscious mental representations through children's verbal and non-verbal behaviors that arise in the context of play, games, and emotional experiences occurring naturally within treatment sessions.

Developmental issues complicate the picture, but are critical to consider when working with children. For example, in addition to defensive processes, children have difficulty cognitively understanding abstract and mixed emotions such as ambivalence (Harter & Whitesell, 1989) and may label emotions differently depending on their developmental level, e.g., sadness in childhood equates to feeling unhappy, while in adolescence is often represented by a blend of negative emotions (Renouf & Harter, 1990). As with adults, on-line emotion processing, in which the therapist and child work together to address emotions that arise in the context of the session, is particularly relevant when working with youth who may otherwise deny the existence of past emotions. Many children experience talking about past emotions as re-experiencing them and when asked to reflect on past emotions, are hesitant to do so. Thus, getting the emotion 'in the room' via play or making use of spontaneous events may be particularly fruitful (Shirk & Russell, 1996).

From a psychodynamic perspective, the emergence of the child's reflective function through the therapist's reflection on the child's emotional experience is central to the development of regulatory structures (Slade, 1999; Target et al., 2005). Therapists, who respond to patients' innermost feelings with empathy, healthy mirroring, and validation, provide a safe base from which patients may begin to tolerate, and eventually explore, their emotional landscape. Patients may come to experience their own emotions first through the eyes of the therapist, and then make sense of, or implicitly mentalize, these emotions as a result. Thus, the therapist serves as a reality test, a corrective relational experience and an attachment figure. In a study among adults, patients who were securely attached to their therapist reported sessions that probed more deeply into emotional issues compared to insecure patients (Mallinckrodt, Porter & Kivlighan, 2005).

Emotion processing in psychodynamic child therapy is grounded in developmental research on attachment formation and parental response to children's emotions (Fonagy & Target, 1997). A parent who is able to accept and 'stay with' a child's needs and negative emotions such as anger, jealousy, and contempt, yet maintain a separate reality, provides the foundation for transforming these feelings into acceptable ones, threatening neither the child nor themselves (Carlson & Sroufe, 1995; Slade, 2005; Zahn-Waxler, Cole & Barrett, 1991). Similarly, a therapist who engages with and mirrors the child and simultaneously maintains a separate sense of self and reality, fosters the child's development of emotional and self-awareness through the therapist's symbolic representation of him (Slade, 2005). The ability to obtain healthy mirroring from a parent or other source, e.g., the therapist) is central to the development of a secure attachment and provides the foundation for the child's own reflective function and later emotion regulation (Fonagy & Target, 1997; Gergely & Watson, 1996). Securely attached children have more synchrony with their mothers (Isabella & Belsky, 1991) and greater awareness of their own and others' emotional states (Laible, 2007; Raikes & Thompson, 2006). In this respect, the therapist's attunement to and reflection of the child's emotional experience is transformed into the child's reflective function. The central psychodynamic hypothesis then, with regard to emotion processing is that the quality of the therapist's attunement and reflection, mirroring, of the child's emotional experience, should facilitate children's awareness of their own and others' emotions, and result in improved emotion regulation.

A growing body of evidence with adults indicates that emotion processing in therapy is linked to better outcomes. For example, it has been shown that depth of in-session emotional processing, rather than content or intensity, is linked to positive therapeutic outcome (Adams & Greenburg, 1996). Further, Pos and colleagues (2003) found that the positive effects of emotional processing occur over and above the role of therapeutic alliance. Others have found, however, that the benefits of emotional arousal and processing are moderated by alliance, e.g., only in the context of a strong alliance does the patient benefit from high arousal (Iwakabe, Rogan & Stalikas, 2000). Finally, Mackay and colleagues (2002) found that relative to patients in cognitive-behavioral treatment, patients in psychodynamic therapy experienced greater distress mid-session, but ended sessions with less distress. These results suggest that emotional processing, that is both confronting difficult emotions and working through them, is core to psychodynamic therapy and represents a target for process research.

From the standpoint of empirical research, very little is known about emotion in child therapy and its relation to treatment outcome. One important development has been the construction and validation of the *Affect in Play Scale* (Russ, 2004) that provides an index of the amount and types of emotion expressed in children's fantasy play. Though developed for coding a standard play task, the scale could be used to measure emotion expression in therapy sessions. However, a child psychodynamic process model of emotion in child therapy requires consideration of the therapist's response to expressed emotion. A number of scales have been developed for the assessment of maternal response to infant affect (e.g., Isabella & Belsky, 1991), which might be adapted to evaluate synchrony and other processes inherent in therapist mirroring. Similarly, a number of measures devised by process researchers in the non-directive, play tradition have reliably assessed therapist empathy and attunement (Shirk & Russell, 1998). Assessment of the interplay between child expression and therapist response thus becomes the unit of analysis. Such a structure might emerge from an examination of behavioral co-variation over time within single cases (P-technique). The identification of a 'mirroring' structure would clearly advance research in this area by providing a window on one of the core emotional change processes in psychodynamic child therapy.

Conclusion

Empirical research on psychodynamic child therapy has been sporadic over the last fifty years. The literature is dotted with relatively few controlled studies of treatment outcome, and even fewer studies of process–outcome relations. However, recent controlled studies of psychodynamic child therapy in Europe indicate that this situation is changing. One of the primary aims of this paper was to build on this development by suggesting that empirical methods can be productively applied to psychodynamic treatment processes as well. Regardless, this will by no means be an easy task; however progress in developmental psychology, particularly within the play and attachment literatures, provides new methods for examining core processes in child therapy. Furthermore, research on psychodynamic adult therapy has shown that it is possible to investigate core processes such as interpretation without losing the richness and uniqueness of individual cases.

In North America, the quest for empirically supported treatments has resulted in an ironic situation. Despite a large and growing number of outcome studies, relatively little is known about specific processes that contribute to positive outcomes for children (Kazdin & Nock, 2003). The relegation of process studies to the periphery of child treatment research is the primary reason for this state of affairs. Conversely, process studies of treatments with limited evidence of efficacy could be viewed as premature, but it is heartening to see new controlled outcome studies of psychodynamic child therapy. Although it could be argued that outcome studies should precede studies of specific processes (Kendall, 2000), we contend that the field will be advanced by integrating process designs into controlled outcome studies. To this end, investigators must be prepared to move beyond randomization and pre to post outcome designs to designs that include process measures and proximal outcomes over the course of therapy. An integrated approach will enable us to answer the question, "Does this treatment work?" as well as, "What makes it work?"

References

Adams, K.E. & Greenburg, L.S. (1996, June). Therapists' influence on depressed clients' therapeutic experiencing and outcome. Paper presented at the 43rd annual convention of the Society for Psychotherapeutic Research, St. Amelia, Fl.

Ainsworth, M., Blehar, M. Waters, E. & Wall, S. (1978). *Patterns of attachment: A study of behavior in the strange situation.* Hillsdale, NJ: Erlbaum.

Alexander, L. & Luborsky, L. (1986). The Penn Helping Alliance Scales. In L. Greenberg & W. Pinsof (Eds.), *The psychotherapeutic process: A research handbook* (pp. 325–366). New York: Guilford Press.

Barber, J., Connolly, M.B., Crits-Christoph, P., Gladis, L. & Siqueland, L. (2000). Alliance predicts outcome beyond in-session change in symptoms. *Journal of Consulting and Clinical Psychology, 68,* 1027–1034.

Baron-Cohen, S., Tager-Flusberg, H. & Cohen, D. (1993). *Understanding other minds: Perspectives from autism.* Oxford: Oxford University Press.

Bordin, E. (1979). The generalizability of the psychoanalytic concept of the working alliance. *Psychotherapy: Theory, Research & Practice, 16,* 252–260.

Bratton, S., Ray, D., Rhine, T. & Jones, L. (2005). The efficacy of play therapy with Children: A meta-analytic review of treatment outcomes. *Professional Psychology: Research and Practice, 36,* 376–390.

Bowlby, J. (1977). The making and breaking of affectional bonds. *British Journal of Psychiatry, 130,* 201–210.

Bowlby, J. (1988). *A secure base: Parent-child attachment and healthy human development.* New York: Basic Books.

Carlson, E.A. & Sroufe, L.A. (1995). Contribution of attachment theory to developmental psychopathology. In D. Cicchetti & D.J. Cohen (Eds.), *Developmental Psychopathology: Theory and Methods (pp. 581–617).* John-Wiley & Sons, Inc.: New York.

Chandler, M., Paget, K. & Koch, D. (1978). The child's demystification of psychological defense mechanisms: A structural and developmental analysis. *Developmental Psychology, 14,* 197–205.

Crits-Christoph, P., Cooper, A. & Luborsky, L. (1988). The accuracy of therapists' interpretations and the outcome of dynamic psychotherapy. *Journal of Consulting and Clinical Psychology, 36,* 490–495.

Crowell, J., Fraley, R. & Shaver, P. (1999). Measurement of individual differences in adolescent and adult attachment. In J. Cassidy & P. Shaver (Eds.), *Handbook of attachment: Theory, research, and clinical applications (pp. 434–465).* New York: Guilford.

Cummings, E.M. & Cicchetti, D. (1990). Towards a transactional model of relations between attachment and depression. In M.T. Greenberg, D. Cicchetti & E.M. Cummings (Eds.), *Attachment in the Preschool Years: Theory, Research & Intervention (pp. 339–372).* University of Chicago Press: Chicago.

Erikson, E. (1964). Clinical observation of play disruption in young children. In M. Haworth (Ed.), *Child psychotherapy* (pp. 264–276). New York; Basic Books.

Estrada. A. & Russell, R. (1999). The development of the *Child Psychotherapy Process Scales. Psychotherapy Research, 9,* 154–166.

Feeley, M., DeRubeis, R. & Gelfand, L. (1999). The temporal relation between adherence and alliance to symptom change in cognitive therapy for depression. *Journal of Consulting and Clinical Psychology, 67,* 578–582.

Fonagy, P. (2004). Psychodynamic therapy with children. In H. Steiner (Ed.), *Handbook of mental health interventions in children and adolescents: An integrated developmental approach,* (pp. 621–658). San Francisco: Jossey-Bass.

Fonagy, P. (1999). Psychodynamic psychotherapy. In S. Russ & T. Ollendick (Eds.), *Handbook of psychotherapies with children and families (pp. 87–106).* New York: Kluwer Academic/Plenum Publishers.

Fonagy, P. (2003). Psychoanalysis today. *World Psychiatry, 2,* 73–80.

Fonagy, P. & Target, M. (1996). Playing with reality: Theory of mind and normal development of psychic reality. *International Journal of Psycho-Analysis, 77,* 217–233.

Fonagy, P. & Target, M. (1997). Attachment and reflective function: Their role in self-organization. *Development and Psychopathology, 9,* 679–700.

Fonagy, P. & Target, M. (2000). The place of psychodynamic theory in developmental psychopathology. *Development and Psychopathology, 12,* 407–425.

Freud, A. (1946). *The psychoanalytic treatment of children.* New York: International Universities Press.

Freud, A. (1965). *The ego and the mechanisms of defense.* New York: International University Press.

Freud, S. (1909). Analysis of a phobia in a five year old boy. In J. Strachey (Ed.), *The standard edition of the complete psychological works of Sigmund Freud,* Vol. 10, (pp. 1–147) London: Hogarth Press.

Freud, S. (1912). The dynamics of transference. In J. Strachey (Ed.), *The standard Edition of the complete psychological works of Sigmund Freud,* (pp. 99–108). London: Hogarth Press.

Freud, S. (1913). On the beginnings of treatment: Further recommendations on the technique of psychoanalysis. In J. Strachey (Ed.), *The standard edition of the complete psychological works of Sigmund Freud.* (pp. 122–144). London: Hogarth.

Furman, W. Simon, V., Shaffer, L. & Bouchey, H. (2002). Adolescents' working models and styles for relationships with parents, friends, and romantic partners. *Child Development, 73,* 241–255.

Gergely, G. & Watson, J.S. (1996). The social biofeedback theory of parental affect-mirroring: The development of emotional self-awareness and self-control in infancy. *International Journal of Psychoanalysis, 77,* 1181–1212.

Harter, S. & Whitesell, N. (1989). Developmental changes in children's understanding of single, multiple, and blended emotion concepts. In C. Saarni & P. Harris (Eds.), *Children's understanding of emotion* (pp. 81–116). New York: Cambridge University Press.

Hawley, K. & Weisz, J. (2005). Youth versus parent working alliance in usual clinical care: Distinctive associations with retention, satisfaction, and treatment outcome. *Journal of Clinical Child and Adolescent Psychology, 34,* 117–128.

Hogland, P. (2004). Analysis of transference in psychodynamic psychotherapy: A review of empirical research. *Canadian Journal of Psychoanalysis, 12,* 280–300.

Horvath, A. & Luborsky, L. (1993). The role of the therapeutic alliance in psychotherapy. *Journal of Consulting and Clinical Psychology, 61,* 561–573.

Hunt, M.G. (1998). The only way out is through: Emotional processing and recovery after a depressing life event. *Behavior Research and Therapy, 36,* 361–384.

Isabella, R.A. & Belsky, J. (1991). Interactional synchrony and the origins of infant-mother attachment: A replication study. *Child Development, 62,* 373–384.

Iwakabe, S., Rogan, K. & Stalikas, A. (2000). The relationship between client emotional expressions, therapist interventions, and the working alliance: An exploration of eight emotional expression events. *Journal of Psychotherapy Integration, 10,* 375–402.

Kazdin, A. & Nock, M. (2003). Delineating mechanisms of change in child and Adolescent therapy: Methodological issues and research recommendations. *Journal of Child Psychology and Psychiatry, 44,* 1116–1129.

Kendall, P.C. (2000). A round of applause for an agenda and report cards for child and adolescent psychotherapy research. *Archives of General Psychiatry, 57*, 839–840.

Kennedy, H. (1971). Problems of reconstruction in child analysis. *The Psycho- analytic Study of the Child, 26*, 386–402.

Kernberg, P. (1995). Child psychiatry: Individual psychotherapy. In H. Kaplan & B. Sadock (Eds.), *Comprehensive textbook of psychiatry* (6th ed., pp. 2399–2412. Baltimore: Williams & Wilkins.

Kernberg, P., Chazan, S. & Normandin, L. (1998). The Children's Play Therapy Instrument: Description, development, and reliability studies. *Journal of Psychotherapy Practice and Research, 7*, 196–207.

Klein, M. (1932). *The psychoanalysis of children*. London: Hogarth Press.

Laible, D. (2007). Attachment with parents and peers in late adolescence: Links with emotional competence and social behavior. *Personality and Individual Differences, 43*, 1185–1197.

Linehan, M.M. (1993). *Cognitive-behavioral treatment of borderline personality disorder*. New York: Guilford Press.

Luborsky, L. & Crits-Christoph, P. (1998). *Understanding transference: The Core Conflictual Relationship Theme method*. Washington, DC: APA.

Mackay, H.C., Barkham, M., Stiles, W.B. & Goldfried, M.R. (2002). Patterns of client emotion in helpful sessions of cognitive-behavioral and psychodynamic-interpersonal therapy. *Journal of Counseling Psychology, 49*, 376–380.

Mallinckrodt, B., Porter, M. & Kivlighan, D.M. (2005). Client attachment to therapist, depth of in-session exploration, and object relations in brief psychotherapy. *Psychotherapy: Theory, Research, Practice, Training, 42*, 85–100.

Main, M., Kaplan, N. & Cassidy, J. (1985). Security in infancy, childhood, and Adulthood: A move to representation. *Monographs of the Society for Research In Child Development, 50*, (1–2, Serial No. 209).

Marmar, C. Weiss, D. & Gaston, L. (1989). Toward the validation of the California therapeutic alliance rating system. *Psychological Assessment, 1*, 46–52.

Martin, D.J., Graske, J.P. & Davis, M.K. (2000). Relation of the therapeutic alliance with outcome and other variables: A meta-analytic review. *Journal of Consulting and Clinical Psychology, 68*, 438–450.

Marziali, E. Marmar, C. & Krupnick, J. (1984). Therapeutic alliance scales: Development And relationship to treatment outcome. *American Journal of Psychiatry, 138*, 361–364.

Moran, G.S. & Fonagy, P. (1987). Psychoanalysis and diabetic control: A single case study. *British Journal of Medical Psychology, 60*, 357–372.

Muratori, F., Picchi, L., Bruni, G., Patarnello, M. & Romagnoli, G. (2003). A two year follow-up of psychodynamic psychotherapy for internalizing disorders in children. *Journal of the American Academy of Child and Adolescent Psychiatry, 42*, 331–339.

Pos, A.E, Greenberg, L.S. & Goldman, R.N. (2003). Emotional processing during experiential treatment of depression. *Journal of Consulting and Clinical Psychology, 71*, 1007–1016.

Raikes, A.H. & Thompson, R. (2006). Family emotional climate, attachment security and young children's emotion knowledge in a high risk sample. *British Journal of Developmental Psychology, 24*, 89–104.

Renouf, A.G. & Harter, S. (1990). Low self-worth and anger as components of the depressive experience in young adolescents. *Development and Psychopathology, 2(3)*, 293–310.

Rogers, A. (1995). *A shining affliction*. New York: Penguin Books.

Russell, R.L. & van den Broek, P. (1988) A cognitive-developmental account of storytelling in child psychotherapy. In S. Shirk (Ed.), *Cognitive development and child psychotherapy* (pp. 19–52). New York: Plenum Press.

Russ, S.W. (2004). *Play in child development and psychotherapy: Toward empirically-supported practice*. London: Lawrence Erlbaum Associates.

Saunders, S., Howard, K. & Orlinsky, D. (1989). The therapeutic bond scales: Psychometric properties and relation to treatment effectiveness. *Psychological Assessment, 1*, 323–330.

Shirk, S.R. (1988). Causal reasoning and children's comprehension of therapeutic interpretations. In S. Shirk (Ed.), *Cognitive development and child Psychotherapy (pp. 53–89)*. New York: Plenum Press.

Shirk, S.R. & Karver, M. (2003). Prediction of treatment outcome from relationship variables in child and adolescent therapy: A meta-analytic review. *Journal of Consulting and Clinical Psychology, 71*, 452–464.

Shirk, S.R. & Karver, M. (2005). Process issues in cognitive-behavioral therapy for youth. In P. Kendall (Ed.), *Child and adolescent therapy: Cognitive- behavioral procedures. (pp. 465–491)*. New York: Guilford Press.

Shirk, S.R. & Russell, R.L. (1996). *Child processes in child psychotherapy: Revitalizing treatment and research*. New York: Guilford Press.

Shirk, S.R. & Russell, R.L. (1998). Process issues in child psychotherapy. In A. Bellack & M. Hersen (Eds.), *Comprehensive clinical psychology, Vol. 15*, (pp. 57–82). Oxford: Pergamon.

Shirk, S.R. & Saiz, C. (1992). The therapeutic alliance in child therapy: Clinical, empirical, and developmental perspectives. *Development and Psychopathology 4*, 713–728.

Slade, A. (1999). Representation, symbolization, and affect regulation in the concomitant treatment of a mother and child: attachment theory and and child psychotherapy, *Psychoanalytic Inquiry, 19*, 824–857.

Slade, A. (2005). Parental reflective functioning: An introduction. *Attachment & Human Development, 7*, 269–281.

Suh, C. Strupp, H. & O'Mally, S. (1986). The Vanderbilt process measures. In L. Greenberg & W. Pinsof (Eds.), *The psychotherapeutic process: A Research handbook.* (pp. 285–323). New York: Guilford Press.

Target, M. Slade, A. Cottrell, D., Fuggle, P. & Fonagy, P. (2005). Psychosocial therapies with children. In G. Gabbard, J. Beck & J. Holmes (Eds.), *Oxford textbook of psychotherapy. (pp. 341–352)* New York: Oxford.

Tsiantis, J., Kolvin, I., Anastasopoulos, D, Trowell, J., Tomaras, V., Miles, G., Papadopoulos, R, Soininen, M., Bostrom, C. & Almqvist, F. (2005). Psychotherapy for early adolescent depression: A comparison of two Psychotherapeutic interventions in three European countries. In E. Hibbs & P. Jensen (Eds.), *Treatments for child and adolescent disorders (2nd Edition)*, (pp. 267–293). Washington, DC: APA.

Weiss, J., Sampson, H. & The Mt. Zion Psychotherapy Research Group (1986). *The psychoanalytic therapeutic process: Theory, clinical observations, and empirical research.* New York: Guildford.

Weisz, J., Weiss, B., Alicke, M. & Klotz, M. (1987). Effectiveness of psychotherapy with children and adolescents: A meta-analysis for clinicians. *Journal of Consulting and Clinical Psychology, 55*, 542–549.

Weisz, J., Weiss, B., Han, S., Granger, D. & Morton, D. (1995). Effects of psychotherapy with children and adolescents revisited. *Psychological Bulletin, 117*, 450–468.

Westen, D. (1991). Social cognition and object relations. *Psychological Bulletin, 109*, 429–455.

Westen, D. (2002). Implications of developments in cognitive neuroscience for psychoanalytic psychotherapy. *Harvard Review of Psychiatry, 10*, 369–373.

Westen, D. (1999). The scientific status of unconscious processes: Is Freud really dead? *Journal of the American Psychoanalytic Association, 47*, 1061–1106.

Winnicott, D. (1958). *Through paediatrics to psychoanalysis.* London: Horgarth Press.

Zahn-Waxler, C., Cole, P.M. & Barrett, K.C. (1991). Guilt and empathy: Sex differences and implications for the development of depression. In J. Garber & K.A. Dodge (Eds.), *The development of emotional regulation and dysregulation* (pp. 243–272). Cambridge, England: Cambridge University Press.

CHAPTER EIGHT

Ethical principles in conducting research with children and adolescents

Euthymia D. Hibbs Ph.D.

> ".....The regimen I adopt (medicine) shall be for the benefit of my patients according to my ability and judgment, and not for their hurt or for any wrong. I will give no deadly drug to any, though it be asked of me, nor will counsel such.... Whatsoever house I enter, there I will go for the benefit of the sick, refraining from all wrong doing, or corruption, and especially from any act of seduction, of male or female, or bond or free. Whatsoever things I see or hear concerning the life of men, in my attendance on the sick or even apart there from, which ought not to be noised abroad, I will keep silence thereon, counting such things to be as sacred secrets."
>
> —The Hippocratic Oath (460 BC).

The need to deliver treatments to patients ethically has concerned health care providers and scientists for over 2000 years. As in 460 BC, current health professionals and specifically investigators confront the same ethical issues. In recent years, research ethics has achieved a higher profile as a result of the emphasis on human rights, and because of well-publicized breaches of research ethics at some prominent institutions. The fundamental principle of modern research focuses on respecting human dignity, which aspires to protect the multiple and interdependent interests of the person from bodily to psychological to cultural integrity (Tricouncil Ethics Statement, 1998). Thus, respect for human dignity entails confidentiality, concern for the welfare of the consumer, the proper handling of human participants, and restraint from exploiting patients or their relatives, when working with research participants.

Advances in medical science and technology, have also contributed in shaping ethical principles to adapt to contemporary needs, became more elaborate, and in some cases, carry legal implications. In Hippocrates' time, the term oath meant an ethical code or ideal, enjoining correct conduct, but it was not a law; to fail to observe it entailed no threat of penalty as might be the case today.

In the last two decades, additional safeguards have been instituted in order to protect research participants from risks while participating in research. Institutional Review Boards (IRB's) were created in order to safeguard the rights and well being of human participants. Initial Review Groups (IRG's) oversee the protection and welfare of research participants as part of their responsibilities. While participation in psychosocial treatment research might be thought of as presenting less of a risk than other forms of treatments because they are not physically invasive, the risks may in fact, be substantial for children with mental disorders. The psychosocial researcher must often base his or her design upon theories of development and of psychosocial functioning which are less well defined than medical principles of physiology or pathology. Thus, research, based on unsubstantiated theories, may bias the investigator's assessment of the morality of research questions and experimental procedures and place participants at risk. For example, if a developmental psychologist subscribes to the theory that children are tough and resilient, he or she may be willing to submit them to more harsh experimental procedures than the investigator, who believes that children are highly vulnerable, would be unwilling even to consider (Keith-Spiegel, 1976). Psychosocial treatment research, like other types of research, involves the pursuit of truth in furthering and advancing knowledge. Clinical research presents unique challenges in part because the relationship between clinical responsibility for the well-being of clients and scientific objectivity, present competing demands to the researcher. Such tensions can be ethically resolved by establishing special precautions to ensure that both clinical and scientific responsibilities can be met.

In this chapter, we will discuss five specific ethical issues that confront the investigators who study the efficacy and effectiveness of psychosocial treatments for children. These issues are competence, informed consent/assent, and confidentiality, use of incentives, and selection and involvement of control subjects.

Clinician/therapist competence

Both Socrates (450 BC–380 BC) and Descartes (1596–1650) considered that rightness of action depends upon certainty of knowledge, and wrongdoing upon ignorance. Investigators conducting psychosocial research need to ensure the competence of the professionals involved in both the scientific and intervention components. Research is an unregulated enterprise and researchers are not required to be board-certified to qualify for performing investigations, thus, peer and self-regulation of research quality and research practice ethics are especially critical (Keith-Spiegel & Koocher, 1985).

On the other hand, scientific investigators work with clinicians who perform the actual therapeutic treatment. Therapists therefore need to be well trained clinicians with experience in childhood psychopathology, and preferably board-certified. However, these credentials imply that their time is highly priced, and most of the time research resources are limited. Thus, the customary practice in research settings is to train graduate students to carry out treatment in the therapeutic modality to be tested. Objectivity and replicability are sought by manualizing the treatment procedure in a regimented treatment protocol. The training, as it is reported in the literature, is usually rigorous. Supervision is carried out directly or through video tapes. Although standardized and focused, this approach to treatment raises some issues of clinical competence. Therapeutic difficulties or crises may arise during the sessions that are not prescribed in the manual. They must be understood and addressed on the spot, not delayed until after consultation with the supervisor, or discussion during a weekly supervisory session. For example, a clinician/therapist is trained to follow a manual for the cognitive treatment of depression. One subject has a co-morbid secondary condition of anxiety disorder. During a session, this child may exhibit distress, difficulty swallowing, breathing, etc., due to an anxiety attack. The therapist needs to be able to diagnose and therapeutically intervene to relieve the child's anguish. Thus, in all studies of psychosocial treatment where specific modalities are being studied, there should always be well-qualified, clinical back-up. Therapist must be competent, fully trained, certified and with adequate clinical experience in carrying out the treatment research, demonstrate integrity and professionalism, and ensure the safety of the research subjects. Otherwise, participants may be harmed if treated by non-competent, non-well trained clinicians.

Informed consent/assent

Informed voluntary consent is an ethical and legal requirement for any research study. The consent form is a written document which explains to an individual who volunteers to participate in a research protocol, the goals, processes, and risks involved. The patient consent form is required to be written in lay terms so as to be understood by individuals not familiar with technical terminology. Beyond obtaining a signature on the written document, the investigator must make appropriate disclosures and ensure that participants have a thorough understanding of the information and their choices, not only at the time of enrollment, but throughout the research process. Information must also be tailored to meet the needs of the participants in the particular research context. Thus, participants and/or parents need to fully understand the significance of their participation before signing the consent document. Investigators should also be ready to answer questions concerning the study to prospective participants. The Ethical Principles of Psychologists (1981) indicate:

> "The investigator establishes a clear and fair agreement with research participants, prior to their participation that clarifies the obligations and responsibilities of each. The investigator has the obligation to honor all promises and commitments included in the agreement. The investigator informs the participants of all aspects of the research that might reasonably be

> expected to influence willingness to participate and explains all other aspects of participants inquire.... Research with children or with participants who have impairments that would limit understanding and/or communication requires special safeguarding procedures."

A revised Code of Federal regulation proposes the following important points to comprise consent forms:

1. Description and purpose of research.
2. Discussion of reasonably foreseeable risks.
3. Expected benefits.
4. Availability of alternative treatments.
5. How and to what extent confidentiality will be maintained.
6. Possible compensation, if injury occurs, from research involving more than minimal risk.
7. Disclosure about who to contact concerning pertinent questions and research-related injury.
8. A statement about the voluntary nature about beginning and continuing with the research (DHHS, 1991).

The National Commission for the Protection of Subjects of Biomedical and Behavioral Research which was established in the 1970s introduced the concept of assent (Hershey & Miller, 1976). Assent means that the child has the right to be informed of and agree to the conditions of research, without necessarily comprehending the information at the level required for legal informed consent. The child's objection supersedes guardian consent, unless the experimental treatment holds out the prospect of direct benefit that can only be achieved through the particular research (Campbell, 1987; Fisher, 1993), and the assent needs to be explained to the child in language that he/she understands. The original cut-off age for obtaining assent was seven, however, currently the age is not specified, is more flexible, and the criteria remain unclear. In obtaining consent, ensuring that the child understands and decides to participate in a study, the investigator must take into consideration the child's developmental level of cognitive and intellectual abilities. For example, for children of any age with developmental disabilities, with impaired cognitive abilities, parental consent only should be sufficient. However, children with internalized disorders, for example, regardless of age, need to be informed explicitly of the goals of the study, what is expected from them, and the procedures involved.

Longitudinal treatment studies present a different consent issue. For example, in studies of longitudinal treatment of chronic disorders, the study's "blanket consent" obtained at the onset would not be sufficient to inform participants of all relevant details of the study. Parents may not remember every procedure that occurs throughout the study and might be surprised at learning that the child was taken out of class to be administered an extensive assessment battery. A recommended procedure is to review the study protocol with parents at certain points during the research, and explain the remaining tasks in the protocol. However, this procedure may present some threat to the research design because some families may need more explanation or coaching than others. Therefore, the recommended procedure is to review the study protocol with parents and children, at certain designated points throughout the research process. The investigator can also provide parents, and children when appropriate, a written schedule or calendar of activities detailing the approximate dates of treatment, assessment, and parent meetings. Periodic parental review and renewed consent to research procedures may however present some threat to research design, because some families would need more explanation or support than others. Although selective clarification may be clinically responsive and alliance-forming, it may also differentially tailor information for some families, potentially skewing the scientific process. However, investigators have by now developed ways of incorporating individual participant responses to consent and debriefing procedures into the experimental design.

The right to withdraw from a research project at any time should be made explicit in the consent form. Withdrawal privilege can only be overridden with parental approval when the participant is legally or mentally incompetent, and when the intervention may provide significant benefit to the person's health and welfare, if it is only available in the research context, and when other alternatives have been exhausted or are unavailable (National Commission or the Protection of Human Subjects in Biomedical and Behavioral Research, 1977).

Confidentiality

Protection against disclosing personally identifiable information

Respect for human dignity also implies respect for privacy and confidentiality. Investigators conducting psychosocial interventions with children and youth need to set up procedures that can adequately protect participant confidentiality. This includes protection of assessment results, treatment outcomes, information about the participant's family members, and ensuring security of information held in electronic media. Protecting confidential information can be particularly difficult when working with minors because there are laws that require the reporting of child abuse and neglect. Accordingly, both parents and prospective child participants must be fully informed about the procedures that will be used to ensure confidentiality, e.g. replacing names with number codes, and security measures for storing files, as well as the limits of confidentiality, e.g. what types of information is required by the law to be reported to outside authorities.

For the most part, individual therapy's data is of little use to others except to the researcher and possibly to the parents who would like to know if there is improvement during treatment. However, there might be some exceptions, for example, in cases of adolescent delinquency, both the assessment and outcome data on a specific individual could be subpoenaed (Wolfgang, 1981), depending on the seriousness of the offense. Legal precedents for researcher's protection of data are not clear. However, one way of providing research participants and investigators immunity from subpoena of research records is through the mechanism of the certificate of confidentiality (Health Omnibus Programs Extension Act, 1988). The certificate of confidentiality provides legal protection for the investigator against being compelled to disclose personal, identifiable information about research subjects and at the same time, assures research participants that they are protected from disclosure of their identity (Hoagwood, 1994).

The use of videotapes and computer technology

Investigators studying psychosocial interventions are increasingly using videotapes to perform complex behavioral analyses or to test hypotheses beyond those directly relevant to treatment efficacy. Take for example, an investigator who is comparing two different therapeutic modes for the treatment of anxiety disorders. A second investigator from another institution has a hypothesis that the therapeutic alliance is established earlier or is stronger with one mode of treatment than the other. The second investigator could use the existing video material to score an alliance measure by reviewing the therapy video-tapes. This approach promises an effective and economical way to examine several hypotheses. However, questions about confidentiality are raised. Does the practice of using existing clinical videotapes for separate research studies fit under the umbrella consent of confidentiality with sharing information on a need-to-know basis? That is, can the second investigator be considered a member of the research team? Does the original consent form adequately address the second analysis procedure and safeguard the rights of the individuals videotaped during the treatment study? Should another consent form be drawn up? If so, what becomes of the clinical material of subjects who are not reachable, those who have moved away? Can the data be used legally or scientifically? If data is missing for the alliance study, would this affect the power or constitute attrition, which in turn biases the sample? From a legal point of view, the specificity of the language in the original consent form may be binding, and it is advisable to write this form with language which allows some generality.

Another threat to confidentiality is computer technology. Should the investigators store data in computer banks? How impenetrable are they? Since investigators can not promise abstinence from advanced technology, the solution may be to ensure that the data is identifiable only to them, and is encrypted or encoded to avoid discovery by unauthorized individuals.

Issues of confidentiality when sharing of information with parents

Aristotle (382–322 BC), in his book on Ethics, described the family as a center of friendship and a powerful force for good. We also recognize that parents are the "gatekeepers" with respect to referral to, and continued "compliance" with the research protocol (Melton & Wilcox, 1989). Therefore, parental involvement is critical in order to assure cooperation for the ongoing treatment of their offspring (Kovacs & Lohr, 1995), and consequently as an opportunity for empowerment of the family to turn into a "powerful force for good."

Usually legal and moral responsibility, in addition to their anxiety and concern, impels parents to want to be informed about ongoing aspects of a treatment study. They may feel they need to know what is happening during the treatment sessions, and may request assessment and therapy material in order to feel part of the process. Because of logistics such as lack of time, incomplete development of comparison norms, or because certain measures can only be scored at the end of the treatment, providing ongoing updates for parents may compromise the integrity of the study. While, of course parents have the right to know what is happening to their child, the question may arise as to how much one can disclose to the parents without threatening the research design and influencing attrition. If their request is not satisfied, they may boycott the treatment or withdraw their child from the study. Consequently, the best way to avoid conflicts would be to work closely at the onset of the study with parents, explaining to them the rules of participation, and the availability of information. For example, may the investigator inform parents after an assessment that their child is improving or not improving? In either case, the parents may withdraw the child. For example, they may reason that because either she or he is doing better there is no need for further treatment, or if they are informed that there is no improvement, they may become disappointed and withdraw from the study.

Another issue related to the sharing of information with parents concerns disclosure about co-morbid conditions. Clinical and research responsibility dictates that the study has foreseen such possibilities and would either provide treatment or make a referral. Since co-morbid conditions are the rule in children more than the exception, the methodological integrity of a study might suffer either because study resources would be diverted to the treatment of the co-morbid conditions, or if the child is referred out for treatment, the information and data may be diluted. The question remains, how much of the protocol's technicalities should parents know? Would they want to participate if they knew of a possible additional referral? Would they be interested in continuing with the study if an outside referral was in order? In such cases attrition may increase, since parents are understandably more interested in obtaining treatment for their child than they are in assisting in accumulating research data. One solution may be, and is actually offered by studies employing new methodologies, to consider parents as an integral part of the treatment of children. These methodologies include parent training or even parent treatment, and often set a schedule for parent feedback during the study. A note of caution would be that trying to specify and rigidly operationalize all clinical guidelines beforehand, may also scare participants away. Therefore, the investigator and clinicians walk on tight rope, trying to maintain flexibility within a rigorous research design.

Confidentiality issues when sharing information with the public

The aim of research is to gain knowledge and to disseminate this knowledge to other professionals for their use. Therapy material gathered through research treatment protocols is always very helpful as a teaching tool to train students or other professionals, especially through the use of videotapes. How can confidentiality be maintained while sharing information with others than parents and the research team? For example, one student of psychology recognized her next door neighbors on a videotaped treatment study which was shown as a teaching example. Assuring confidentiality in discussion with students should always occur, if concealment of parents' identity is not possible.

The general public also has a right to research findings, because of their tax contributions to research studies, the expressed value of shared knowledge, and their freedom to access and apply new knowledge. The media can be a major communicator of research breakthrough, since only a few people read professional journals. However, because the media seeks material to disseminate rapidly to wide audiences, videotapes are used for this purpose. The issues arises for investigators how to maintain confidentiality for research participants whose faces appear on camera.

For example, an investigator developed and tested a therapy manual which seemed to be effective in treating a specific mental disorder. The media learned of it through the investigator's publications and requested permission to present the videotaped treatment on national television. What should the investigators' responsibilities be concerning public dissemination? One possibility is for the investigators to draw up a new consent form, explaining in detail to the participants the meaning and the consequences of being viewed in a classroom filming or on national T.V. Some research participants may not fully understand the consequences, and may even feel proud to be seen on T.V. On the other hand, they may be angry when unflattering excerpts of the video are shown.

A second example further illustrates this point. An investigator foresaw that his interview/assessment instrument for differential diagnosis, developed to assign participants to treatment groups, would be of interest to the public. At the outset of the study he explained to potential participants the possibility that videotaped sessions might be seen by psychology and psychiatry students or be shown eventually on T.V. The investigator drew up a separate consent form at that time for the participants to sign. A few years later, when the study was in its final stages and data analyses showed significant results, excerpts of a video interview of one study participant were shown on T.V. The participant was enraged because he had forgotten signing the consent form, his life had changed to the better, and he did not want to "expose" his past problems to the public. He threatened to sue the institution and the investigator conducting the study. Therefore, study participants not only need to be reminded of what they agreed to, but also be given another opportunity to decide whether to agree to public exposure. They must also know what choices they have about how this will be done. They may choose to allow to be shown in full, to conceal their identities by screening their features, or to refuse to sign the consent, so the video may not be shown. The investigator must respect their wishes fully and abide by the principles of confidentiality.

Incentives for participation

Psychosocial treatment research, like any other clinical research, will seek volunteer participants with specific mental disorders to participate in treatment studies. Investigators may advertise in newspapers, doctors' offices, schools, in the media, and in other ways. Although participation is defined as voluntary, it has been documented that voluntariness is relative. The potential for incentives to be a coercive influence on children needs to be carefully considered by investigators. Is it simplistic to think that voluntary consent is always obtained without coercion, pressure, or undue inducement? At what level of reimbursement is remuneration potentially great enough to influence participants to consent to participate in a study? For individuals in great financial need, there may be little likelihood they will reject the offer to participate; does this imply coercion? If the investigator appeals to an individual's altruism, e.g. "This study will help us understand how to treat this disorder and your participation will help people in the future", is he or she exerting moral coercion? If the study offers treatment which is otherwise unaffordable, will a potential subject feel compelled to participate?

Remuneration for participation in a study is permissible and is used extensively, not as an incentive but as a token (a) to express the investigator's appreciation for the child's/parent effort, and (b) to reimburse the subjects for travel or other expenses due to their participation in research (Small, Campbell, Shay & Goodman, 1994).

In addition to ethical concerns, a threat to the research design may be posed by using incentives. Some participant volunteers may be distraught individuals who either could not find treatment elsewhere or who cannot afford it. Others may be responding to an advertisement, but not be as symptomatic as they claim; some are merely seeking novelty. It also happens that philanthropic organizations or churches encourage their constituents to volunteer and then donate the remuneration to the institution.

In all of the above conditions, there is a risk of selective recruitment of a subject of the population who reads newspapers, attends church or responds to advertisements. Selection bias may put the generalizability of the study at risk. To avoid such problems, a systematic outreach and effort to include a representative sample from all SES, ethnic/cultural groups, is crucial. In summary, caution should be exercised in developing recruitment strategies for research participants, and as such, advice from ethics consultants is encouraged.

Control participants

In order for the study to be scientifically valid and for its results to be interpretable, a comparison/control group is usually necessary. Control groups may vary, depending upon the hypothesis tested, including individuals without psychopathology, those with physical illness only, or subjects with a different diagnosis than the one under investigation. In the case of psychosocial treatment research, individuals also falling within the same diagnostic category, but receiving a different treatment modality, are often used for the control condition. How the control condition is applied depends on the research design of the study. All conditions, as we will see below, potentially encounter ethical dilemmas.

No-treatment control: No-treatment control groups help in discerning to what extent participants would improve without treatment. These groups are controlled for history, maturational level and the effects of repeated testing, and so on. The control and experimental groups are usually equivalent in all independent variables. Conversely, withholding treatment is ethically undesirable (Hibbs, 1993). For example, in the treatment of school phobia, it might be unethical to allow a phobic child to remain in fear of, and away from school, for a prolonged period of time. In addition, participation in a no-treatment control group may lead to differential attrition. If parents, in order to alleviate their child's suffering, seek treatment elsewhere without informing the investigator, the results of the study will be compromised. If they drop out of the study, the remaining participants will comprise a select group (Kazdin & Wilson, 1978) whose selection did not fit the study design.

Wait-list control group. A wait-list control group has several advantages. An intake interview is usually performed prior to placement on the waiting list, and patients expect an appointment in the near future. Patient expectancy, the improvement that occurs in anticipation of treatment, provides important information on the natural history of the disorder (O'Leary & Borcovec, 1978). However, there are several problems associated with wait-list controls. Participants may differ in characteristics such as severity of disorder and rate of attrition, as they are not often randomly assigned. Delaying treatment is unethical unless the participants are assigned to the wait-list control group on the basis of their ability to wait for treatment. In this case the research design is in trouble because of selection bias and the study's generalizability is thrown into question. Attrition may occur when treatment is readily available in subjects' locality. It is also unethical to delay treatment in situations when treatment is unavailable except through the research study.

Placebo control group. Placebo control typically includes components and other mechanisms that account for treatment effects, such as expectation of improvement, and controlling for frequency of contacts (attentional control), since both control and experimental participants receive the same number of sessions. Process research which attempts to investigate and isolate the active components of therapy is best controlled by using placebo treatment groups. Participants in the control group should be equivalent in every way to the experimental group, except for the active components of therapy to be isolated and investigated. However, the placebo condition necessitates deception, which presents ethical problems. While in drug studies it is explained to subjects that at some point during their treatment they will receive an "inert pill", in psychosocial treatment "placebo/inert" conditions are not usually explained. Hence, important information is withheld from the subject in the consent process (Hibbs, 1993). The Ethical guidelines of psychologists (1981) state that when methodological requirements make use of deception necessary, the investigator has a special responsibility to determine whether the use of such techniques is justified by the study's prospective scientific, educational, or applied value, to determine whether alternative procedures are available, and to ensure that the participants are provided with sufficient explanation as soon as possible.

Conclusion

Democritus (470 BC), an ancient Greek physical philosopher, wrote that Prudence, which is the outcome of nature and education, enables the right decision to be made. The best ethical approach underlying scientific research is that the research be of the best quality, so that the energies of both the scientist and the participants are justly expended. Thus, a good design is the first principle requirement of good science. This chapter addressed the challenges of carrying out psychosocial research and preserving a good research design while treating subjects with honesty and fairness.

Although "non-invasive" physiologically, psychosocial interventions may be psychologically invasive, and may have a powerful impact upon patients, therefore minimal risk should not be assumed. Five challenges to ethically conducting high quality psychosocial research with children and adolescents have been discussed in this chapter. These are summarized below.

First, funding constraints may compromise research design either by necessitating the employment of less experienced assistants or by limiting the accommodation available for addressing co-morbid conditions and/or clinical crises. Clinicians carrying out treatment within a research protocol must employ well trained staff, even if the cost of employing such individuals is higher. Therapeutic effectiveness is known to depend upon therapist-patient factors which are difficult to operationalize and quantify and which potentially threaten the objectivity and interchangeability of treatment units. For example, treatment effectiveness increases if the therapist feels invested in the patient's well-being however, this may be seen as therapeutic bias, jeopardizing objectivity. Flexibility of therapist response to patients is a feature of clinical competence, as is the ability to perceive subtle behaviors and patterns which cannot be quantified in treatment manuals. Therefore, there may be a negative trade-off of clinical information for quantifiable data, unless investigators are able to apply both clinical mastery and rigor of research design.

A second challenge is posed by the problem of obtaining informed consent with proxy consenters, parents or other responsible adults, and determining children's assent to participation. In this chapter we discussed the difficulties of obtaining consent at one point in time for treatment which extends over time, the necessity to consider developmental factors, and the constant possibility for undue inducement or actual coercion of subjects to participate. Consent may need to be obtained at multiple points over the course of a longitudinal study. These are examples of ethical problems in treatment research of children that have been explored elsewhere in the literature (Krener & Mancina, 1994).

A third challenge when conducting psychosocial research is that of ensuring patient confidentiality while collecting data which is intended for dissemination. Troubled individuals may find many ways via their families and communities to assist themselves with overcoming their symptoms and solving their problems with living. If participation in psychosocial research causes a patient to limit his or her search for assistance to one standardized intervention, then that patient may be walled off from other sorts of social assistance. Data from treatment in a research project may be confounded by other therapeutic experiences which had been discovered outside the project. The increase of videotape data necessitates additional protection. Investigators need to create procedures for management of videotaped data including obtaining additional consent from participants and developing policies for access to these data. A related threat to the ethical treatment of participants is presented by the question of preserving confidentiality while also meeting the scientific obligation to disseminate data and teach the next generation of researchers and clinicians. The power of the media to widely broadcast images which are one person's personal experiences and another person's data points magnifies this threat. The investigator needs to anticipate potential distortions and abuses, and both protect the patient from unwanted surprises by adequate informed consent, while protecting the data from distortion in transmission by carefully controlling how it is exposed.

A fourth problem concerns the differential effects of specific incentives upon various patients. Clinical judgment, skill, and foresight should be brought to bear on the question as to whether the incentive structure will exert a differential effect upon selection, or retention, or whether it constitutes by undue inducement.

Finally, the selection of appropriate control groups and the optimal design for their involvement are often accompanied by a variety of ethical dilemmas. In psychosocial research, this is a crucial feature of study design, extending beyond the analytical problem of controlling for independent variables, because the control persons' life experiences and their psychosocial parameters are potential study confounds to a greater extent than in other treatment trials. No-treatment control group designs are the most problematic because withholding treatment from individuals, who, by definition, may require intervention, is clearly unacceptable. Such a design also risks loss of study participants. Wait-list control group designs do not pose the same problem as withholding treatment, but attrition of participants is a risk. Placebo control designs, while offering the advantage of rigor, generally involve deception, and this of course requires careful thought and justification.

Although these five ethical issues tend to arise in many studies of psychosocial treatments, there are creative ways to engage with the problems presented. As the field of psychosocial treatment research with children continues to grow, one can expect dilemmas to recur. Several approaches will facilitate sound ethical decision making, for example, strengthening the role of clinicians in such research; delineating the separate responsibilities for the clinician and the scientific components of these studies; ensuring that new technology, which can strengthen scientific contribution, is accompanied by foresight and caution; and involving families in multiple aspects of the research process. Above all we must remember integrity, objectivity, special responsibility in respecting human dignity, are the cornerstones of successful research outcomes.

References

American Psychologist. (1981). *Ethical Principles of Psychologists 36 (6)*: 633–638.

Campbell, M. (1987). Consent Issues with Disturbed and/or Retarded Children, *Psychopharmacology Bulletin, 23 (3)*: 379–381.

Department of Health and Human Services (DHHS). (1991). Title 45 Public Welfare, Part 46 *Code of Federal Regulations, Protection of Human Subjects.*

Fisher, C.B. (1993). Integrating Science and Ethics in Research with High Risk Children and Youth. *Society for Research in Child development: Social Policy Report, (4)*: 1–27.

Health Omnibus Program Extension Act of 1988. Paragraph 242a, 42 U.S.C. Paragraph 301(d) (1988).

Hershey, N. & Miller, R.D. (1976). *Human Experimentation and the Law,* Germantown, Maryland: Aspen Systems Corp.

Hibbs, E.D. (1993). Psychosocial Treatment Research with Children and Adolescents: Methodological Issues. *Psychopharmacology Bulletin, 29 (1)*: 27–33.

Hoagwood, K. (1994). The Certificate of Confidentiality at the National Institute of Mental Health: Discretionary Considerations in its Applicability in Research on Child and Adolescent Mental Disorders. *Ethics & Behavior, 4 (2)*: 123–131.

Kazdin, A.E. & Wilson, G.T. (1978). *Evaluation of Behavior Therapy: Issues, Evidence, and Research Strategies.* Cambridge, MA: Ballinger Publishing Co.

Keith-Spiegel, P. (1976). Children's Rights as Participants in Research. In: G.P. Koocher (Ed.), *Children's Rights and the Mental Health Professions.* New York: Wiley.

Keith-Spiegel, P. & Koocher, G.P. (1985). *Ethics in Psychology: Professional Standards and Cases*, pp. 383–431, Random House, New York.

Kovacs, M. & Lohr, W.D. (1995). Research on Psychotherapy with Children and Adolescents: An Overview of Evolving Trends and Current Issues. *Journal of Abnormal Psychology, 23 (1)*, 11–30.

Krener, P.K. & Mancina, R.A. (1994). Informed Consent or Informed Coercion? Decision-making in Pediatric Psychopharmacology. *Journal of Child and Adolescent Psychopharmacology, 4 (3)*: 183–200.

Melton, G.B. & Wilcox, B.L. (1989). Changes in Family Law and Family Life. *American Psychologist, 44*: 1213–1216.

National Commission for the Protection of Human Subjects of Biomedical and Behavioral Research. (1977). *Research Involving Children.* (Publication No. 0577-004). Washington, D.C.: Department of Health, Education and Welfare.

O'Leary, K.D. & Borkovec, T.D. Conceptual, Methodological, and Ethical Problems in Placebo Groups in Psychotherapy Research. (1978). *American Psychologist*, 9: 821–830.

Small, A.M., Campbell, M., Shay, J. & Goodman, I.S. (1994). Ethical Guidelines for Psychopharmacological Research in Children. In: J.Y. Hattab (Ed.), *Ethics and Child Mental Health*, Hewlett, NY: Gefen Books.

Tricouncil Ethics Statement. *Ethical Conduct for Research Involving Humans.* (1998).

Wolfgang, M.E. (1981). Confidentiality in Criminological Research and Other Ethical Issues. *Journal of Criminal Law and Criminology*, 72: 345–361.

INDEX

Kolibri 360 GmbH
Ferdinand-Jühlke-Straße 7
99095 Erfurt, Deutschland
produktsicherheit@kolibri360.de